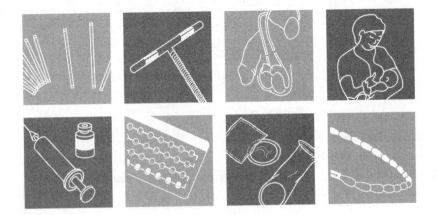

Family Planning

A GLOBAL HANDBOOK FOR PROVIDERS

Evidence-based guidance developed
through worldwide collaboration

A WHO Family Planning Cornerstone

W9-BZW-660

World Health Organization
Department of
Reproductive Health and Research

Johns Hopkins
Bloomberg School of Public Health
Center for Communication Programs
Knowledge for Health Project

United States Agency for International Development
Bureau for Global Health
Office of Population and Reproductive Health

2011

Family Planning
A GLOBAL HANDBOOK FOR PROVIDERS

Contents

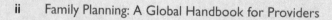

Searchable online at www.fphandbook.org

Forewords

From the World Health Organization

The job of family planning remains unfinished. Despite great progress over the last several decades, more than 120 million women worldwide want to prevent pregnancy, but they and their partners are not using contraception. Reasons for unmet need are many: Services and supplies are not yet available everywhere or choices are limited. Fear of social disapproval or partner's opposition pose formidable barriers. Worries of side effects and health concerns hold some people back; others lack knowledge about contraceptive options and their use. These people need help now.

Millions more are using family planning to avoid pregnancy but fail, for a variety of reasons. They may not have received clear instructions on how to use the method properly, could not get a method better suited to them, were not properly prepared for side effects, or supplies ran out. These people need better help now.

Moreover, the job of family planning never will be finished. In the next 5 years about 60 million girls and boys will reach sexual maturity. Generation after generation, there will always be people needing family planning and other health care.

While current challenges to health throughout the world are many and serious, the need to control one's own fertility probably touches more lives than any other health issue. It is crucial to people's well-being, particularly that of women—and fundamental to their self-determination.

How can this book help? By enabling health care providers to give better care to more people. In a straightforward, easily used way, this book translates scientific evidence into practical guidance on all major contraceptive methods. This guidance reflects the consensus of experts from the world's leading health organizations. With this book in hand, a provider can confidently serve clients with many different needs and knowledgeably offer a wide range of methods.

The World Health Organization (WHO) appreciates the many contributions to this book made by people from around the world. The collaboration to develop, by consensus, an evidence-based book of this scope and depth is a remarkable achievement. WHO would like to thank particularly the Johns Hopkins Bloomberg School of Public Health/Center for Communication Programs for its invaluable partnership in the preparation of this book. WHO also appreciates the commitment of the many organizations—United Nations agencies, members of the Implementing Best Practices Consortium, and many others—that are adopting this handbook and disseminating it to health care providers throughout the world with the financial support of a wide range of government agencies and other development partners. These concerted efforts attest that the job of improving the world's health lies in good hands.

Paul F.A. Van Look, MD PhD FRCOG
Former Director, Department of Reproductive Health and Research
World Health Organization

From the United States Agency for International Development

The practical, up-to-date guidance in this new handbook will help to improve the quality of family planning services and maximize people's access to them. It can help family planning providers to assist clients choosing a family planning method, to support effective use, and to solve clients' problems. Managers and trainers can use this book, too.

While this handbook covers many topics, 4 overall themes emerge:

1. Almost everyone can safely use almost any method, and providing most methods is usually not complicated. Thus, methods can be made widely available and offered even where health care resources are quite limited. This book defines and explains the many opportunities for people to choose, start, and change family planning methods appropriately.

2. Family planning methods can be effective when properly provided. For greatest effectiveness some methods, such as pills and condoms, require the user's conscientious action. The provider's help and support often can make the difference, such as discussing common possible side effects. Some methods require the provider to perform a procedure correctly, such as sterilization or IUD insertion. Short of giving instructions on performing procedures, this handbook offers the guidance and information that providers need to support effective and continuing contraceptive use.

3. New clients usually come for services with a method already in mind, and this is usually the best choice for them. Within the broad range of methods that a client can use safely, the client's purposes and preferences should govern family planning decisions. To find and use the most suitable method, a client needs good information and, often, help thinking through choices. This book provides information that client and provider may want to consider together.

4. Many continuing clients need little support, and for them convenient access is key. For ongoing clients who encounter problems or concerns, help and support are vital. This handbook provides counseling and treatment recommendations for these clients.

With the collaboration of the World Health Organization and many organizations, many experts worked together to create this book. The United States Agency for International Development is proud to support the work of many of the contributors' organizations and the publication of this book, as well as to have participated in developing its content. Together with the providers of family planning who use this book, we all endeavor to make the world a better place.

James D. Shelton, MD
Science Advisor, Bureau for Global Health
United States Agency for International Development

Acknowledgements

Vera Zlidar, Ushma Upadhyay, and Robert Lande of the INFO Project, Center for Communication Programs at Johns Hopkins Bloomberg School of Public Health were the principal technical writers and led the handbook development process, together with Ward Rinehart from the INFO Project and Sarah Johnson of the World Health Organization, who also served as editors. Other contributors to the research and writing from the INFO Project include Fonda Kingsley, Sarah O'Hara, Hilary Schwandt, Ruwaida Salem, Vidya Setty, Deepa Ramchandran, Catherine Richey, Mahua Mandal, and Indu Adhikary.

Key technical advisors throughout the development of the book include Robert Hatcher, Roy Jacobstein, Enriquito Lu, Herbert Peterson, James Shelton, and Irina Yacobson. Kathryn Curtis, Anna Glasier, Robert Hatcher, Roy Jacobstein, Herbert Peterson, James Shelton, Paul Van Look, and Marcel Vekemans conducted final technical review of this book.

The following people provided their expertise during expert meetings in Baltimore in October 2004, Geneva in June 2005, or both: Yasmin Ahmed, Marcos Arevalo, Luis Bahamondes, Miriam Chipimo, Maria del Carmen Cravioto, Kathryn Curtis, Juan Diaz, Soledad Diaz, Mohammad Eslami, Anna Glasier, John Guillebaud, Ezzeldin Othman Hassan, Robert Hatcher, Mihai Horga, Douglas Huber, Carlos Huezo, Roy Jacobstein, Enriquito Lu, Pisake Lumbiganon, Pamela Lynam, Trent MacKay, Olav Meirik, Isaiah Ndong, Herbert Peterson, John Pile, Robert Rice, Roberto Rivera, Lois Schaefer, Markku Seppala, James Shelton, Bulbul Sood, Markus Steiner, James Trussell, Marcel Vekemans, and Wu Shangchun.

The key contributors to this handbook, who are listed above, declared no conflicts of interest.

The following organizations made extraordinary technical contributions to the creation of this handbook: The Centre for Development and Population Activities, EngenderHealth, Family Health International, Georgetown University Institute for Reproductive Health, JHPIEGO, Management Sciences for Health, Population Council, and the United States Agency for International Development.

Many others also contributed their expertise on specific topics and participated in the development of consensus on technical content. Contributors include Christopher Armstrong, Mark Barone, Mags Beksinska, Yemane Berhane, Ann Blouse, Julia Bluestone, Paul Blumenthal, Annette Bongiovanni, Débora Bossemeyer, Nathalie Broutet, Ward

Cates, Venkatraman Chandra-Mouli, Kathryn Church, Samuel Clark, Carmela Cordero, Vanessa Cullins, Kelly Culwell, Johannes van Dam, Catherine d'Arcangues, Barbara Kinzie Deller, Sibongile Dludlu, Mary Drake, Paul Feldblum, Ron Frezieres, Claudia Garcia-Moreno, Kamlesh Giri, Patricia Gómez, Pio Iván Gómez Sánchez, Vera Halpern, Robert Hamilton, Theresa Hatzell, Helena von Hertzen, John Howson, Carol Joanis, Robert Johnson, Adrienne Kols, Deborah Kowal, Jan Kumar, Anne MacGregor, Luann Martin, Matthews Mathai, Noel McIntosh, Manisha Mehta, Kavita Nanda, Ruchira Tabassum Naved, Francis Ndowa, Nuriye Ortayli, Elizabeth Raymond, Heidi Reynolds, Mandy Rose, Sharon Rudy, Joseph Ruminjo, Dana Samu, Julia Samuelson, Harshad Sanghvi, George Schmid, Judith Senderowitz, Jacqueline Sherris, Nono Simelela, Irving Sivin, Jenni Smit, David Sokal, Jeff Spieler, Kay Stone, Maryanne Stone-Jimenez, Fatiha Terki, Kathleen Vickery, Lee Warner, Mary Nell Wegner, Peter Weis, and Tim Williams.

Family planning providers in Bangladesh, Brazil, China, Ghana, India, Indonesia, Kenya, Pakistan, the Philippines, and Zambia offered comments on draft covers and chapters of the book in sessions organized by Yasmin Ahmed, Ekta Chandra, Miriam Chipimo, Sharmila Das, Juan Diaz, Carlos Huezo, Enriquito Lu, Isaiah Ndong, Samson Radeny, Mary Segall, Sarbani Sen, Nina Shalita, Bulbul Sood, and Wu Shangchun.

John Fiege, Linda Sadler, and Rafael Avila created the layout of the book. Mark Beisser created the cover and initial design along with Linda Sadler, the staff at Prographics, and John Fiege. Rafael Avila managed the photographs and illustrations. Ushma Upadhyay, Vera Zlidar, and Robert Jacoby managed the book's production. Heather Johnson managed printing and distribution of the handbook along with Mandy Liberto, Tre Turner, Roslyn Suite-Parham, and Quan Wynder.

ISBN 13: 978-0-9788563-7-3
ISBN 10: 0-9788563-0-9

Suggested citation: World Health Organization Department of Reproductive Health and Research (WHO/RHR) and Johns Hopkins Bloomberg School of Public Health/Center for Communication Programs (CCP), Knowledge for Health Project. Family Planning: A Global Handbook for Providers (2011 update). Baltimore and Geneva: CCP and WHO, 2011.

Published with support from the United States Agency for International Development, Global, GH/SPBO/OPS, under the terms of Grant No. GPO-A-00-08-00006-00. Opinions expressed herein are those of the authors and do not necessarily reflect the views of USAID, The Johns Hopkins University, or the World Health Organization.

What's New in This Handbook?

This new handbook on family planning methods and related topics is the first of its kind: Through an organized, collaborative process, experts from around the world have come to consensus on practical guidance that reflects the best available scientific evidence. The World Health Organization (WHO) convened this process. Many major technical assistance and professional organizations have endorsed and adopted this guidance.

This book serves as a quick-reference resource for all levels of health care workers. It is the successor to *The Essentials of Contraceptive Technology*, first published in 1997 by the Center for Communication Programs at Johns Hopkins Bloomberg School of Public Health. In format and organization it resembles the earlier handbook. At the same time, all of the content of *Essentials* has been re-examined, new evidence has been gathered, guidance has been revised where needed, and gaps have been filled. This handbook reflects the family planning guidance developed by WHO. Also, this book expands on the coverage of *Essentials:* It addresses briefly other needs of clients that come up in the course of providing family planning.

New WHO Guidance Since 2007

Since the handbook was first published in 2007, the Department of Reproductive Health and Research of WHO convened an expert Working Group in April 2008 and two technical consultations in October 2008 and January 2010 to address questions for the Medical Eligibility Criteria (MEC) and the Selected Practice Recommendations and a technical consultation in June 2009 on the provision of progestin-only injectables by community health workers. Also, the HIV Department of WHO convened an expert Working Group in October 2009 to update guidance on infant feeding and HIV. This 2011 printing of the Global Handbook reflects new guidance developed in these meetings. (See p. 354.) Updates include:

- A woman may have a repeat injection of depot-medroxyprogesterone acetate (DMPA) up to 4 weeks late. (Previous guidance said that she could have her DMPA reinjection up to 2 weeks late.) The guidance for reinjection of norethisterone enanthate (NET-EN) remains at up to 2 weeks late. (See p. 74.)

- During breastfeeding, antiretroviral (ARV) therapy for the mother, for the HIV-exposed infant, or for both can significantly reduce the chances of HIV transmission through breast milk. HIV-infected mothers should receive the appropriate ARV therapy and should exclusively breastfeed their infants for the first 6 months of life, then introduce appropriate complementary foods and continue breastfeeding for the first 12 months of life. (See p. 294.)

- Postpartum women who are not breastfeeding can generally start combined hormonal methods at 3 weeks (MEC category 2). However, some women who have additional risk factors for venous thromboembolism (VTE) generally should not start combined hormonal methods until 6 weeks after childbirth, depending on the number, severity, and combination of the risk factors (MEC category 2/3). These additional risk factors include previous VTE, thrombophilia, caesarean delivery, blood transfusion at delivery, postpartum hemorrhage, pre-eclampsia, obesity, smoking, and being bedridden. (See p. 325.)

- Women with deep vein thrombosis who are established on anticoagulant therapy generally can use progestin-only contraceptives (MEC category 2) but not combined hormonal methods (MEC category 4). (See p. 327.)

- Women with systemic lupus erythematosus generally can use any contraceptive except that: (a) A woman with positive (or unknown) antiphospholipid antibodies should not use combined hormonal methods (MEC category 4) and generally should not use progestin-only methods (MEC category 3). (b) A woman with severe thrombocytopenia generally should not start a progestin-only injectable or have a copper-bearing IUD inserted (MEC category 3). (See p. 328.)

- Women with AIDS who are treated with ritonavir-boosted protease inhibitors, a class of ARV drugs, generally should not use combined hormonal methods or progestin-only pills (MEC category 3). These ARV drugs may make these contraceptive methods less effective. These women can use progestin-only injectables, implants, and other methods. Women taking only other classes of ARVs can use any hormonal method. (See p. 330.)

- Women with chronic hepatitis or mild cirrhosis of the liver can use any contraceptive method (MEC category 1). (See p. 331.)

- Women taking medicines for seizures or rifampicin or rifabutin for tuberculosis or other conditions generally can use implants. (See p. 332.)

New Guidance for Community-Based Provision of Injectables

- Community-based provision of progestin-only injectable contraceptives by appropriately trained community health workers is safe, effective, and acceptable. Such services should be part of a family planning program offering a range of contraceptive methods. (See p. 63.)

Other Content Addressing Important Questions

World Health Organization's 4 Cornerstones of Family Planning Guidance

This handbook is one of the World Health Organization's (WHO) 4 cornerstones of family planning guidance. Together, the 4 cornerstones support the safe and effective provision and use of family planning methods.

The first 2 cornerstones provide policy-makers and program managers with recommendations that can be used to establish or update national guidelines and program policies. The *Medical Eligibility Criteria for Contraceptive Use* (4th edition, 2010) provides guidance on whether people with certain medical conditions can safely and effectively use specific contraceptive methods. The *Selected Practice Recommendations for Contraceptive Use* (2nd edition, 2005) and the *Selected Practice Recommendations for Contraceptive Use: 2008 Update* answer specific questions about how to use various contraceptive methods. Both sets of guidance come from expert Working Group meetings convened by WHO.

The third cornerstone, the *Decision-Making Tool for Family Planning Clients and Providers,* incorporates the guidance of the first 2 cornerstones and reflects evidence on how best to meet clients' family planning needs. It is intended for use during counseling. The tool leads the provider and client through a structured yet tailored process that facilitates choosing and using a family planning method. The *Decision-Making Tool* also helps to guide return visits.

As the fourth cornerstone, *Family Planning: A Global Handbook for Providers* offers technical information to help health care providers deliver family planning methods appropriately and effectively. A thorough reference guide, the handbook provides specific guidance on 20 family planning methods and addresses many of providers' different needs, from correcting misunderstandings to managing side effects. Like the *Decision-Making Tool,* this handbook incorporates the guidance of the first 2 cornerstones. It also covers related health issues that may arise in the context of family planning.

The 4 cornerstones can be found on the WHO Web site at http://www.who.int/reproductionhealth/publications/family_planning/. The handbook can also be found on the Knowledge for Health Project Web site at http://www.fphandbook.org. Updates to the handbook and news about translations are posted on these Web sites. For information on ordering printed copies, see next page.

How to Obtain More Copies of This Book

The Knowledge for Health Project at Johns Hopkins Bloomberg School of Public Health/Center for Communication Programs offers copies of *Family Planning: A Global Handbook for Providers* free of charge to readers in developing countries. All others, please contact the Knowledge for Health Project for more information. To order, please send your name, mailing address, e-mail address, and telephone number.

To order by e-mail: orders@jhuccp.org
To order by fax: +1 410 659-6266
To order by phone: +1 410 659-6315
To order via the Web: http://www.fphandbook.org/
To order by mail:
Orders, Knowledge for Health Project
Center for Communication Programs
Johns Hopkins Bloomberg School of Public Health
111 Market Place, Suite 310
Baltimore, MD 21202, USA

CHAPTER 1

Combined Oral Contraceptives

Key Points for Providers and Clients

- **Take one pill every day.** For greatest effectiveness a woman must take pills daily and start each new pack of pills on time.

- **Bleeding changes are common but not harmful.** Typically, irregular bleeding for the first few months and then lighter and more regular bleeding.

- **Take any missed pill as soon as possible.** Missing pills risks pregnancy and may make some side effects worse.

- **Can be given to women at any time to start later.** If pregnancy cannot be ruled out, a provider can give her pills to take later, when her monthly bleeding begins.

What Are Combined Oral Contraceptives?

- Pills that contain low doses of 2 hormones—a progestin and an estrogen—like the natural hormones progesterone and estrogen in a woman's body.

- Combined oral contraceptives (COCs) are also called "the Pill," low-dose combined pills, OCPs, and OCs.

- Work primarily by preventing the release of eggs from the ovaries (ovulation).

How Effective?

Effectiveness depends on the user: Risk of pregnancy is greatest when a woman starts a new pill pack 3 or more days late, or misses 3 or more pills near the beginning or end of a pill pack.

- As commonly used, about 8 pregnancies per 100 women using COCs over the first year. This means that 92 of every 100 women using COCs will not become pregnant.

- When no pill-taking mistakes are made, less than 1 pregnancy per 100 women using COCs over the first year (3 per 1,000 women).

Return of fertility after COCs are stopped: No delay

Protection against sexually transmitted infections (STIs): None

Side Effects, Health Benefits, and Health Risks

Side Effects (see Managing Any Problems, p. 17)

Some users report the following:

- Changes in bleeding patterns including:
  - Lighter bleeding and fewer days of bleeding
  - Irregular bleeding
  - Infrequent bleeding
  - No monthly bleeding
- Headaches
- Dizziness
- Nausea
- Breast tenderness
- Weight change (see Question 6, p. 22)
- Mood changes
- Acne (can improve or worsen, but usually improves)

Other possible physical changes:

- Blood pressure increases a few points (mm Hg). When increase is due to COCs, blood pressure declines quickly after use of COCs stops.

Why Some Women Say They Like Combined Oral Contraceptives

- Are controlled by the woman
- Can be stopped at any time without a provider's help
- Do not interfere with sex

Known Health Benefits

Help protect against:

- Risks of pregnancy
- Cancer of the lining of the uterus (endometrial cancer)
- Cancer of the ovary
- Symptomatic pelvic inflammatory disease

May help protect against:

- Ovarian cysts
- Iron-deficiency anemia

Reduce:

- Menstrual cramps
- Menstrual bleeding problems
- Ovulation pain
- Excess hair on face or body
- Symptoms of polycystic ovarian syndrome (irregular bleeding, acne, excess hair on face or body)
- Symptoms of endometriosis (pelvic pain, irregular bleeding)

Known Health Risks

Very rare:

- Blood clot in deep veins of legs or lungs (deep vein thrombosis or pulmonary embolism)

Extremely rare:

- Stroke
- Heart attack

See also Facts About Combined Oral Contraceptives and Cancer, p. 4.

Correcting Misunderstandings (see also Questions and Answers, p. 22)

Combined oral contraceptives:

- Do not build up in a woman's body. Women do not need a "rest" from taking COCs.
- Must be taken every day, whether or not a woman has sex that day.
- Do not make women infertile.
- Do not cause birth defects or multiple births.
- Do not change women's sexual behavior.
- Do not collect in the stomach. Instead, the pill dissolves each day.
- Do not disrupt an existing pregnancy.

Facts About Combined Oral Contraceptives and Cancer

Ovarian and endometrial cancer

- Use of COCs helps *protect* users from 2 kinds of cancer—cancer of the ovaries and cancer of the lining of the uterus (endometrial cancer).

- This protection continues for 15 or more years after stopping use.

Breast cancer

- Research findings about COCs and breast cancer are difficult to interpret:

  - Studies find that women who have used COCs more than 10 years ago face the same risk of breast cancer as similar women who have never used COCs. In contrast, current users of COCs and women who have used COCs within the past 10 years are slightly more likely to be diagnosed with breast cancer.

  - When a current or former COC user is diagnosed with breast cancer, the cancers are less advanced than cancers diagnosed in other women.

  - It is unclear whether these findings are explained by earlier detection of existing breast cancers among COC users or by a biologic effect of COCs on breast cancer.

Cervical cancer

- Cervical cancer is caused by certain types of human papillomavirus (HPV). HPV is a common sexually transmitted infection that usually clears on its own without treatment, but sometimes persists.

- Use of COCs for 5 years or more appears to speed up the development of persistent HPV infection into cervical cancer. The number of cervical cancers associated with COC use is thought to be very small.

- If cervical screening is available, providers can advise COC users—and all other women—to be screened every 3 years (or as national guidelines recommend) to detect any precancerous changes on the cervix, which can be removed. Factors known to increase cervical cancer risk include having many children and smoking (see Cervical Cancer, p. 284.)

Who Can and Cannot Use Combined Oral Contraceptives

Safe and Suitable for Nearly All Women

Nearly all women can use COCs safely and effectively, including women who:

- Have or have not had children
- Are not married
- Are of any age, including adolescents and women over 40 years old
- Have just had an abortion or miscarriage
- Smoke cigarettes—if under 35 years old
- Have anemia now or had in the past
- Have varicose veins
- Are infected with HIV, whether or not on antiretroviral therapy, unless that therapy includes ritonavir (see Combined Oral Contraceptives for Women With HIV, p. 9)

Women can begin using COCs:

- Without a pelvic examination
- Without any blood tests or other routine laboratory tests
- Without cervical cancer screening
- Without a breast examination
- Even when a woman is not having monthly bleeding at the time, if it is reasonably certain she is not pregnant (see Pregnancy Checklist, p. 372)

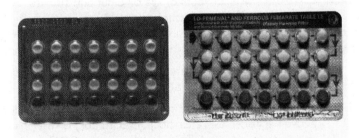

Combined Oral Contraceptives

Ask the client the questions below about known medical conditions. Examinations and tests are not necessary. If she answers "no" to all of the questions, then she can start COCs if she wants. If she answers "yes" to a question, follow the instructions. In some cases she can still start COCs. These questions also apply for the combined patch (see p. 102) and the combined vaginal ring (see p. 106).

---

1. **Are you breastfeeding a baby less than 6 months old?**

❑ NO ❑ YES

- If fully or nearly fully breastfeeding: Give her COCs and tell her to start taking them 6 months after giving birth or when breast milk is no longer the baby's main food—whichever comes first (see Fully or nearly fully breastfeeding, p. 10).

- If partially breastfeeding: She can start COCs as soon as 6 weeks after childbirth (see Partially breastfeeding, p. 11).

2. **Have you had a baby in the last 3 weeks and you are not breastfeeding?**

❑ NO ❑ YES Give her COCs now and tell her to start taking them 3 weeks after childbirth. (If there is an additional risk that she might develop a blood clot in a deep vein (deep vein thrombosis, or VTE), then she should not start COCs at 3 weeks after childbirth, but start at 6 weeks instead. These additional risk factors include previous VTE, thrombophilia, caesarean delivery, blood transfusion at delivery, postpartum hemorrhage, pre-eclampsia, obesity ($\geq$30 kg/m^2), smoking, and being bedridden for a prolonged time.)

3. **Do you smoke cigarettes?**

❑ NO ❑ YES If she is 35 years of age or older and smokes, do not provide COCs. Urge her to stop smoking and help her choose another method.

4. **Do you have cirrhosis of the liver, a liver infection, or liver tumor? (Are her eyes or skin unusually yellow? [signs of jaundice]) Have you ever had jaundice when using COCs?**

❑ NO ❑ YES If she reports serious active liver disease (jaundice, active hepatitis, severe cirrhosis, liver tumor) or ever had jaundice while using COCs, do not provide COCs. Help her choose a method without hormones. (She can use monthly injectables if she has had jaundice only with past COC use.)

5. Do you have high blood pressure?

❏ NO ❏ YES If you cannot check blood pressure and she reports a history of high blood pressure, or if she is being treated for high blood pressure, do not provide COCs. Refer her for a blood pressure check if possible or help her choose a method without estrogen.

Check blood pressure if possible:

- If her blood pressure is below 140/90 mm Hg, provide COCs.
- If her systolic blood pressure is 140 mm Hg or higher or diastolic blood pressure is 90 or higher, do not provide COCs. Help her choose a method without estrogen, but not progestin-only injectables if systolic blood pressure is 160 or higher or diastolic pressure is 100 or higher.

(One blood pressure reading in the range of 140–159/90–99 mm Hg is not enough to diagnose high blood pressure. Give her a backup method* to use until she can return for another blood pressure check, or help her choose another method now if she prefers. If her blood pressure at next check is below 140/90, she can use COCs.)

6. Have you had diabetes for more than 20 years or damage to your arteries, vision, kidneys, or nervous system caused by diabetes?

❏ NO ❏ YES Do not provide COCs. Help her choose a method without estrogen but not progestin-only injectables.

7. Do you have gallbladder disease now or take medication for gallbladder disease?

❏ NO ❏ YES Do not provide COCs. Help her choose another method but not the combined patch or combined vaginal ring.

8. Have you ever had a stroke, blood clot in your legs or lungs, heart attack, or other serious heart problems?

❏ NO ❏ YES If she reports heart attack, heart disease due to blocked or narrowed arteries, or stroke, do not provide COCs. Help her choose a method without estrogen but not progestin-only injectables. If she reports a current blood clot in the deep veins of the legs or lungs (not superficial clots), help her choose a method without hormones.

(Continued on next page)

* Backup methods include abstinence, male and female condoms, spermicides, and withdrawal. Tell her that spermicides and withdrawal are the least effective contraceptive methods. If possible, give her condoms.

9. Do you have or have you ever had breast cancer?

❑ NO ❑ YES Do not provide COCs. Help her choose a method without hormones.

10. Do you sometimes see a bright area of lost vision in the eye before a very bad headache (migraine aura)? Do you get throbbing, severe head pain, often on one side of the head, that can last from a few hours to several days and can cause nausea or vomiting (migraine headaches)? Such headaches are often made worse by light, noise, or moving about.

❑ NO ❑ YES If she has migraine aura at any age, do not provide COCs. If she has migraine headaches *without* aura *and* is age 35 or older, do not provide COCs. Help these women choose a method without estrogen. If she is under 35 and has migraine headaches without aura, she can use COCs (see Identifying Migraine Headaches and Auras, p. 368).

11. Are you taking medications for seizures? Are you taking rifampicin or rifabutin for tuberculosis or other illness?

❑ NO ❑ YES If she is taking barbiturates, carbamazepine, lamotrigine, oxcarbazepine, phenytoin, primidone, topiramate, rifampicin, rifabutin, or ritonavir, do not provide COCs. They can make COCs less effective. Help her choose another method but not progestin-only pills. If she is taking lamotrigine, help her choose a method without estrogen.

12. Are you planning major surgery that will keep you from walking for one week or more?

❑ NO ❑ YES If so, she can start COCs 2 weeks after the surgery. Until she can start COCs, she should use a backup method.

13. Do you have several conditions that could increase your chances of heart disease (coronary artery disease) or stroke, such as older age, smoking, high blood pressure, or diabetes?

❑ NO ❑ YES Do not provide COCs. Help her choose a method without estrogen but not progestin-only injectables.

Also, women should not use COCs if they report having thrombogenic mutations or lupus with positive (or unknown) antiphospholipid antibodies. For complete classifications, see Medical Eligibility Criteria for Contraceptive Use, p. 324. Be sure to explain the health benefits and risks and the side effects of the method that the client will use. Also, point out any conditions that would make the method inadvisable, when relevant to the client.

Using Clinical Judgment in Special Cases

Usually, a woman with any of the conditions listed below should not use COCs. In special circumstances, however, when other, more appropriate methods are not available or acceptable to her, a qualified provider who can carefully assess a specific woman's condition and situation may decide that she can use COCs. The provider needs to consider the severity of her condition and, for most conditions, whether she will have access to follow-up.

- Not breastfeeding and less than 3 weeks since giving birth
- Not breastfeeding and between 3 and 6 weeks postpartum with additional risk that she might develop a blood clot in a deep vein (VTE)
- Primarily breastfeeding between 6 weeks and 6 months since giving birth
- Age 35 or older and smokes fewer than 15 cigarettes a day
- High blood pressure (systolic blood pressure between 140 and 159 mm Hg or diastolic blood pressure between 90 and 99 mm Hg)
- Controlled high blood pressure, where continuing evaluation is possible
- History of high blood pressure, where blood pressure cannot be taken (including pregnancy-related high blood pressure)
- History of jaundice while using COCs in the past
- Gall bladder disease (current or medically treated)
- Age 35 or older and has migraine headaches without aura
- Younger than age 35 and has migraine headaches without aura that have developed or have gotten worse while using COCs
- Had breast cancer more than 5 years ago, and it has not returned
- Diabetes for more than 20 years or damage to arteries, vision, kidneys, or nervous system caused by diabetes
- Multiple risk factors for arterial cardiovascular disease such as older age, smoking, diabetes, and high blood pressure
- Taking barbiturates, carbamazepine, oxcarbazepine, phenytoin, primidone, topiramate, rifampicin, rifabutin, or ritonavir or ritonavir-boosted protease inhibitors. A backup contraceptive method should also be used because these medications reduce the effectiveness of COCs.
- Taking lamotrigine. Combined hormonal methods may make lamotrigine less effective.

Combined Oral Contraceptives for Women With HIV

- Women can safely use COCs even if they are infected with HIV, have AIDS, or are on antiretroviral (ARV) therapy unless their therapy includes ritonavir. Ritonavir may reduce the effectiveness of COCs. (See Medical Eligibility Criteria, p. 330.)

- Urge these women to use condoms along with COCs. Used consistently and correctly, condoms help prevent transmission of HIV and other STIs. Condoms also provide extra contraceptive protection for women on ARV therapy.

Providing Combined Oral Contraceptives

When to Start

IMPORTANT: A woman can start using COCs any time she wants if it is reasonably certain she is not pregnant. To be reasonably certain she is not pregnant, use the Pregnancy Checklist (see p. 372). Also, a woman can be given COCs at any time and told when to start taking them.

Woman's situation	When to start
Having menstrual cycles or switching from a nonhormonal method	**Any time of the month** • If she is starting within 5 days after the start of her monthly bleeding, no need for a backup method. • If it is more than 5 days after the start of her monthly bleeding, she can start COCs any time it is reasonably certain she is not pregnant. She will need a backup method* for the first 7 days of taking pills. (If you cannot be reasonably certain, give her COCs now and tell her to start taking them during her next monthly bleeding.) • If she is switching from an IUD, she can start COCs immediately (see Copper-Bearing IUD, Switching From an IUD to Another Method, p. 148).
Switching from a hormonal method	• Immediately, if she has been using the hormonal method consistently and correctly or if it is otherwise reasonably certain she is not pregnant. No need to wait for her next monthly bleeding. No need for a backup method. • If she is switching from injectables, she can begin taking COCs when the repeat injection would have been given. No need for a backup method.
Fully or nearly fully breastfeeding Less than 6 months after giving birth	• Give her COCs and tell her to start taking them 6 months after giving birth or when breast milk is no longer the baby's main food—whichever comes first.

* Backup methods include abstinence, male and female condoms, spermicides, and withdrawal. Tell her that spermicides and withdrawal are the least effective contraceptive methods. If possible, give her condoms.

Fully or nearly fully breastfeeding
(continued)

More than 6 months after giving birth	• If her monthly bleeding has not returned, she can start COCs any time it is reasonably certain she is not pregnant. She will need a backup method for the first 7 days of taking pills. (If you cannot be reasonably certain, give her COCs now and tell her to start taking them during her next monthly bleeding.)
	• If her monthly bleeding has returned, she can start COCs as advised for women having menstrual cycles (see previous page).

Partially breastfeeding

Less than 6 weeks after giving birth	• Give her COCs and tell her to start taking them 6 weeks after giving birth.
	• Also give her a backup method to use until 6 weeks since giving birth if her monthly bleeding returns before this time.
More than 6 weeks after giving birth	• If her monthly bleeding has not returned, she can start COCs any time it is reasonably certain she is not pregnant.† She will need a backup method for the first 7 days of taking pills. (If you cannot be reasonably certain, give her COCs now and tell her to start taking them during her next monthly bleeding.)
	• If her monthly bleeding has returned, she can start COCs as advised for women having menstrual cycles (see previous page).

Not breastfeeding

Less than 4 weeks after giving birth	• She can start COCs at any time on days 21–28 after giving birth. Give her pills any time to start during these 7 days. No need for a backup method. (If additional risk for VTE, wait until 6 weeks. See p. 6, Question 2.)

---

† *Where a visit 6 weeks after childbirth is routinely recommended and other opportunities to obtain contraception limited, some providers and programs may give COCs at the 6-week visit, without further evidence that the woman is not pregnant, if her monthly bleeding has not yet returned.*

Combined Oral Contraceptives

Woman's situation	When to start
Not breastfeeding (continued)	
More than 4 weeks after giving birth	• If her monthly bleeding has not returned, she can start COCs any time it is reasonably certain she is not pregnant.[†] She will need a backup method for the first 7 days of taking pills. (If you cannot be reasonably certain, give her COCs now and tell her to start taking them during her next monthly bleeding.) • If her monthly bleeding has returned, she can start COCs as advised for women having menstrual cycles (see p. 10).
No monthly bleeding (not related to childbirth or breastfeeding)	• She can start COCs any time it is reasonably certain she is not pregnant. She will need a backup method for the first 7 days of taking pills.
After miscarriage or abortion	• Immediately. If she is starting within 7 days after first- or second-trimester miscarriage or abortion, no need for a backup method. • If it is more than 7 days after first- or second-trimester miscarriage or abortion, she can start COCs any time it is reasonably certain she is not pregnant. She will need a backup method for the first 7 days of taking pills. (If you cannot be reasonably certain, give her COCs now and tell her to start taking them during her next monthly bleeding.)

After taking emergency contraceptive pills (ECPs)	• She can start COCs the day after she finishes taking the ECPs. There is no need to wait for her next monthly bleeding to start her pills.
	
	  – A new COC user should begin a new pill pack.
	
	  – A continuing user who needed ECPs due to pill-taking errors can continue where she left off with her current pack.
	
	  – All women will need to use a backup method for the first 7 days of taking pills.

[†] *Where a visit 6 weeks after childbirth is routinely recommended and other opportunities to obtain contraception limited, some providers and programs may give COCs at the 6-week visit, without further evidence that the woman is not pregnant, if her monthly bleeding has not yet returned.*

Giving Advice on Side Effects

IMPORTANT: Thorough counseling about bleeding changes and other side effects is an important part of providing the method. Counseling about bleeding changes may be the most important help a woman needs to keep using the method.

Describe the most common side effects	• In the first few months, bleeding at unexpected times (irregular bleeding). Then lighter, shorter, and more regular monthly bleeding. • Headaches, breast tenderness, weight change, and possibly other side effects.
Explain about these side effects	• Side effects are not signs of illness. • Most side effects usually become less or stop within the first few months of using COCs. • Common, but some women do not have them.
Explain what to do in case of side effects	• Keep taking COCs. Skipping pills risks pregnancy and can make some side effects worse. • Take each pill at the same time every day to help reduce irregular bleeding and also help with remembering. • Take pills with food or at bedtime to help avoid nausea. • The client can come back for help if side effects bother her.

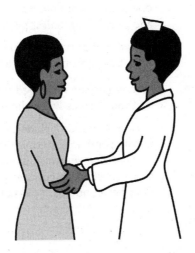

Explaining How to Use

1. Give pills	• Give as many packs as possible—even as much as a year's supply (13 packs).
2. Explain pill pack	• Show which kind of pack—21 pills or 28 pills. With 28-pill packs, point out that the last 7 pills are a different color and do not contain hormones. • Show how to take the first pill from the pack and then how to follow the directions or arrows on the pack to take the rest of the pills.
3. Give key instruction	• **Take one pill each day—** until the pack is empty. • Discuss cues for taking a pill every day. Linking pill-taking to a daily activity—such as cleaning her teeth—may help her remember. • Taking pills at the same time each day helps to remember them. It also may help reduce some side effects.
4. Explain starting next pack	• 28-pill packs: When she finishes one pack, she should take the first pill from the next pack on the very next day. • 21-pill packs: After she takes the last pill from one pack, she should wait 7 days—no more—and then take the first pill from the next pack. • It is very important to start the next pack on time. Starting a pack late risks pregnancy.
5. Provide backup method and explain use	• Sometimes she may need to use a backup method, such as when she misses pills. • Backup methods include abstinence, male or female condoms, spermicides, and withdrawal. Tell her that spermicides and withdrawal are the least effective contraceptive methods. Give her condoms, if possible.

Supporting the User

Managing Missed Pills

It is easy to forget a pill or to be late in taking it. COC users should know what to do if they forget to take pills. **If a woman misses one or more pills, she should follow the instructions below.** Use the tool on the inside back cover to help explain these instructions to the client.

Making Up Missed Pills With 30–35 µg Estrogen[‡]

Key message	• **Take a missed hormonal pill as soon as possible.** • Keep taking pills as usual, one each day. (She may take 2 pills at the same time or on the same day.)
Missed 1 or 2 pills? **Started new pack 1 or 2 days late?**	• Take a hormonal pill as soon as possible. • Little or no risk of pregnancy.
Missed pills 3 or more days in a row in the first or second week? Started new pack 3 or more days late?	• Take a hormonal pill as soon as possible. • Use a backup method for the next 7 days. • Also, if she had sex in the past 5 days, can consider ECPs (see Emergency Contraceptive Pills, p. 45).
Missed 3 or more pills in the third week?	• Take a hormonal pill as soon as possible. • Finish all hormonal pills in the pack. Throw away the 7 nonhormonal pills in a 28-pill pack. • Start a new pack the next day. • Use a backup method for the next 7 days. • Also, if she had sex in the past 5 days, can consider ECPs (see Emergency Contraceptive Pills, p. 45).
Missed any non-hormonal pills? (last 7 pills in 28-pill pack)	• Discard the missed nonhormonal pill(s). • Keep taking COCs, one each day. Start the new pack as usual.
Severe vomiting or diarrhea	• If she vomits within 2 hours after taking a pill, she should take another pill from her pack as soon as possible, then keep taking pills as usual. • If she has vomiting or diarrhea for more than 2 days, follow instructions for 3 or more missed pills, above.

[‡] *For pills with 20 µg of estrogen or less, women missing one pill should follow the same guidance as for missing one or two 30–35 µg pills. Women missing 2 or more pills should follow the same guidance as for missing 3 or more 30–35 µg pills.*

"Come Back Any Time": Reasons to Return

Assure every client that she is welcome to come back any time—for example, if she has problems, questions, or wants another method; she has any major change in health status; or she thinks she might be pregnant. Also if:

- She lost her pills or started a new pack more than 3 days late and also had sex during this time. She may wish to consider ECPs (see Emergency Contraceptive Pills, p. 45).

General health advice: Anyone who suddenly feels that something is seriously wrong with her health should immediately seek medical care from a nurse or doctor. Her contraceptive method is most likely not the cause of the condition, but she should tell the nurse or doctor what method she is using.

Planning the Next Visit

1. Encourage her to come back for more pills before she uses up her supply of pills.

2. An annual visit is recommended.

3. Some women can benefit from contact after 3 months of COC use. This offers an opportunity to answer any questions, help with any problems, and check on correct use.

Helping Continuing Users

1. Ask how the client is doing with the method and whether she is satisfied. Ask if she has any questions or anything to discuss.

2. Ask especially if she is concerned about bleeding changes. Give her any information or help that she needs (see Managing Any Problems, next page).

3. Ask if she often has problems remembering to take a pill every day. If so, discuss ways to remember, making up missed pills, and ECPs, or choosing another method.

4. Give her more pill packs—a full year's supply (13 packs), if possible. Plan her next resupply visit before she will need more pills.

5. Every year or so, check blood pressure if possible (see Medical Eligibility Criteria, Question 5, p. 7).

6. Ask a long-term client if she has had any new health problems since her last visit. Address problems as appropriate. For new health problems that may require switching methods, see p. 19.

7. Ask a long-term client about major life changes that may affect her needs—particularly plans for having children and STI/HIV risk. Follow up as needed.

Managing Any Problems

Problems Reported as Side Effects or Problems With Use

May or may not be due to the method.

- Problems with side effects affect women's satisfaction and use of COCs. They deserve the provider's attention. If the client reports side effects or problems, listen to her concerns, give her advice, and, if appropriate, treat.

- Encourage her to keep taking a pill every day even if she has side effects. Missing pills can risk pregnancy and may make some side effects worse.

- Many side effects will subside after a few months of use. For a woman whose side effects persist, give her a different COC formulation, if available, for at least 3 months.

- Offer to help the client choose another method—now, if she wishes, or if problems cannot be overcome.

Missed pills

- See Managing Missed Pills, p. 15.

Irregular bleeding (bleeding at unexpected times that bothers the client)

- Reassure her that many women using COCs experience irregular bleeding. It is not harmful and usually becomes less or stops after the first few months of use.

- Other possible causes of irregular bleeding include:
  - Missed pills
  - Taking pills at different times every day
  - Vomiting or diarrhea
  - Taking anticonvulsants or rifampicin (see Starting treatment with anticonvulsants or rifampicin, p. 20)

- To reduce irregular bleeding:
  - Urge her to take a pill each day and at the same time each day.
  - Teach her to make up for missed pills properly, including after vomiting or diarrhea (see Managing Missed Pills, p. 15).
  - For modest short-term relief, she can try 800 mg ibuprofen 3 times daily after meals for 5 days or other nonsteroidal anti-inflammatory drug (NSAID), beginning when irregular bleeding starts. NSAIDs provide some relief of irregular bleeding for implants, progestin-only injectables, and IUDs, and they may also help for COCs.
  - If she has been taking the pills for more than a few months and NSAIDs do not help, give her a different COC formulation, if available. Ask her to try the new pills for at least 3 months.

- If irregular bleeding continues or starts after several months of normal or no monthly bleeding, or you suspect that something may be wrong for other reasons, consider underlying conditions unrelated to method use (see Unexplained vaginal bleeding, next page).

No monthly bleeding

- Ask if she is having any bleeding at all. (She may have just a small stain on her underclothing and not recognize it as monthly bleeding.) If she is, reassure her.

- Reassure her that some women using COCs stop having monthly bleeding, and this is not harmful. There is no need to lose blood every month. It is similar to not having monthly bleeding during pregnancy. She is not infertile. Blood is not building up inside her. (Some women are happy to be free from monthly bleeding.)

- Ask if she has been taking a pill every day. If so, reassure her that she is not likely to be pregnant. She can continue taking her COCs as before.

- Did she skip the 7-day break between packs (21-day packs) or skip the 7 nonhormonal pills (28-day pack)? If so, reassure her that she is not pregnant. She can continue using COCs.

- If she has missed hormonal pills or started a new pack late:
  - She can continue using COCs.
  - Tell a woman who has missed 3 or more pills or started a new pack 3 or more days late to return if she has signs and symptoms of early pregnancy (see p. 371 for common signs and symptoms of pregnancy).
  - See p. 15 for instructions on how to make up for missed pills.

Ordinary headaches (nonmigrainous)

- Try the following (one at a time):
  - Suggest aspirin (325–650 mg), ibuprofen (200–400 mg), paracetamol (325–1000 mg), or other pain reliever.
  - Some women get headaches during the hormone-free week (the 7 days a woman does not take hormonal pills). Consider extended use (see Extended and Continuous Use of Combined Oral Contraceptives, p. 21).

- Any headaches that get worse or occur more often during COC use should be evaluated.

Nausea or dizziness

- For nausea, suggest taking COCs at bedtime or with food.

If symptoms continue:

- Consider locally available remedies.

- Consider extended use if her nausea comes after she starts a new pill pack (see Extended and Continuous Use of Combined Oral Contraceptives, p. 21).

Breast tenderness

- Recommend that she wear a supportive bra (including during strenuous activity and sleep).
- Try hot or cold compresses.
- Suggest aspirin (325–650 mg), ibuprofen (200–400 mg), paracetamol (325–1000 mg), or other pain reliever.
- Consider locally available remedies.

Weight change

- Review diet and counsel as needed.

Mood changes or changes in sex drive

- Some women have changes in mood during the hormone-free week (the 7 days when a woman does not take hormonal pills). Consider extended use (see Extended and Continuous Use of Combined Oral Contraceptives, p. 21).
- Ask about changes in her life that could affect her mood or sex drive, including changes in her relationship with her partner. Give her support as appropriate.
- Clients who have serious mood changes such as major depression should be referred for care.
- Consider locally available remedies.

Acne

- Acne usually improves with COC use. It may worsen for a few women.
- If she has been taking pills for more than a few months and acne persists, give her a different COC formulation, if available. Ask her to try the new pills for at least 3 months.
- Consider locally available remedies.

New Problems That May Require Switching Methods

May or may not be due to the method.

Unexplained vaginal bleeding (that suggests a medical condition not related to the method) or heavy or prolonged bleeding

- Refer or evaluate by history and pelvic examination. Diagnose and treat as appropriate.
- She can continue using COCs while her condition is being evaluated.
- If bleeding is caused by sexually transmitted infection or pelvic inflammatory disease, she can continue using COCs during treatment.

Starting treatment with anticonvulsants, rifampicin, rifabutin, or ritonavir

- Barbiturates, carbamazepine, oxcarbazepine, phenytoin, primidone, topiramate, rifampicin, rifabutin, and ritonavir may make COCs less effective. Combined hormonal methods, including combined pills and monthly injectables, may make lamotrigine less effective. If using these medications long-term, she may want a different method, such as a progestin-only injectable or a copper-bearing or LNG-IUD.

- If using these medications short-term, she can use a backup method along with COCs for greater protection from pregnancy.

Migraine headaches (see Identifying Migraine Headaches and Auras, p. 368)

- Regardless of her age, a woman who develops migraine headaches, with or without aura, or whose migraine headaches become worse while using COCs should stop using COCs.

- Help her choose a method without estrogen.

Circumstances that will keep her from walking for one week or more

- If she is having major surgery, or her leg is in a cast, or for other reasons she will be unable to move about for several weeks, she should:
  - Tell her doctors that she is using COCs.
  - Stop taking COCs and use a backup method during this period.
  - Restart COCs 2 weeks after she can move about again.

Certain serious health conditions (suspected heart or serious liver disease, high blood pressure, blood clots in deep veins of legs or lungs, stroke, breast cancer, damage to arteries, vision, kidneys, or nervous system caused by diabetes, or gall bladder disease). See Signs and Symptoms of Serious Health Conditions, p. 320.

- Tell her to stop taking COCs.
- Give her a backup method to use until the condition is evaluated.
- Refer for diagnosis and care if not already under care.

Suspected pregnancy

- Assess for pregnancy.
- Tell her to stop taking COCs if pregnancy is confirmed.
- There are no known risks to a fetus conceived while a woman is taking COCs (see Question 5, p. 22).

Extended and Continuous Use of Combined Oral Contraceptives

Some COC users do not follow the usual cycle of 3 weeks taking hormonal pills followed by one week without hormones. Some women take hormonal pills for 12 weeks without a break, followed by one week of nonhormonal pills (or no pills). This is extended use. Other women take hormonal pills without any breaks at all. This is continuous use. Monophasic pills are recommended for such use (see Question 16, p. 24).

Women easily manage taking COCs in different ways when properly advised how to do so. Many women value controlling when they have monthly bleeding—if any—and tailoring pill use as they wish.

Benefits of Extended and Continuous Use

- Women have vaginal bleeding only 4 times a year or not at all.
- Reduces how often some women suffer headaches, premenstrual syndrome, mood changes, and heavy or painful bleeding during the week without hormonal pills.

Disadvantages of Extended and Continuous Use

- Irregular bleeding may last as long as the first 6 months of use—especially among women who have never before used COCs.
- More supplies needed—15 to 17 packs every year instead of 13.

Extended Use Instructions

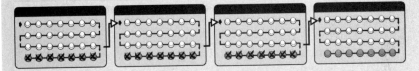

- Skip the last week of pills (without hormones) in 3 packs in a row. (21-day users skip the 7-day waits between the first 3 packs.) No backup method is needed during this time.
- Take all 4 weeks of pills in the 4th pack. (21-day users take all 3 weeks of pills in the 4th pack.) Expect some bleeding during this 4th week.
- Start the next pack of pills the day after taking the last pill in the 4th pack. (21-day users wait 7 days before starting the next pack.)

Continuous Use Instructions

Take one hormonal pill every day for as long as she wishes to use COCs. If bothersome irregular bleeding occurs, a woman can stop taking pills for 3 or 4 days and then start taking hormonal pills continuously again.

Questions and Answers About Combined Oral Contraceptives

1. **Should a woman take a "rest" from COCs after taking them for a time?**

   No. There is no evidence that taking a "rest" is helpful. In fact, taking a "rest" from COCs can lead to unintended pregnancy. COCs can safely be used for many years without having to stop taking them periodically.

2. **If a woman has been taking COCs for a long time, will she still be protected from pregnancy after she stops taking COCs?**

   No. A woman is protected only as long as she takes her pills regularly.

3. **How long does it take to become pregnant after stopping COCs?**

   Women who stop using COCs can become pregnant as quickly as women who stop nonhormonal methods. COCs do not delay the return of a woman's fertility after she stops taking them. The bleeding pattern a woman had before she used COCs generally returns after she stops taking them. Some women may have to wait a few months before their usual bleeding pattern returns.

4. **Do COCs cause abortion?**

   No. Research on COCs finds that they do not disrupt an existing pregnancy. They should not be used to try to cause an abortion. They will not do so.

5. **Do COCs cause birth defects? Will the fetus be harmed if a woman accidentally takes COCs while she is pregnant?**

   No. Good evidence shows that COCs will not cause birth defects and will not otherwise harm the fetus if a woman becomes pregnant while taking COCs or accidentally starts to take COCs when she is already pregnant.

6. **Do COCs cause women to gain or lose a lot of weight?**

   No. Most women do not gain or lose weight due to COCs. Weight changes naturally as life circumstances change and as people age. Because these changes in weight are so common, many women think that COCs cause these gains or losses in weight. Studies find, however, that, on average, COCs do not affect weight. A few women experience sudden changes in weight when using COCs. These changes reverse after they stop taking COCs. It is not known why these women respond to COCs in this way.

7. **Do COCs change women's mood or sex drive?**

Generally, no. Some women using COCs report these complaints. The great majority of COC users do not report any such changes, however, and some report that both mood and sex drive improve. It is difficult to tell whether such changes are due to the COCs or to other reasons. Providers can help a client with these problems (see Mood changes or changes in sex drive, p. 19). There is no evidence that COCs affect women's sexual behavior.

8. **What can a provider say to a client asking about COCs and breast cancer?**

The provider can point out that both COC users and women who do not use COCs can have breast cancer. In scientific studies breast cancer was slightly more common among women using COCs and those who had used COCs in the past 10 years than among other women. Scientists do not know whether or not COCs actually caused the slight increase in breast cancers. It is possible that the cancers were already there before COC use but were found sooner in COC users (see Facts About Combined Oral Contraceptives and Cancer, p. 4).

9. **Can COCs be used as a pregnancy test?**

No. A woman may experience some vaginal bleeding (a "withdrawal bleed") as a result of taking several COCs or one full cycle of COCs, but studies suggest that this practice does not accurately identify who is or is not pregnant. Thus, giving a woman COCs to see if she has bleeding later is not recommended as a way to tell if she is pregnant. COCs should not be given to women as a pregnancy test of sorts because they do not produce accurate results.

10. **Must a woman have a pelvic examination before she can start COCs or at follow-up visits?**

No. Instead, asking the right questions usually can help to make reasonably certain that a woman is not pregnant (see Pregnancy Checklist, p. 372). No condition that could be detected by a pelvic examination rules out COC use.

11. **Can women with varicose veins use COCs?**

Yes. COCs are safe for women with varicose veins. Varicose veins are enlarged blood vessels close to the surface of the skin. They are not dangerous. They are not blood clots, nor are these veins the deep veins in the legs where a blood clot can be dangerous (deep vein thrombosis). A woman who has or has had deep vein thrombosis should not use COCs.

12. Can a woman safely take COCs throughout her life?

Yes. There is no minimum or maximum age for COC use. COCs can be an appropriate method for most women from onset of monthly bleeding (menarche) to menopause (see Women Near Menopause, p. 272).

13. Can women who smoke use COCs safely?

Women younger than age 35 who smoke can use low-dose COCs. Women age 35 and older who smoke should choose a method without estrogen or, if they smoke fewer than 15 cigarettes a day, monthly injectables. Older women who smoke can take the progestin-only pill if they prefer pills. All women who smoke should be urged to stop smoking.

14. What if a client wants to use COCs but it is not reasonably certain that she is not pregnant after using the pregnancy checklist?

If pregnancy tests are not available, a woman can be given COCs to take home with instructions to begin their use within 5 days after the start of her next monthly bleeding. She should use a backup method until then.

15. Can COCs be used as emergency contraceptive pills (ECPs) after unprotected sex?

Yes. As soon as possible, but no more than 5 days after unprotected sex, a woman can take COCs as ECPs (see Emergency Contraceptive Pills, Pill Formulations and Dosing, p. 56). Progestin-only pills, however, are more effective and cause fewer side effects such as nausea and stomach upset.

16. What are the differences among monophasic, biphasic, and triphasic pills?

Monophasic pills provide the same amount of estrogen and progestin in every hormonal pill. Biphasic and triphasic pills change the amount of estrogen and progestin at different points of the pill-taking cycle. For biphasic pills, the first 10 pills have one dosage, and then the next 11 pills have another level of estrogen and progestin. For triphasic pills, the first 7 or so pills have one dosage, the next 7 pills have another dosage, and the last 7 hormonal pills have yet another dosage. All prevent pregnancy in the same way. Differences in side effects, effectiveness, and continuation appear to be slight.

17. Is it important for a woman to take her COCs at the same time each day?

Yes, for 2 reasons. Some side effects may be reduced by taking the pill at the same time each day. Also, taking a pill at the same time each day can help women remember to take their pills more consistently. Linking pill taking with a daily activity also helps women remember to take their pills.

CHAPTER 2

Progestin-Only Pills

This chapter focuses on progestin-only pills for breastfeeding women. Women who are not breastfeeding also can use progestin-only pills. Guidance that differs for women who are not breastfeeding is noted.

Key Points for Providers and Clients

- **Take one pill every day.** No breaks between packs.

- **Safe for breastfeeding women and their babies.** Progestin-only pills do not affect milk production.

- **Add to the contraceptive effect of breastfeeding.** Together, they provide effective pregnancy protection.

- **Bleeding changes are common but not harmful**. Typically, pills lengthen how long breastfeeding women have no monthly bleeding. For women having monthly bleeding, frequent or irregular bleeding is common.

- **Can be given to a woman at any time to start later.** If pregnancy cannot be ruled out, a provider can give her pills to take later, when her monthly bleeding begins.

What Are Progestin-Only Pills?

- Pills that contain very low doses of a progestin like the natural hormone progesterone in a woman's body.

- Do not contain estrogen, and so can be used throughout breastfeeding and by women who cannot use methods with estrogen.

- Progestin-only pills (POPs) are also called "minipills" and progestin-only oral contraceptives.

- Work primarily by:

  - Thickening cervical mucus (this blocks sperm from meeting an egg)

  - Disrupting the menstrual cycle, including preventing the release of eggs from the ovaries (ovulation)

How Effective?

Effectiveness depends on the user: For women who have monthly bleeding, risk of pregnancy is greatest if pills are taken late or missed completely.

Breastfeeding women:

- As commonly used, about 1 pregnancy per 100 women using POPs over the first year. This means that 99 of every 100 women will not become pregnant.

- When pills are taken every day, less than 1 pregnancy per 100 women using POPs over the first year (3 per 1,000 women).

Less effective for women not breastfeeding:

- As commonly used, about 3 to 10 pregnancies per 100 women using POPs over the first year. This means that 90 to 97 of every 100 women will not become pregnant.

- When pills are taken every day at the same time, less than 1 pregnancy per 100 women using POPs over the first year (9 per 1,000 women).

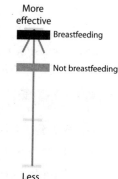

More effective

Breastfeeding

Not breastfeeding

Less effective

Return of fertility after POPs are stopped: No delay

Protection against sexually transmitted infections (STIs): None

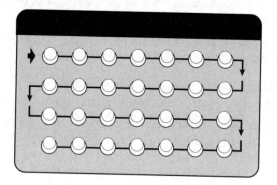

Why Some Women Say They Like Progestin-Only Pills

- Can be used while breastfeeding
- Can be stopped at any time without a provider's help
- Do not interfere with sex
- Are controlled by the woman

Side Effects, Health Benefits, and Health Risks

Side Effects (see Managing Any Problems, p. 38)

Some users report the following:

- Changes in bleeding patterns including:
  - For breastfeeding women, longer delay in return of monthly bleeding after childbirth (lengthened postpartum amenorrhea)
  - Frequent bleeding
  - Irregular bleeding
  - Infrequent bleeding
  - Prolonged bleeding
  - No monthly bleeding

  Breastfeeding also affects a woman's bleeding patterns.
- Headaches
- Dizziness
- Mood changes
- Breast tenderness
- Abdominal pain
- Nausea

Other possible physical changes:

- For women not breastfeeding, enlarged ovarian follicles

Known Health Benefits	*Known Health Risks*
Help protect against:	None
• Risks of pregnancy	

Correcting Misunderstandings (see also Questions and Answers, p. 42)

Progestin-only pills:

- Do not cause a breastfeeding woman's milk to dry up.
- Must be taken every day, whether or not a woman has sex that day.
- Do not make women infertile.
- Do not cause diarrhea in breastfeeding babies.
- Reduce the risk of ectopic pregnancy.

Who Can and Cannot Use Progestin-Only Pills

Safe and Suitable for Nearly All Women

Nearly all women can use POPs safely and effectively, including women who:

- Are breastfeeding (starting as soon as 6 weeks after childbirth)
- Have or have not had children
- Are not married
- Are of any age, including adolescents and women over 40 years old
- Have just had an abortion, miscarriage, or ectopic pregnancy
- Smoke cigarettes, regardless of woman's age or number of cigarettes smoked
- Have anemia now or had in the past
- Have varicose veins
- Are infected with HIV, whether or not on antiretroviral therapy, unless that therapy includes ritonavir (see Progestin-Only Pills for Women With HIV, p. 30)

Women can begin using POPs:

- Without a pelvic examination
- Without any blood tests or other routine laboratory tests
- Without cervical cancer screening
- Without a breast examination
- Even when a woman is not having monthly bleeding at the time, if it is reasonably certain she is not pregnant (see Pregnancy Checklist, p. 372)

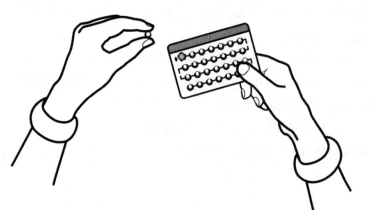

Medical Eligibility Criteria for
Progestin-Only Pills

Ask the client the questions below about known medical conditions. Examinations and tests are not necessary. If she answers "no" to all of the questions, then she can start POPs if she wants. If she answers "yes" to a question, follow the instructions. In some cases she can still start POPs.

1. **Are you breastfeeding a baby less than 6 weeks old?**

   ❑ NO ❑ **YES** She can start taking POPs as soon as 6 weeks after childbirth. Give her POPs now and tell her when to start taking them (see Fully or nearly fully breastfeeding or Partially breastfeeding, p. 31).

2. **Do you have severe cirrhosis of the liver, a liver infection, or liver tumor? (Are her eyes or skin unusually yellow? [signs of jaundice])**

   ❑ NO ❑ **YES** If she reports serious active liver disease (jaundice, severe cirrhosis, liver tumor), do not provide POPs. Help her choose a method without hormones.

3. **Do you have a serious problem now with a blood clot in your legs or lungs?**

   ❑ NO ❑ **YES** If she reports a current blood clot (not superficial clots), and she is not on anticoagulant therapy, do not provide POPs. Help her choose a method without hormones.

4. **Are you taking medication for seizures? Are you taking rifampicin or rifabutin for tuberculosis or other illness?**

   ❑ NO ❑ **YES** If she is taking barbiturates, carbamazepine, oxcarbazepine, phenytoin, primidone, topiramate, rifampicin, rifabutin, or ritonavir, do not provide POPs. They can make POPs less effective. Help her choose another method but not combined oral contraceptives.

5. **Do you have or have you ever had breast cancer?**

   ❑ NO ❑ **YES** Do not provide POPs. Help her choose a method without hormones.

Be sure to explain the health benefits and risks and the side effects of the method that the client will use. Also, point out any conditions that would make the method inadvisable, when relevant to the client.

Using Clinical Judgment in Special Cases

Usually, a woman with any of the conditions listed below should not use POPs. In special circumstances, however, when other, more appropriate methods are not available or acceptable to her, a qualified provider who can carefully assess a specific woman's condition and situation may decide that she can use POPs. The provider needs to consider the severity of her condition and, for most conditions, whether she will have access to follow-up.

- Breastfeeding and less than 6 weeks since giving birth
- Acute blood clot in deep veins of legs or lungs
- Had breast cancer more than 5 years ago, and it has not returned
- Severe liver disease, infection, or tumor
- Systemic lupus erythematosus with positive (or unknown) antiphospho-lipid antibodies
- Taking barbiturates, carbamazepine, oxcarbazepine, phenytoin, primidone, topiramate, rifampicin, rifabutin. or ritonavir or ritonavir-boosted protease inhibitors. A backup contraceptive method should also be used because these medications reduce the effectiveness of POPs.

Progestin-Only Pills for Women With HIV

- Women can safely use POPs even if they are infected with HIV, have AIDS, or are on antiretroviral (ARV) therapy unless their therapy includes ritonavir. Ritonavir may reduce the effectiveness of POPs. (See Medical Eligibility Criteria, p. 330.)

- Urge these women to use condoms along with POPs. Used consistently and correctly, condoms help prevent transmission of HIV and other STIs. Condoms also provide extra contraceptive protection for women on ARV therapy.

- For appropriate breastfeeding practices for women with HIV, see Maternal and Newborn Health, Preventing Mother-to-Child Transmission of HIV, p. 294.

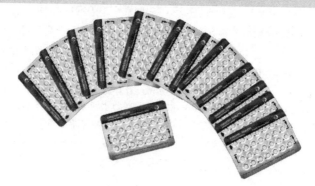

Providing Progestin-Only Pills

When to Start

IMPORTANT: A woman can start using POPs any time she wants if it is reasonably certain she is not pregnant. To be reasonably certain she is not pregnant, use the Pregnancy Checklist (see p. 372). Also, a woman can be given POPs at any time and told when to start taking them.

Woman's situation	When to start
Fully or nearly fully breastfeeding	
Less than 6 months after giving birth	• If she gave birth less than 6 weeks ago, give her POPs and tell her to start taking them 6 weeks after giving birth.
	• If her monthly bleeding has not returned, she can start POPs any time between 6 weeks and 6 months. No need for a backup method.
	• If her monthly bleeding has returned, she can start POPs as advised for women having menstrual cycles (see p. 33).
More than 6 months after giving birth	• If her monthly bleeding has not returned, she can start POPs any time it is reasonably certain she is not pregnant. She will need a backup method* for the first 2 days of taking pills. (If you cannot be reasonably certain, give her POPs now and tell her to start taking them during her next monthly bleeding.)
	• If her monthly bleeding has returned, she can start POPs as advised for women having menstrual cycles (see p. 33).
Partially breastfeeding	
Less than 6 weeks after giving birth	• Give her POPs and tell her to start taking them 6 weeks after giving birth.
	• Also give her a backup method to use until 6 weeks since giving birth if her monthly bleeding returns before this time.

---

* *Backup methods include abstinence, male and female condoms, spermicides, and withdrawal. Tell her that spermicides and withdrawal are the least effective contraceptive methods. If possible, give her condoms.*

Woman's situation	When to start

Partially breastfeeding
(continued)

More than 6 weeks after giving birth	• If her monthly bleeding has not returned, she can start POPs any time it is reasonably certain she is not pregnant.† She will need a backup method for the first 2 days of taking pills. (If you cannot be reasonably certain, give her POPs now and tell her to start taking them during her next monthly bleeding.) • If her monthly bleeding has returned, she can start POPs as advised for women having menstrual cycles (see next page).

Not breastfeeding

Less than 4 weeks after giving birth	• She can start POPs at any time. No need for a backup method.
More than 4 weeks after giving birth	• If her monthly bleeding has not returned, she can start POPs any time it is reasonably certain she is not pregnant.† She will need a backup method for the first 2 days of taking pills. (If you cannot be reasonably certain, give her POPs now and tell her to start taking them during her next monthly bleeding.) • If her monthly bleeding has returned, she can start POPs as advised for women having menstrual cycles (see next page).
Switching from a hormonal method	• Immediately, if she has been using the hormonal method consistently and correctly or if it is otherwise reasonably certain she is not pregnant. No need to wait for her next monthly bleeding. No need for a backup method. • If she is switching from injectables, she can begin taking POPs when the repeat injection would have been given. No need for a backup method.

† Where a visit 6 weeks after childbirth is routinely recommended and other opportunities to obtain contraception limited, some providers and programs may allow a woman to start POPs at the 6-week visit, without further evidence that the woman is not pregnant, if her monthly bleeding has not yet returned.

Woman's situation	When to start
Having menstrual cycles or switching from a nonhormonal method	**Any time of the month** • If she is starting within 5 days after the start of her monthly bleeding, no need for a backup method. • If it is more than 5 days after the start of her monthly bleeding, she can start POPs any time it is reasonably certain she is not pregnant. She will need a backup method for the first 2 days of taking pills. (If you cannot be reasonably certain, give her POPs now and tell her to start taking them during her next monthly bleeding.) • If she is switching from an IUD, she can start POPs immediately (see Copper-Bearing IUD, Switching From an IUD to Another Method, p. 148).
No monthly bleeding (not related to childbirth or breastfeeding)	• She can start POPs any time it is reasonably certain she is not pregnant. She will need a backup method for the first 2 days of taking pills.
After miscarriage or abortion	• Immediately. If she is starting within 7 days after first- or second-trimester miscarriage or abortion, no need for a backup method. • If it is more than 7 days after first- or second-trimester miscarriage or abortion, she can start POPs any time it is reasonably certain she is not pregnant. She will need a backup method for the first 2 days of taking pills. (If you cannot be reasonably certain, give her POPs now and tell her to start taking them during her next monthly bleeding.)
After taking emergency contraceptive pills (ECPs)	• She can start POPs the day after she finishes taking the ECPs. There is no need to wait for her next monthly bleeding to start her pills. — A new POP user should begin a new pill pack. — A continuing user who needed ECPs due to pill-taking errors can continue where she left off with her current pack. — All women will need to use a backup method for the first 2 days of taking pills.

Giving Advice on Side Effects

IMPORTANT: Thorough counseling about bleeding changes and other side effects is an important part of providing the method. Counseling about bleeding changes may be the most important help a woman needs to keep using the method.

Describe the most common side effects	• Breastfeeding women normally do not have monthly bleeding for several months after giving birth. POPs lengthen this period of time.
	• Women who are not breastfeeding may have frequent or irregular bleeding for the first several months, followed by regular bleeding or continued irregular bleeding.
	• Headaches, dizziness, breast tenderness, and possibly other side effects.
Explain about these side effects	• Side effects are not signs of illness.
	• Usually become less or stop within the first few months of using POPs. Bleeding changes, however, usually persist.
	• Common, but some women do not have them.
Explain what to do in case of side effects	• Keep taking POPs. Skipping pills risks pregnancy.
	• Try taking pills with food or at bedtime to help avoid nausea.
	• The client can come back for help if side effects bother her.

Explaining How to Use

1. Give pills	• Give as many packs as possible—even as much as a year's supply (11 or 13 packs).
2. Explain pill pack	• Show which kind of pack—28 pills or 35 pills.
	• Explain that all pills in POP packs are the same color and all are active pills, containing a hormone that prevents pregnancy.
	• Show how to take the first pill from the pack and then how to follow the directions or arrows on the pack to take the rest of the pills.
3. Give key instruction	• **Take one pill each day**— until the pack is empty.
	• Discuss cues for taking a pill every day. Linking pill-taking to a daily activity—such as cleaning her teeth— may help her remember.
	• Taking pills at the same time each day helps to remember them.
4. Explain starting next pack	• When she finishes one pack, she should take the first pill from the next pack on the very next day.
	• It is very important to start the next pack on time. Starting a pack late risks pregnancy.
5. Provide backup method and explain use	• Sometimes she may need to use a backup method, such as when she misses pills.
	• Backup methods include abstinence, male or female condoms, spermicides, and withdrawal. Tell her that spermicides and withdrawal are the least effective contraceptive methods. Give her condoms, if possible.
6. Explain that effectiveness decreases when breastfeeding stops	• Without the additional protection of breastfeeding itself, POPs are not as effective as most other hormonal methods.
	• When she stops breastfeeding, she can continue taking POPs if she is satisfied with the method, or she is welcome to come back for another method.

Supporting the User

Managing Missed Pills

It is easy to forget a pill or to be late in taking it. POP users should know what to do if they forget to take pills. **If a woman is 3 or more hours late taking a pill (12 or more hours late taking a POP containing desogestrel 75 mg), or if she misses a pill completely, she should follow the instructions below.** For breastfeeding women, whether missing a pill places her at risk of pregnancy depends on whether or not her monthly bleeding has returned.

Making Up Missed Progestin-Only Pills

Key message	• **Take a missed pill as soon as possible.** • Keep taking pills as usual, one each day. (She may take 2 pills at the same time or on the same day.)
Do you have monthly bleeding regularly?	• If yes, she also should use a backup method for the next 2 days. • Also, if she had sex in the past 5 days, can consider taking ECPs (see Emergency Contraceptive Pills, p. 45).
Severe vomiting or diarrhea	• If she vomits within 2 hours after taking a pill, she should take another pill from her pack as soon as possible, and keep taking pills as usual. • If her vomiting or diarrhea continues, follow the instructions for making up missed pills above.

"Come Back Any Time": Reasons to Return

Assure every client that she is welcome to come back any time—for example, if she has problems, questions, or wants another method; she has a major change in health status; or she thinks she might be pregnant. Also if:

- She has stopped breastfeeding and wants to switch to another method.

- For a woman who has monthly bleeding: If she took a pill more than 3 hours late or missed one completely, and also had sex during this time, she may wish to consider ECPs (see Emergency Contraceptive Pills, p. 45).

General health advice: Anyone who suddenly feels that something is seriously wrong with her health should immediately seek medical care from a nurse or doctor. Her contraceptive method is most likely not the cause of the condition, but she should tell the nurse or doctor what method she is using.

Planning the Next Visit

1. Encourage her to come back for more pills before she uses up her supply of pills.

2. Contacting women after the first 3 months of POP use is recommended. This offers an opportunity to answer any questions, help with any problems, and check on correct use.

Helping Continuing Users

1. Ask how the client is doing with the method and whether she is satisfied. Ask if she has any questions or anything to discuss.

2. Ask especially if she is concerned about bleeding changes. Give her any information or help that she needs (see Managing Any Problems, p. 38).

3. Ask if she often has problems remembering to take a pill every day. If so, discuss ways to remember, making up for missed pills, and ECPs, or choosing another method.

4. Give her more pill packs—as much as a full year's supply (11 or 13 packs), if possible. Plan her next resupply visit before she will need more pills.

5. Ask a long-term client if she has had any new health problems since her last visit. Address problems as appropriate. For new health problems that may require switching methods, see p. 41.

6. Ask a long-term client about major life changes that may affect her needs—particularly plans for having children and STI/HIV risk. Follow up as needed.

Managing Any Problems

Problems Reported as Side Effects or Problems With Use

May or may not be due to the method.

- Problems with side effects affect women's satisfaction and use of POPs. They deserve the provider's attention. If the client reports side effects or problems, listen to her concerns, give her advice, and, if appropriate, treat.

- Encourage her to keep taking a pill every day even if she has side effects. Missing pills can risk pregnancy.

- Many side effects will subside after a few months of use. For a woman whose side effects persist, give her a different POP formulation, if available, for at least 3 months.

- Offer to help the client choose another method—now, if she wishes, or if problems cannot be overcome.

No monthly bleeding

- Breastfeeding women:

  - Reassure her that this is normal during breastfeeding. It is not harmful.

- Women not breastfeeding:

  - Reassure her that some women using POPs stop having monthly bleeding, and this is not harmful. There is no need to lose blood every month. It is similar to not having monthly bleeding during pregnancy. She is not infertile. Blood is not building up inside her. (Some women are happy to be free from monthly bleeding.)

Irregular bleeding (bleeding at unexpected times that bothers the client)

- Reassure her that many women using POPs experience irregular bleeding—whether breastfeeding or not. (Breastfeeding itself also can cause irregular bleeding.) It is not harmful and sometimes becomes less or stops after the first several months of use. Some women have irregular bleeding the entire time they are taking POPs, however.

- Other possible causes of irregular bleeding include:

  - Vomiting or diarrhea

  - Taking anticonvulsants or rifampicin (see Starting treatment with anticonvulsants or rifampicin, p. 41)

- To reduce irregular bleeding:

  - Teach her to make up for missed pills properly, including after vomiting or diarrhea (see Managing Missed Pills, p. 36).

  - For modest short-term relief she can try 800 mg ibuprofen 3 times daily after meals for 5 days or other nonsteroidal anti-inflammatory drug (NSAID), beginning when irregular bleeding starts. NSAIDs provide some relief of irregular bleeding for implants, progestin-only injectables, and IUDs, and they may also help POP users.

- If she has been taking the pills for more than a few months and NSAIDs do not help, give her a different POP formulation, if available. Ask her to try the new pills for at least 3 months.

- If irregular bleeding continues or starts after several months of normal or no monthly bleeding, or you suspect that something may be wrong for other reasons, consider underlying conditions unrelated to method use (see Unexplained vaginal bleeding, p. 41).

Heavy or prolonged bleeding (twice as much as usual or longer than 8 days)

- Reassure her that some women using POPs experience heavy or prolonged bleeding. It is generally not harmful and usually becomes less or stops after a few months.

- For modest short-term relief she can try NSAIDs, beginning when heavy bleeding starts. Try the same treatments as for irregular bleeding (see previous page).

- To help prevent anemia, suggest she take iron tablets and tell her it is important to eat foods containing iron, such as meat and poultry (especially beef and chicken liver), fish, green leafy vegetables, and legumes (beans, bean curd, lentils, and peas).

- If heavy or prolonged bleeding continues or starts after several months of normal or no monthly bleeding, or you suspect that something may be wrong for other reasons, consider underlying conditions unrelated to method use (see Unexplained vaginal bleeding, p. 41).

Missed pills

- See Managing Missed Pills, p. 36.

Ordinary headaches (nonmigrainous)

- Suggest aspirin (325–650 mg), ibuprofen (200–400 mg), paracetamol (325–1000 mg), or other pain reliever.

- Any headaches that get worse or occur more often during POP use should be evaluated.

Mood changes or changes in sex drive

- Ask about changes in her life that could affect her mood or sex drive, including changes in her relationship with her partner. Give her support as appropriate.

- Some women experience depression in the year after giving birth. This is not related to POPs. Clients who have serious mood changes such as major depression should be referred for care.

- Consider locally available remedies.

Breast tenderness

- Breastfeeding women:
  - See Maternal and Newborn Health, Sore Breasts, p. 295.
- Women not breastfeeding:
  - Recommend that she wear a supportive bra (including during strenuous activity and sleep).
  - Try hot or cold compresses.
  - Suggest aspirin (325–650 mg), ibuprofen (200–400 mg), paracetamol (325–1000 mg), or other pain reliever.
  - Consider locally available remedies.

Severe pain in lower abdomen

- Abdominal pain may be due to various problems, such as enlarged ovarian follicles or cysts.
  - A woman can continue to use POPs during evaluation and treatment.
  - There is no need to treat enlarged ovarian follicles or cysts unless they grow abnormally large, twist, or burst. Reassure the client that they usually disappear on their own. To be sure the problem is resolving, see the client again in 6 weeks, if possible.
- With severe abdominal pain, be particularly alert for additional signs or symptoms of ectopic pregnancy, which is rare and not caused by POPs, but it can be life-threatening (see p. 44, Question 12).
- In the early stages of ectopic pregnancy, symptoms may be absent or mild, but eventually they will become severe. A combination of these signs or symptoms should increase suspicion of ectopic pregnancy:
  - Unusual abdominal pain or tenderness
  - Abnormal vaginal bleeding or no monthly bleeding—especially if this is a change from her usual bleeding pattern
  - Light-headedness or dizziness
  - Fainting
- If ectopic pregnancy or other serious health condition is suspected, refer at once for immediate diagnosis and care. (See Female Sterilization, Managing Ectopic Pregnancy, p. 179, for more on ectopic pregnancies.)

Nausea or dizziness

- For nausea, suggest taking POPs at bedtime or with food.
- If symptoms continue, consider locally available remedies.

New Problems That May Require Switching Methods

May or may not be due to the method.

Unexplained vaginal bleeding (that suggests a medical condition not related to the method)

- Refer or evaluate by history and pelvic examination. Diagnose and treat as appropriate.
- She can continue using POPs while her condition is being evaluated.
- If bleeding is caused by a sexually transmitted infection or pelvic inflammatory disease, she can continue using POPs during treatment.

Starting treatment with anticonvulsants, rifampicin, rifabutin, or ritonavir

- Barbiturates, carbamazepine, oxcarbazepine, phenytoin, primidone, topiramate, rifampicin, rifabutin, and ritonavir may make POPs less effective. If using these medications long-term, she may want a different method, such as progestin-only injectables or a copper-bearing IUD or LNG-IUD.
- If using these medications short-term, she can use a backup method along with POPs.

Migraine headaches (see Identifying Migraine Headaches and Auras, p. 368)

- If she has migraine headaches without aura, she can continue to use POPs if she wishes.
- If she has migraine aura, stop POPs. Help her choose a method without hormones.

Certain serious health conditions (suspected blood clots in deep veins of legs or lungs, liver disease, or breast cancer). See Signs and Symptoms of Serious Health Conditions, p. 320.

- Tell her to stop taking POPs.
- Give her a backup method to use until the condition is evaluated.
- Refer for diagnosis and care if not already under care.

Heart disease due to blocked or narrowed arteries (ischemic heart disease) **or stroke**

- A woman who has one of these conditions can safely start POPs. If, however, the condition develops after she starts using POPs, she should stop. Help her choose a method without hormones.
- Refer for diagnosis and care if not already under care.

Suspected pregnancy

- Assess for pregnancy, including ectopic pregnancy.
- Tell her to stop taking POPs if pregnancy is confirmed.
- There are no known risks to a fetus conceived while a woman is taking POPs (see Question 3, p. 42).

Questions and Answers About Progestin-Only Pills

1. **Can a woman who is breastfeeding safely use POPs?**

    Yes. This is a good choice for a breastfeeding mother who wants to use pills. POPs are safe for both the mother and the baby, starting as early as 6 weeks after giving birth. They do not affect milk production.

2. **What should a woman do when she stops breastfeeding her baby? Can she continue taking POPs?**

    A woman who is satisfied with using POPs can continue using them when she has stopped breastfeeding. She is less protected from pregnancy than when breastfeeding, however. She can switch to another method if she wishes.

3. **Do POPs cause birth defects? Will the fetus be harmed if a woman accidentally takes POPs while she is pregnant?**

    No. Good evidence shows that POPs will not cause birth defects and will not otherwise harm the fetus if a woman becomes pregnant while taking POPs or accidentally takes POPs when she is already pregnant.

4. **How long does it take to become pregnant after stopping POPs?**

    Women who stop using POPs can become pregnant as quickly as women who stop nonhormonal methods. POPs do not delay the return of a woman's fertility after she stops taking them. The bleeding pattern a woman had before she used POPs generally returns after she stops taking them. Some women may have to wait a few months before their usual bleeding pattern returns.

5. **If a woman does not have monthly bleeding while taking POPs, does this mean that she is pregnant?**

Probably not, especially if she is breastfeeding. If she has been taking her pills every day, she is probably not pregnant and can keep taking her pills. If she is still worried after being reassured, she can be offered a pregnancy test, if available, or referred for one. If not having monthly bleeding bothers her, switching to another method may help—but not to a progestin-only injectable.

6. **Must the POP be taken every day?**

Yes. All of the pills in the POP package contain the hormone that prevents pregnancy. If a woman does not take a pill every day— especially a woman who is not breastfeeding—she could become pregnant. (In contrast, the last 7 pills in a 28-pill pack of combined oral contraceptives are not active. They contain no hormones.)

7. **Is it important for a woman to take her POPs at the same time each day?**

Yes, for 2 reasons. POPs contain very little hormone, and taking a pill more than 3 hours late (more than 12 hours late with POPs containing desogestrel 75 mg) could reduce their effectiveness for women who are not breastfeeding. (Breastfeeding women have the additional protection from pregnancy that breastfeeding provides, so taking pills late is not as risky.) Also, taking a pill at the same time each day can help women remember to take their pills more consistently. Linking pill taking with a daily activity also helps women remember to take their pills.

8. **Do POPs cause cancer?**

No. Few large studies exist on POPs and cancer, but smaller studies of POPs are reassuring. Larger studies of implants have not shown any increased risk of cancer. Implants contain hormones similar to those used in POPs, and, during the first few years of implant use, at about twice the dosage.

9. **Can POPs be used as emergency contraceptive pills (ECPs) after unprotected sex?**

Yes. As soon as possible, but no more than 5 days after unprotected sex, a woman can take POPs as ECPs (see Emergency Contraceptive Pills, Pill Formulations and Dosing, p. 56). Depending on the type of POP, she will have to take 40 to 50 pills. This is many pills, but it is safe because there is very little hormone in each pill.

10. Do POPs change women's mood or sex drive?

Generally, no. Some women using POPs report these complaints. The great majority of POP users do not report any such changes, however, and some report that both mood and sex drive improve. It is difficult to tell whether such changes are due to the POPs or to other reasons. Providers can help a client with these problems (see Mood changes or changes in sex drive, p. 39). There is no evidence that POPs affect women's sexual behavior.

11. What should be done if a POP user has an ovarian cyst?

The great majority of cysts are not true cysts but actually fluid-filled structures in the ovary (follicles) that continue to grow beyond the usual size in a normal menstrual cycle. They may cause some mild abdominal pain, but they only require treatment if they grow abnormally large, twist, or burst. These follicles usually go away without treatment (see Severe pain in lower abdomen, p. 40).

12. Do POPs increase the risk of ectopic pregnancy?

No. On the contrary, POPs reduce the risk of ectopic pregnancy. Ectopic pregnancies are rare among POP users. The rate of ectopic pregnancy among women using POPs is 48 per 10,000 women per year. The rate of ectopic pregnancy among women in the United States using no contraceptive method is 65 per 10,000 women per year.

On the uncommon occasions that POPs fail and pregnancy occurs, 5 to 10 of every 100 of these pregnancies are ectopic. Thus, the great majority of pregnancies after POPs fail are not ectopic. Still, ectopic pregnancy can be life-threatening, so a provider should be aware that ectopic pregnancy is possible if POPs fail.

CHAPTER 3

Emergency Contraceptive Pills

Key Points for Providers and Clients

- **Emergency contraceptive pills help to prevent pregnancy when taken up to 5 days after unprotected sex.** The sooner they are taken, the better.

- **Do not disrupt an existing pregnancy.**

- **Safe for all women**—even women who cannot use ongoing hormonal contraceptive methods.

- **Provide an opportunity for women to start using an ongoing family planning method.**

- **Many options can be used as emergency contraceptive pills.** Dedicated products, progestin-only pills, and combined oral contraceptives all can act as emergency contraceptives.

What Are Emergency Contraceptive Pills?

- Pills that contain a progestin alone, or a progestin and an estrogen together—hormones like the natural hormones progesterone and estrogen in a woman's body.

- Emergency contraceptive pills (ECPs) are sometimes called "morning after" pills or postcoital contraceptives.

- Work primarily by preventing or delaying the release of eggs from the ovaries (ovulation). They do not work if a woman is already pregnant (see Question 1, p. 54).

What Pills Can Be Used as Emergency Contraceptive Pills?

- A special ECP product with levonorgestrel only, or estrogen and levonorgestrel combined, or ulipristal acetate
- Progestin-only pills with levonorgestrel or norgestrel
- Combined oral contraceptives with estrogen and a progestin— levonorgestrel, norgestrel, or norethindrone (also called norethisterone)

When to Take Them?

- *As soon as possible* after unprotected sex. The sooner ECPs are taken after unprotected sex, the better they prevent pregnancy.
- Can prevent pregnancy when taken any time up to 5 days after unprotected sex.

How Effective?

- If 100 women each had sex once during the second or third week of the menstrual cycle without using contraception, 8 would likely become pregnant.
- If all 100 women used progestin-only ECPs, one would likely become pregnant.
- If all 100 women used estrogen and progestin ECPs, 2 would likely become pregnant.

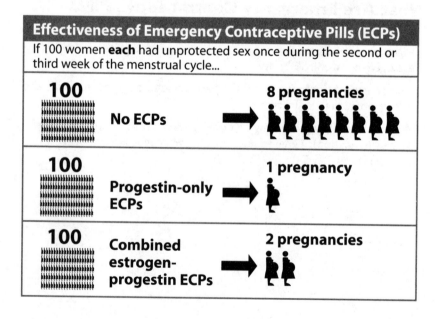

Effectiveness of Emergency Contraceptive Pills (ECPs)

If 100 women **each** had unprotected sex once during the second or third week of the menstrual cycle...

100 No ECPs	→	**8 pregnancies**
100 Progestin-only ECPs	→	**1 pregnancy**
100 Combined estrogen-progestin ECPs	→	**2 pregnancies**

Return of fertility after taking ECPs: No delay. A woman can become pregnant immediately after taking ECPs. Taking ECPs prevents pregnancy only from acts of sex that took place in the 5 days before. They will not protect a woman from pregnancy from acts of sex *after* she takes ECPs—not even on the next day. To stay protected from pregnancy, women must begin to use another contraceptive method at once (see Planning Ongoing Contraception, p. 51).

Protection against sexually transmitted infections (STIs): None

Side Effects, Health Benefits, and Health Risks

Side Effects (see Managing Any Problems, p. 53)

Some users report the following:

- Changes in bleeding patterns including:
  - Slight irregular bleeding for 1–2 days after taking ECPs
  - Monthly bleeding that starts earlier or later than expected

In the week after taking ECPs:

- Nausea[‡]
- Abdominal pain
- Fatigue
- Headaches
- Breast tenderness
- Dizziness
- Vomiting[‡]

Known Health Benefits	*Known Health Risks*
Help protect against:	None
• Risks of pregnancy	

[‡] *Women using progestin-only ECP formulations are much less likely to experience nausea and vomiting than women using estrogen and progestin ECP formulations.*

Correcting Misunderstandings (see also Questions and Answers, p. 54)

Emergency contraceptive pills:

- Do not cause abortion.
- Do not cause birth defects if pregnancy occurs.
- Are not dangerous to a woman's health.
- Do not promote sexual risk-taking.
- Do not make women infertile.

Why Some Women Say They Like Emergency Contraceptive Pills

- Offer a second chance at preventing pregnancy
- Are controlled by the woman
- Reduce seeking out abortion in the case of contraceptive errors or if contraception is not used
- Can have on hand in case an emergency arises

Who Can Use Emergency Contraceptive Pills

Safe and Suitable for All Women

Tests and examinations are not necessary for using ECPs. They may be appropriate for other reasons—especially if sex was forced (see Violence Against Women, Provide Appropriate Care, p. 302).

Medical Eligibility Criteria for

Emergency Contraceptive Pills

All women can use ECPs safely and effectively, including women who cannot use ongoing hormonal contraceptive methods. Because of the short-term nature of their use, there are no medical conditions that make ECPs unsafe for any woman.

Providing Emergency Contraceptive Pills

ECPs may be needed in many different situations. Therefore, if possible, give all women who want ECPs a supply in advance. A woman can keep them in case she needs them. Women are more likely to use ECPs if they already have them when needed. Also, having them on hand enables women to take them as soon as possible after unprotected sex.

When to Use

- Any time within 5 days after unprotected sex. The sooner after unprotected sex that ECPs are taken, the more effective they are.

ECPs Appropriate in Many Situations

ECPs can be used any time a woman is worried that she might become pregnant. For example, after:

- Sex was forced (rape) or coerced

- Any unprotected sex

- Contraceptive mistakes, such as:

  - Condom was used incorrectly, slipped, or broke

  - Couple incorrectly used a fertility awareness method (for example, failed to abstain or to use another method during the fertile days)

  - Man failed to withdraw, as intended, before he ejaculated

  - Woman has missed 3 or more combined oral contraceptive pills or has started a new pack 3 or more days late

  - IUD has come out of place

  - Woman is more than 4 weeks late for her repeat injection of DMPA, more than 2 weeks late for her repeat injection of NET-EN, or more than 7 days late for her repeat monthly injection

Dosing Information

For specific products and number of pills to provide, see Pill Formulations and Dosing, p. 56.

Pill type	Total dosage to provide
Levonorgestrel-only dedicated product	• 1.5 mg of levonorgestrel in a single dose.[§]
Estrogen-progestin dedicated product	• 0.1 mg ethinyl estradiol + 0.5 mg levonorgestrel. Follow with same dose 12 hours later.
Progestin-only pills with levonorgestrel or norgestrel	• Levonorgestrel pills: 1.5 mg levonorgestrel in a single dose. • Norgestrel pills: 3 mg norgestrel in a single dose.
Combined (estrogen-progestin) oral contraceptives containing levonorgestrel, norgestrel, or norethindrone	• Estrogen and levonorgestrel pills: 0.1 mg ethinyl estradiol + 0.5 mg levonorgestrel. Follow with same dose 12 hours later. • Estrogen and norgestrel pills: 0.1 mg ethinyl estradiol + 1 mg norgestrel. Follow with same dose 12 hours later. • Estrogen and norethindrone pills: 0.1 mg ethinyl estradiol + 2 mg norethindrone. Follow with same dose 12 hours later.
Ulipristal acetate dedicated product	• 30 mg of ulipristal acetate in a single dose.

Giving Emergency Contraceptive Pills

1. Give pills	• She can take them at once. • If she is using a 2-dose regimen, tell her to take the next dose in 12 hours.
2. Describe the most common side effects	• Nausea, abdominal pain, possibly others. • Slight bleeding or change in timing of monthly bleeding. • Side effects are not signs of illness.

[§] *Alternatively, clients can be given 0.75 mg levonorgestrel at once, followed by the same dose 12 hours later. One dose is easier for the client to take and works just as well as 2 doses.*

3. Explain what to do about side effects	• Nausea:
	
	  – Routine use of anti-nausea medications is not recommended.
	
	  – Women who have had nausea with previous ECP use or with the first dose of a 2-dose regimen can take anti-nausea medication such as 50 mg meclizine (Agyrax, Antivert, Bonine, Postafene) one-half to one hour before taking ECPs.
	
	• Vomiting:
	
	  – If the woman vomits within 2 hours after taking ECPs, she should take another dose. (She can use anti-nausea medication with this repeat dose, as above.) If vomiting continues, she can take the repeat dose by placing the pills high in her vagina. If vomiting occurs more than 2 hours after taking ECPs, she does not need to take any extra pills.

4. Give more ECPs and help her start an ongoing method	• If possible, give her more ECPs to take home in case she needs them in the future. • See Planning Ongoing Contraception, below.

"Come Back Any Time": Reasons to Return

No routine return visit is required. Assure every client that she is welcome to come back any time, however, and also if:

• She thinks she might be pregnant, especially if she has no monthly bleeding or her next monthly bleeding is delayed by more than one week.

Planning Ongoing Contraception

1. Explain that ECPs will not protect her from pregnancy for any future sex—even the next day. Discuss the need for and choice of ongoing pregnancy prevention and, if at risk, protection from STIs including HIV (see Sexually Transmitted Infections, Including HIV, p. 275).

2. If she does not want to start a contraceptive method now, give her condoms or oral contraceptives and ask her to use them if she changes her mind. Give instructions on use. Invite her to come back any time if she wants another method or has any questions or problems.

3. If possible, give her more ECPs to use in the future in case of unprotected sex.

When to Start Contraception After ECP Use

Method	When to start

Combined oral contraceptives, progestin-only pills, combined patch, combined vaginal ring	Can begin the day after she takes the ECPs. *No need to wait for her next monthly bleeding.*
	
	• Oral contraceptives and vaginal ring:
	  – New users should begin a new pill pack or ring.
	  – A continuing user who needed ECPs due to error can resume use as before.
	• Patch:
	  – All users should begin a new patch.
	• All women need to use a backup method* for the first 7 days of using their method.

Progestin-only injectables	• She can start progestin-only injectables on the same day as the ECPs, or if preferred, within 7 days after the start of her monthly bleeding. She will need a backup method for the first 7 days after the injection. She should return if she has signs or symptoms of pregnancy other than not having monthly bleeding (see p. 371 for common signs and symptoms of pregnancy).
Monthly injectables	• She can start monthly injectables on the same day as the ECPs. There is no need to wait for her next monthly bleeding to have the injection. She will need a backup method for the first 7 days after the injection.
Implants	• After her monthly bleeding has returned. Give her a backup method or oral contraceptives to use until then, starting the day after she finishes taking the ECPs.
Intrauterine device (copper-bearing or hormonal IUDs)	• A copper-bearing IUD can be used for emergency contraception. This is a good option for a woman who wants an IUD as her long-term method (see Copper-Bearing IUD, p. 131). • If she decides to use an IUD after taking ECPs, the IUD can be inserted on the same day she takes the ECPs. No need for a backup method.

* Backup methods include abstinence, male and female condoms, spermicides, and withdrawal. Tell her that spermicides and withdrawal are the least effective contraceptive methods. If possible, give her condoms.

Method	When to start
Male and female condoms, spermicides, diaphragms, cervical caps, withdrawal	• Immediately.
Fertility awareness methods	• Standard Days Method: With the start of her next monthly bleeding. • Symptoms-based methods: Once normal secretions have returned. • Give her a backup method or oral contraceptives to use until she can begin the method of her choice.

Helping Users

Managing Any Problems

Problems Reported as Side Effects or Method Failure

May or may not be due to the method.

Slight irregular bleeding

• Irregular bleeding due to ECPs will stop without treatment.

• Assure the woman that this is not a sign of illness or pregnancy.

Change in timing of next monthly bleeding or suspected pregnancy

• Monthly bleeding may start earlier or later than expected. This is not a sign of illness or pregnancy.

• If her next monthly bleeding is more than one week later than expected after taking ECPs, assess for pregnancy. There are no known risks to a fetus conceived if ECPs fail to prevent pregnancy (see Question 2, p. 54).

Questions and Answers About Emergency Contraceptive Pills

1. **Do ECPs disrupt an existing pregnancy?**

   No. ECPs do not work if a woman is already pregnant. When taken before a woman has ovulated, ECPs prevent the release of an egg from the ovary or delay its release by 5 to 7 days. By then, any sperm in the woman's reproductive tract will have died, since sperm can survive there for only about 5 days.

2. **Do ECPs cause birth defects? Will the fetus be harmed if a woman accidentally takes ECPs while she is pregnant?**

   No. Good evidence shows that ECPs will not cause birth defects and will not otherwise harm the fetus if a woman is already pregnant when she takes ECPs or if ECPs fail to prevent pregnancy.

3. **How long do ECPs protect a woman from pregnancy?**

   Women who take ECPs should understand that they could become pregnant the next time they have sex unless they begin to use another method of contraception at once. Because ECPs delay ovulation in some women, *she may be most fertile soon after taking ECPs.* If she wants ongoing protection from pregnancy, she must start using another contraceptive method at once.

4. **What oral contraceptive pills can be used as ECPs?**

   Many combined (estrogen-progestin) oral contraceptives and progestin-only pills can be used as ECPs. Any pills containing the hormones used for emergency contraception—levonorgestrel, norgestrel, norethindrone, and these progestins together with estrogen (ethinyl estradiol)—can be used. (See Pill Formulations and Dosing, p. 56, for examples of what pills can be used.)

5. **Is it safe to take 40 or 50 progestin-only pills as ECPs?**

   Yes. Progestin-only pills contain very small amounts of hormone. Thus, it is necessary to take many pills in order to receive the total ECP dose needed. In contrast, the ECP dosage with combined (estrogen-progestin) oral contraceptives is generally only 2 to 5 pills in each of 2 doses 12 hours apart. Women should not take 40 or 50 combined (estrogen-progestin) oral contraceptive pills as ECPs.

6. **Are ECPs safe for women with HIV or AIDS? Can women on antiretroviral therapy safely use ECPs?**

   Yes. Women with HIV, AIDS, and those on antiretroviral therapy can safely use ECPs.

7. **Are ECPs safe for adolescents?**

   Yes. A study of ECP use among girls 13 to 16 years old found it safe. Furthermore, all of the study participants were able to use ECPs correctly.

8. **Can a woman who cannot use combined (estrogen-progestin) oral contraceptives or progestin-only pills as an ongoing method still safely use ECPs?**

   Yes. This is because ECP treatment is very brief.

9. **If ECPs failed to prevent pregnancy, does a woman have a greater chance of that pregnancy being an ectopic pregnancy?**

   No. To date, no evidence suggests that ECPs increase the risk of ectopic pregnancy. Worldwide studies of progestin-only ECPs, including a United States Food and Drug Administration review, have not found higher rates of ectopic pregnancy after ECPs failed than are found among pregnancies generally.

10. **Why give women ECPs before they need them? Won't that discourage or otherwise affect contraceptive use?**

    No. Studies of women given ECPs in advance report these findings:

    - Women who have ECPs on hand took them sooner after having unprotected sex than women who had to seek out ECPs. Taken sooner, the ECPs are more likely to be effective.

    - Women given ECPs ahead of time were more likely to use ECPs than women who had to go to a provider to get ECPs.

    - Women continued to use other contraceptive methods as they did before obtaining ECPs in advance.

11. **Should women use ECPs as a regular method of contraception?**

    No. Nearly all other contraceptive methods are more effective in preventing pregnancy. A woman who uses ECPs regularly for contraception is more likely to have an unintended pregnancy than a woman who uses another contraceptive regularly. Still, women using other methods of contraception should know about ECPs and how to obtain them if needed—for example, if a condom breaks or a woman misses 3 or more combined oral contraceptive pills.

12. **If a woman buys ECPs over the counter, can she use them correctly?**

    Yes. Taking ECPs is simple, and medical supervision is not needed. Studies show that young and adult women find the label and instructions easy to understand. ECPs are approved for over-the-counter sales or nonprescription use in many countries.

Pill Formulations and Dosing
for Emergency Contraception

Hormonal and Pill Type	Formulation	Common Brand Names	Pills to Take	
			At First	12 Hours Later
Progestin-only				
Progestin-only dedicated ECPs	1.5 mg LNG	An Ting 1.5, Anlitin 1.5, Bao Shi Ting, D-Sigyent 1, Dan Mei, Emkit DS, Emkit Plus, Escapel, Escapel-1, Escapelle, Escapelle 1.5, Escinor 1.5, Glanique 1, Hui Ting 1.5, i-pill, Impreviat 1500, Jin Yu Ting, Jin Xiao, Ka Rui Ding, Ladiades 1.5, Levonelle 1500, Levonelle-1, Levonelle One Step, Levonorgestrel Biogaran 1500, Mergynex Plus, Nogestrol 1, Norgestrel Max Unidosis, NorLevo 1.5, Ovulol UD, Plan B One Step, PostDay 1, Postinor-1, Postinor 1.5, Postinor 1500, Postinor 2 SD, Postinor-2 Unidosis, Postinor New, Postinor Uno, Pozato Uni, Pregnon 1.5, Prikul 1, Secufem Plus, Segurite UD, Silogen 1.5, Tace 1.5, Tibex 1.5, Unlevo 1500, Unofem, Velor 1.5, Vikela, Xian Ju	1	0
	0.75 mg LNG	Ai Wu You, Alterna, An Ting 0.75, Anthia, Auxxil, Bao Shi Ting (Postinor-2), Ceciora T, Contraplan II, D-Sigyent, Dan Mei, Dia-Post, Dia-Post Gold, Diad, Duet, E Pills, EC, ECee2, ECP, Escinor 0.75, Emergyn, Emkit, Escapel-2, Estinor, Evital, Evitarem, Glanique, Glanix, Gynotrel 2, Hui Ting, Imediat, Imediat-N, Impreviat 750, Jin Xiao, L Novafem, Ladiades 0.75, Le Ting, Lenor 72, Levogynon, Levonelle, Levonelle-2, LNG-Method 5, Longil, Madonna, Me Tablet, Minipil 2, Next Choice, Nogestrol, Nogravide, Norgestrel-Max, NorLevo 0.75, Nortrel 2, Novanor 2, Nuo Shuang, Optinor, Ovocease, Ovulol, P2, Pilem, Pill 72, Pillex, Plan B, Poslov, PostDay, Postinor, Postinor-2, Postinor Duo, Postpill, Pozato, PPMS, Pregnon, Prevemb, Preventol, Prevyol, Prikul, Pronta, Rigesoft, Safex, Secufem, Seguidet, Segurité, Silogin 0.75, Smart Lady (Pregnon), Tace, Tibex, Velor 72, Vermagest, Vika, Yi Ting, Yu Ping, Yu Ting, Zintemore	2	0

LNG = levonorgestrel   EE = ethinyl estradiol

Hormonal and Pill Type	Formu- lation	Common Brand Names	Pills to Take	
			At First	12 Hours Later
Progestin- only pills	0.03 mg LNG	28 Mini, Follistrel, Microlut, Microlut 35, Microluton, Microval, Mikro-30, Norgeston, Nortrel	50*	0
	0.0375 mg LNG	Neogest, Norgeal	40*	0
	0.075 mg norgestrel	Minicon, Ovrette	40*	0
Estrogen and Progestin				
Estrogen- progestin dedicated ECPs	0.05 mg EE + 0.25 mg LNG	Control NF, Fertilan, Tetragynon	2	2
Combined (estrogen- progestin) oral contra- ceptives	0.02 mg EE + 0.1 mg LNG	Alesse, Anulette 20, April, Aviane, Femexin, Leios, Lessina, Levlite, Loette, Loette-21, Loette-28, Loette Suave, LoSeasonique, Lovette, Lowette, Lutera, Microgynon 20, Microgynon Suave, Microlevlen, Microlite, Miranova, Norvetal 20, Sronyx	5	5
	0.03 mg EE + 0.15 mg LNG	Anna, Anovulatorios Microdosis, Anulette CD, Anulit, Charlize, Ciclo 21, Ciclon, Combination 3, Confiance, Contraceptive L.D., Eugynon 30ED, Famila-28, Femigoa, Femranette mikro, Follimin, Gestrelan, Gynatrol, Innova CD, Jolessa, Lady, Levlen, Levlen 21, Levlen 28, Levonorgestrel Pill, Levora, Logynon (take ochre pills only), Lorsax, Ludéal Gé, Mala-D, Microfemin, Microfemin CD, Microgest, Microgest ED, Microgyn, Microgynon, Microgynon-21, Microgynon-28, Microgynon-30, Microgynon 30ED, Microgynon CD, Microgynon ED, Microgynon ED 28, Microsoft CD, Microvlar, Minidril, Minigynon, Minigynon 30, Minivlar, Mithuri, Monofeme, Neomonovar, Neovletta, Nociclin, Nordet, Nordette, Nordette 150/30, Nordette-21, Nordette-28, Norgylene, Norvetal, Nouvelle Duo,	4	4

*Many pills, but safe. See p. 54, Q&A 5.

LNG = levonorgestrel   EE = ethinyl estradiol

(continued)

Hormonal and Pill Type	Formu-lation	Common Brand Names	Pills to Take	
			At First	12 Hours Later
Combined (estrogen-progestin) oral contra-ceptives *(continued)*	0.03 mg EE + 0.15 mg LNG	Ologyn-micro, Ovoplex 3, Ovoplex 30/50, Ovranet, Ovranette, Ovranette 30, Perle Ld, Portia, Primafem, Quasense, R-den, Reget 21+7, Riget, Rigevidon, Rigevidon 21, Rigevidon 21+7, Roselle, Seasonale, Seasonique, Seif, Sexcon, Stediril 30, Suginor	4	4
	0.03 mg EE + 0.125 mg LNG	Enpresse, Minisiston, Mono Step, Trivora, Trust Pills	4	4
	0.05 mg EE + 0.25 mg LNG	Contraceptive H.D., Control, D-Norginor, Denoval, Denoval-Wyeth, Duoluton, Duoluton L, Dystrol, Evanor, Evanor-d, FMP, Follinette, Neogentrol, Neogynon, Neogynon 21, Neogynon 50, Neogynon CD, Neogynona, Neovlar, Noral, Nordiol, Nordiol 21, Normamor, Novogyn 21, Ogestrel, Ologyn, Ovidon, Ovoplex, Ovran, Stediril-D	2	2
	0.03 mg EE + 0.3 mg norgestrel	Anulette, Cryselle, Lo-Femenal, Lo-Gentrol, Low-Ogestrel, Lo/Ovral, Lo-Rondal, Minovral, Min-Ovral, Segura	4	4
	0.05 mg EE + 0.5 mg norgestrel	Anfertil, Eugynon, Eugynon CD, Femenal, Jeny FMP, Ovral, Planovar, Stediril	2	2
Ulipristal acetate				
Ulipristal acetate dedicated ECPs	30 mg ulipristal acetate	ella, ellaOne	1	0

LNG = levonorgestrel   EE = ethinyl estradiol
Sources: The Emergency Contraception Web site, the International Planned Parenthood Federation Directory of Hormonal Contraceptives, and the International Consortium for Emergency Contraception

CHAPTER 4

Progestin-Only Injectables

Key Points for Providers and Clients

- **Bleeding changes are common but not harmful.** Typically, irregular bleeding for the first several months and then no monthly bleeding.
- **Return for injections regularly.** Coming back every 3 months (13 weeks) for DMPA or every 2 months for NET-EN is important for greatest effectiveness.
- **Injection can be as much as 4 weeks late for DMPA or 2 weeks late for NET-EN.** Client should come back even if later.
- **Gradual weight gain is common.**
- **Return of fertility is often delayed.** It takes several months longer on average to become pregnant after stopping progestin-only injectables than after other methods.

What Are Progestin-Only Injectables?

- The injectable contraceptives depot medroxyprogesterone acetate (DMPA) and norethisterone enanthate (NET-EN) each contain a progestin like the natural hormone progesterone in a woman's body. (In contrast, monthly injectables contain both estrogen and progestin. See Monthly Injectables, p. 81.)
- Do not contain estrogen, and so can be used throughout breastfeeding and by women who cannot use methods with estrogen.
- DMPA, the most widely used progestin-only injectable, is also known as "the shot," "the jab," the injection, Depo, Depo-Provera, Megestron, and Petogen.
- NET-EN is also known as norethindrone enanthate, Noristerat, and Syngestal. (See Comparing Injectables, p. 359, for differences between DMPA and NET-EN.)

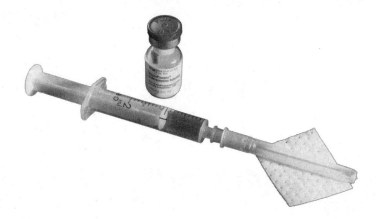

- Given by injection into the muscle (intramuscular injection). The hormone is then released slowly into the bloodstream. A different formulation of DMPA can be injected just under the skin (subcutaneous injection). See New Formulation of DMPA, p. 63.

- Work primarily by preventing the release of eggs from the ovaries (ovulation).

How Effective?

More effective

Effectiveness depends on getting injections regularly: Risk of pregnancy is greatest when a woman misses an injection.

- As commonly used, about 3 pregnancies per 100 women using progestin-only injectables over the first year. This means that 97 of every 100 women using injectables will not become pregnant.

- When women have injections on time, less than 1 pregnancy per 100 women using progestin-only injectables over the first year (3 per 1,000 women).

Return of fertility after injections are stopped: An average of about 4 months longer for DMPA and 1 month longer for NET-EN than with most other methods (see Question 7, p. 79).

Less effective

Protection against sexually transmitted infections (STIs): None

Side Effects, Health Benefits, and Health Risks

Side Effects (see Managing Any Problems, p. 75)

Some users report the following:

- Changes in bleeding patterns including, with DMPA:

  First 3 months:
  - Irregular bleeding
  - Prolonged bleeding

  At one year:
  - No monthly bleeding
  - Infrequent bleeding
  - Irregular bleeding

- NET-EN affects bleeding patterns less than DMPA. NET-EN users have fewer days of bleeding in the first 6 months and are less likely to have no monthly bleeding after one year than DMPA users.

- Weight gain (see Question 4, p. 78)

- Headaches

- Dizziness

- Abdominal bloating and discomfort

- Mood changes

- Less sex drive

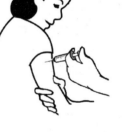

Other possible physical changes:

- Loss of bone density (see Question 10, p. 80)

Why Some Women Say They Like Progestin-Only Injectables

- Do not require daily action
- Do not interfere with sex
- Are private: No one else can tell that a woman is using contraception
- Cause no monthly bleeding (for many women)
- May help women to gain weight

Known Health Benefits	Known Health Risks

DMPA

Helps protect against:

- Risks of pregnancy
- Cancer of the lining of the uterus (endometrial cancer)
- Uterine fibroids

May help protect against:

- Symptomatic pelvic inflammatory disease
- Iron-deficiency anemia

Reduces:

- Sickle cell crises among women with sickle cell anemia
- Symptoms of endometriosis (pelvic pain, irregular bleeding)

Known Health Risks (DMPA): None

NET-EN

Helps protect against:

- Risks of pregnancy
- Iron-deficiency anemia

Known Health Risks (NET-EN): None

NET-EN may offer many of the same health benefits as DMPA, but this list of benefits includes only those for which there is available research evidence.

Correcting Misunderstandings (see also Questions and Answers, p. 78)

Progestin-only injectables:

- Can stop monthly bleeding, but this is not harmful. It is similar to not having monthly bleeding during pregnancy. Blood is not building up inside the woman.
- Do not disrupt an existing pregnancy.
- Do not make women infertile.

Delivering injectable contraception in the community

More and more women are asking for injectable contraceptives. This method can be more widely available when it is offered in the community as well as in clinics.

A WHO technical consultation in 2009 reviewed evidence and program experience and concluded that "community-based provision of progestin-only injectable contraceptives by appropriately trained community health workers is safe, effective, and acceptable" to clients.

Community-based providers of injectables should be able to screen clients for pregnancy and for medical eligibility. Also, they should be able to give injections safely and to inform women about delayed return of fertility and common side effects, including irregular bleeding, no monthly bleeding, and weight gain. They also should be able to counsel women about their choice of methods, including methods available at the clinic. All providers of injectables need specific performance-based training and supportive supervision to carry out these tasks.

It is desirable, if possible, to check blood pressure before a woman starts an injectable (see p. 65, Question 3). However, in areas where the risks of pregnancy are high and few other methods are available, blood pressure measurement is not required.

For success, clinic-based providers and community-based providers must work closely together. Programs vary, but these are some ways that clinic-based providers can support community-based providers: treating side effects (see pp. 75–77), using clinical judgment concerning medical eligibility in special cases (see p. 67), ruling out pregnancy in women who are more than 4 weeks late for an injection of DMPA or 2 weeks late for NET-EN, and responding to any concerns of clients referred by the community-based providers.

The clinic also can serve as "home" for the community-based providers, where they go for resupply, for supervision, training, and advice, and to turn in their records.

New formulation of DMPA

A new type of prefilled, single-use syringe could be particularly useful to provide DMPA in the community. These syringes have a short needle meant for subcu-taneous injection (that is, injec-tion just below the skin). They contain a special formulation of DMPA, called DMPA-SC. It is

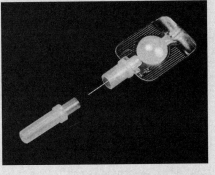

(Continued on next page)

meant only for subcutaneous injection and not for injection into muscle. This formulation of DMPA is available in conventional prefilled auto-disable syringes and in the Uniject system, in which squeezing a bulb pushes the fluid through the needle (see photo on previous page). Like all single-use syringes, these syringes should be placed in a sharps box after use, and then the sharps box should be disposed of properly (see Infection Prevention in the Clinic, p. 312).

Who Can and Cannot Use Progestin-Only Injectables

Safe and Suitable for Nearly All Women

Nearly all women can use progestin-only injectables safely and effectively, including women who:

- Have or have not had children
- Are not married
- Are of any age, including adolescents and women over 40 years old
- Have just had an abortion or miscarriage
- Smoke cigarettes, regardless of woman's age or number of cigarettes smoked
- Are breastfeeding (starting as soon as 6 weeks after childbirth; however, see p. 129, Q&A 8)
- Are infected with HIV, whether or not on antiretroviral therapy (see Progestin-Only Injectables for Women With HIV, p. 67)

Women can begin using progestin-only injectables:

- Without a pelvic examination
- Without any blood tests or other routine laboratory tests
- Without cervical cancer screening
- Without a breast examination
- Even when a woman is not having monthly bleeding at the time, if it is reasonably certain she is not pregnant (see Pregnancy Checklist, p. 372)

Progestin-Only Injectables

Ask the client the questions below about known medical conditions. Examinations and tests are not necessary. If she answers "no" to all of the questions, then she can start progestin-only injectables if she wants. If she answers "yes" to a question, follow the instructions. In some cases she can still start progestin-only injectables.

1. **Are you breastfeeding a baby less than 6 weeks old?**

   ❑ NO   ❑ **YES** She can start using progestin-only injectables as soon as 6 weeks after childbirth (see Fully or nearly fully breastfeeding or Partially breastfeeding, p. 69).

2. **Do you have severe cirrhosis of the liver, a liver infection, or liver tumor? (Are her eyes or skin unusually yellow? [signs of jaundice])**

   ❑ NO   ❑ **YES** If she reports serious active liver disease (jaundice, severe cirrhosis, liver tumor), do not provide progestin-only injectables. Help her choose a method without hormones.

3. **Do you have high blood pressure?**

   ❑ NO   ❑ **YES** If you cannot check blood pressure and she reports having high blood pressure in the past, provide progestin-only injectables.

   Check her blood pressure if possible:

   - If she is currently being treated for high blood pressure and it is adequately controlled, or her blood pressure is below 160/100 mm Hg, provide progestin-only injectables.

   - If systolic blood pressure is 160 mm Hg or higher or diastolic blood pressure 100 or higher, do not provide progestin-only injectables. Help her choose another method without estrogen.

4. **Have you had diabetes for more than 20 years or damage to your arteries, vision, kidneys, or nervous system caused by diabetes?**

   ❑ NO   ❑ **YES** Do not provide progestin-only injectables. Help her choose another method without estrogen.

(Continued on next page)

5. Have you ever had a stroke, blood clot in your legs or lungs, heart attack, or other serious heart problems?

❑ NO ❑ YES If she reports heart attack, heart disease due to blocked or narrowed arteries, or stroke, do not provide progestin-only injectables. Help her choose another method without estrogen. If she reports a current blood clot in the deep veins of the leg or in the lung (not superficial clots), and she is not on anticoagulant therapy, help her choose a method without hormones.

6. Do you have vaginal bleeding that is unusual for you?

❑ NO ❑ YES If she has unexplained vaginal bleeding that suggests pregnancy or an underlying medical condition, progestin-only injectables could make diagnosis and monitoring of any treatment more difficult. Help her choose a method to use while being evaluated and treated (but not implants or a copper-bearing or hormonal IUD). After treatment, re-evaluate for use of progestin-only injectables.

7. Do you have or have you ever had breast cancer?

❑ NO ❑ YES Do not provide progestin-only injectables. Help her choose a method without hormones.

8. Do you have several conditions that could increase your chances of heart disease (coronary artery disease) or stroke, such as high blood pressure and diabetes?

❑ NO ❑ YES Do not provide progestin-only injectables. Help her choose another method without estrogen.

Be sure to explain the health benefits and risks and the side effects of the method that the client will use. Also, point out any conditions that would make the method inadvisable, when relevant to the client.

Using Clinical Judgment in Special Cases

Usually, a woman with any of the conditions listed below should not use progestin-only injectables. In special circumstances, however, when other, more appropriate methods are not available or acceptable to her, a qualified provider who can carefully assess a specific woman's condition and situation may decide that she can use progestin-only injectables. The provider needs to consider the severity of her condition and, for most conditions, whether she will have access to follow-up.

- Breastfeeding and less than 6 weeks since giving birth (considering the risks of another pregnancy and that a woman may have limited further access to injectables)
- Severe high blood pressure (systolic 160 mm Hg or higher or diastolic 100 mm Hg or higher)
- Acute blood clot in deep veins of legs or lungs
- History of heart disease or current heart disease due to blocked or narrowed arteries (ischemic heart disease)
- History of stroke
- Multiple risk factors for arterial cardiovascular disease such as diabetes and high blood pressure
- Unexplained vaginal bleeding before evaluation for possible serious underlying condition
- Had breast cancer more than 5 years ago, and it has not returned
- Diabetes for more than 20 years or damage to arteries, vision, kidneys, or nervous system caused by diabetes
- Severe liver disease, infection, or tumor
- Systemic lupus erythematosus with positive (or unknown) antiphospholipid antibodies or, if starting a progestin-only injectable, severe thrombocytopenia

Progestin-Only Injectables for Women With HIV

- Women who are infected with HIV, have AIDS, or are on antiretroviral (ARV) therapy can safely use progestin-only injectables.
- Urge these women to use condoms along with progestin-only injectables. Used consistently and correctly, condoms help prevent transmission of HIV and other STIs.

Providing Progestin-Only Injectables

When to Start

IMPORTANT: A woman can start injectables any time she wants if it is reasonably certain she is not pregnant. To be reasonably certain she is not pregnant, use the Pregnancy Checklist (see p. 372).

Woman's situation	When to start
Having menstrual cycles or switching from a nonhormonal method	**Any time of the month** • If she is starting within 7 days after the start of her monthly bleeding, no need for a backup method. • If it is more than 7 days after the start of her monthly bleeding, she can start injectables any time it is reasonably certain she is not pregnant. She will need a backup method* for the first 7 days after the injection. • If she is switching from an IUD, she can start injectables immediately (see Copper-Bearing IUD, Switching From an IUD to Another Method, p. 148).
Switching from a hormonal method	• Immediately, if she has been using the hormonal method consistently and correctly or if it is otherwise reasonably certain she is not pregnant. No need to wait for her next monthly bleeding. No need for a backup method. • If she is switching from another injectable, she can have the new injectable when the repeat injection would have been given. No need for a backup method.

---

* Backup methods include abstinence, male and female condoms, spermicides, and withdrawal. Tell her that spermicides and withdrawal are the least effective contraceptive methods. If possible, give her condoms.

Woman's situation	When to start

Fully or nearly fully breastfeeding

Less than 6 months after giving birth

- If she gave birth less than 6 weeks ago, delay her first injection until at least 6 weeks after giving birth. (See p. 129, Q&A 8.)
- If her monthly bleeding has not returned, she can start injectables any time between 6 weeks and 6 months. No need for a backup method.
- If her monthly bleeding has returned, she can start injectables as advised for women having menstrual cycles (see previous page).

More than 6 months after giving birth

- If her monthly bleeding has not returned, she can start injectables any time it is reasonably certain she is not pregnant. She will need a backup method for the first 7 days after the injection.
- If her monthly bleeding has returned, she can start injectables as advised for women having menstrual cycles (see previous page).

Partially breastfeeding

Less than 6 weeks after giving birth

- Delay her first injection until at least 6 weeks after giving birth. (See p. 129, Q&A 8.)

More than 6 weeks after giving birth

- If her monthly bleeding has not returned, she can start injectables any time it is reasonably certain she is not pregnant.[†] She will need a backup method for the first 7 days after the injection.
- If her monthly bleeding has returned, she can start injectables as advised for women having menstrual cycles (see previous page).

[†] *Where a visit 6 weeks after childbirth is routinely recommended and other opportunities to obtain contraception limited, some providers and programs may give the first injection at the 6-week visit, without further evidence that the woman is not pregnant, if her monthly bleeding has not yet returned.*

Progestin-Only Injectables

Woman's situation	When to start
Not breastfeeding	
Less than 4 weeks after giving birth	• She can start injectables at any time. No need for a backup method.
More than 4 weeks after giving birth	• If her monthly bleeding has not returned, she can start injectables any time it is reasonably certain she is not pregnant.[†] She will need a backup method for the first 7 days after the injection.
	• If her monthly bleeding has returned, she can start injectables as advised for women having menstrual cycles (see p. 68).
No monthly bleeding (not related to childbirth or breastfeeding)	• She can start injectables any time it is reasonably certain she is not pregnant. She will need a backup method for the first 7 days after the injection.
After miscarriage or abortion	• Immediately. If she is starting within 7 days after first- or second-trimester miscarriage or abortion, no need for a backup method.
	• If it is more than 7 days after first- or second-trimester miscarriage or abortion, she can start injectables any time it is reasonably certain she is not pregnant. She will need a backup method for the first 7 days after the injection.
After taking emergency contraceptive pills (ECPs)	• She can start injectables on the same day as the ECPs, or if preferred, within 7 days after the start of her monthly bleeding. She will need a backup method for the first 7 days after the injection. She should return if she has signs or symptoms of pregnancy other than not having monthly bleeding (see p. 371 for common signs and symptoms of pregnancy).

[†] *Where a visit 6 weeks after childbirth is routinely recommended and other opportunities to obtain contraception limited, some providers and programs may give the first injection at the 6-week visit, without further evidence that the woman is not pregnant, if her monthly bleeding has not yet returned.*

Giving Advice on Side Effects

IMPORTANT: Thorough counseling about bleeding changes and other side effects must come before giving the injection. Counseling about bleeding changes may be the most important help a woman needs to keep using the method.

Describe the most common side effects	• For the first several months, irregular bleeding, prolonged bleeding, frequent bleeding. Later, no monthly bleeding. • Weight gain (about 1–2 kg per year), headaches, dizziness, and possibly other side effects.
Explain about these side effects	• Side effects are not signs of illness. • Common, but some women do not have them. • The client can come back for help if side effects bother her.

Giving the Injection

1. Obtain one dose of injectable, needle, and syringe	• DMPA: 150 mg for injections into the muscle (intramuscular injection). NET-EN: 200 mg for injections into the muscle. • If possible, use single-dose vials. Check expiration date. If using an open multidose vial, check that the vial is not leaking. • DMPA: A 2 ml syringe and a 21–23 gauge intramuscular needle. • NET-EN: A 2 or 5 ml syringe and a 19-gauge intramuscular needle. A narrower needle (21–23 gauge) also can be used. • For each injection use a disposable auto-disable syringe and needle from a new, sealed package (within expiration date and not damaged), if available.
2. Wash	• Wash hands with soap and water, if possible. • If injection site is dirty, wash it with soap and water. • No need to wipe site with antiseptic.

3. Prepare vial	• DMPA: Gently shake the vial.
	• NET-EN: Shaking the vial is not necessary.
	• No need to wipe top of vial with antiseptic.
	• If vial is cold, warm to skin temperature before giving the injection.
4. Fill syringe	• Pierce top of vial with sterile needle and fill syringe with proper dose.
5. Inject formula	• Insert sterile needle deep into the hip (ventrogluteal muscle), the upper arm (deltoid muscle), or the buttocks (gluteal muscle, upper outer portion), whichever the woman prefers. Inject the contents of the syringe.
	• Do not massage injection site.

| **6. Dispose of disposable syringes and needles safely** | • Do not recap, bend, or break needles before disposal. |
| | • Place in a puncture-proof sharps container. |

• Do not reuse disposable syringes and needles. They are meant to be destroyed after a single use. Because of their shape, they are very difficult to disinfect. Therefore, reuse might transmit diseases such as HIV and hepatitis.

• If reusable syringe and needle are used, they must be sterilized again after each use (see Infection Prevention in the Clinic, p. 312).

Supporting the User

Give specific instructions	• Tell her not to massage the injection site.
	• Tell the client the name of the injection and agree on a date for her next injection.

"Come Back Any Time": Reasons to Return Before the Next Injection

Assure every client that she is welcome to come back any time—for example, if she has problems, questions, or wants another method; she has a major change in health status; or she thinks she might be pregnant.

General health advice: Anyone who suddenly feels that something is seriously wrong with her health should immediately seek medical care from a nurse or doctor. Her contraceptive method is most likely not the cause of the condition, but she should tell the nurse or doctor what method she is using.

Planning the Next Injection

1. Agree on a date for her next injection in 3 months (13 weeks) for DMPA, or in 2 months (8 weeks) for NET-EN. Discuss how to remember the date, perhaps tying it to a holiday or other event.

2. Ask her to try to come on time. With DMPA she may come up to 4 weeks late and still get an injection. With NET-EN she may come up to 2 weeks late and still get an injection. With either DMPA or NET-EN, she can come up to 2 weeks early.

3. She should come back no matter how late she is for her next injection. If more than 4 weeks late for DMPA or 2 weeks late for NET-EN, she should abstain from sex or use condoms, spermicides, or withdrawal until she can get an injection. Also, if she has had sex in the past 5 days without using another contraceptive method, she can consider emergency contraceptive pills (see Emergency Contraceptive Pills, p. 45).

Helping Continuing Users

Repeat Injection Visits

1. Ask how the client is doing with the method and whether she is satisfied. Ask if she has any questions or anything to discuss.

2. Ask especially if she is concerned about bleeding changes. Give her any information or help that she needs (see Managing Any Problems, next page).

3. Give her the injection. Injection of DMPA can be given up to 4 weeks late. Injection of NET-EN can be given up to 2 weeks late.

4. Plan for her next injection. Agree on a date for her next injection (in 3 months or 13 weeks for DMPA, 2 months for NET-EN). Remind her that she should try to come on time, but she should come back no matter how late she is.

5. Every year or so, check her blood pressure if possible (see Medical Eligibility Criteria, Question 3, p. 65).

6. Ask a long-term client if she has had any new health problems. Address problems as appropriate. For new health problems that may require switching methods, see p. 77.

7. Ask a long-term client about major life changes that may affect her needs— particularly plans for having children and STI/HIV risk. Follow up as needed.

Managing Late Injections

- If the client is less than 4 weeks late for a repeat injection of DMPA, or less than 2 weeks late for a repeat injection of NET-EN, she can receive her next injection. No need for tests, evaluation, or a backup method.

- A client who is more than 4 weeks late for DMPA, or more than 2 weeks late for NET-EN, can receive her next injection if:

  – She has not had sex since *2 weeks after* she should have had her last injection, or

  – She has used a backup method or has taken emergency contraceptive pills (ECPs) after any unprotected sex since *2 weeks after* she should have had her last injection, or

  – She is fully or nearly fully breastfeeding and she gave birth less than 6 months ago.

  She will need a backup method for the first 7 days after the injection.

- If the client is more than 4 weeks late for DMPA, or more than 2 weeks late for NET-EN, and she does not meet these criteria, additional steps can be taken to be reasonably certain she is not pregnant (see Further Options to Assess for Pregnancy, p. 370). These steps are helpful because many women who have been using progestin-only injectables will have no monthly bleeding for at least a few months, even after discontinuation. Thus, asking her to come back during her next monthly bleeding means her next injection could be unnecessarily delayed. She may be left without contraceptive protection.

- Discuss why the client was late and solutions. Remind her that she should keep trying to come back every 3 months for DMPA, or every 2 months for NET-EN. If coming back on time is often a problem, discuss using a backup method when she is late for her next injection, taking ECPs, or choosing another method.

Managing Any Problems

Problems Reported as Side Effects

May or may not be due to the method.

- Problems with side effects affect women's satisfaction and use of injectables. They deserve the provider's attention. If the client reports side effects, listen to her concerns, give her advice, and, if appropriate, treat.
- Offer to help the client choose another method—now, if she wishes, or if problems cannot be overcome.

No monthly bleeding

- Reassure her that most women using progestin-only injectables stop having monthly bleeding over time, and this is not harmful. There is no need to lose blood every month. It is similar to not having monthly bleeding during pregnancy. She is not infertile. Blood is not building up inside her. (Some women are happy to be free from monthly bleeding.)
- If not having monthly bleeding bothers her, she may want to switch to monthly injectables, if available.

Irregular bleeding (bleeding at unexpected times that bothers the client)

- Reassure her that many women using progestin-only injectables experience irregular bleeding. It is not harmful and usually becomes less or stops after the first few months of use.
- For modest short-term relief, take 500 mg mefenamic acid 2 times daily after meals for 5 days or 40 mg of valdecoxib daily for 5 days, beginning when irregular bleeding starts.
- If irregular bleeding continues or starts after several months of normal or no monthly bleeding, or you suspect that something may be wrong for other reasons, consider underlying conditions unrelated to method use (see Unexplained vaginal bleeding, p. 77).

Weight gain

- Review diet and counsel as needed.

Abdominal bloating and discomfort

- Consider locally available remedies.

Heavy or prolonged bleeding (twice as much as usual or longer than 8 days)

- Reassure her that some women using progestin-only injectables experience heavy or prolonged bleeding. It is not harmful and usually becomes less or stops after a few months.

- For modest short-term relief she can try (one at a time), beginning when heavy bleeding starts:
  - 500 mg of mefenamic acid twice daily after meals for 5 days.
  - 40 mg of valdecoxib daily for 5 days.
  - 50 μg of ethinyl estradiol daily for 21 days, beginning when heavy bleeding starts.

- If bleeding becomes a health threat or if the woman wants, help her choose another method. In the meantime, she can use one of the treatments listed above to help reduce bleeding.

- To help prevent anemia, suggest she take iron tablets and tell her it is important to eat foods containing iron, such as meat and poultry (especially beef and chicken liver), fish, green leafy vegetables, and legumes (beans, bean curd, lentils, and peas).

- If heavy or prolonged bleeding continues or starts after several months of normal or no monthly bleeding, or you suspect that something may be wrong for other reasons, consider underlying conditions unrelated to method use (see Unexplained vaginal bleeding, next page).

Ordinary headaches (nonmigrainous)

- Suggest aspirin (325–650 mg), ibuprofen (200–400 mg), paracetamol (325–1000 mg), or other pain reliever.

- Any headaches that get worse or occur more often during use of injectables should be evaluated.

Mood changes or changes in sex drive

- Ask about changes in her life that could affect her mood or sex drive, including changes in her relationship with her partner. Give support as appropriate.

- Clients who have serious mood changes such as major depression should be referred for care.

- Consider locally available remedies.

Dizziness

- Consider locally available remedies.

New Problems That May Require Switching Methods

May or may not be due to the method.

Migraine headaches (see Identifying Migraine Headaches and Auras, p. 368)

- If she has migraine headaches without aura, she can continue to use the method if she wishes.
- If she has migraine aura, do not give the injection. Help her choose a method without hormones.

Unexplained vaginal bleeding (that suggests a medical condition not related to the method)

- Refer or evaluate by history and pelvic examination. Diagnose and treat as appropriate.
- If no cause of bleeding can be found, consider stopping progestin-only injectables to make diagnosis easier. Provide another method of her choice to use until the condition is evaluated and treated (not implants or a copper-bearing or hormonal IUD).
- If bleeding is caused by sexually transmitted infection or pelvic inflammatory disease, she can continue using progestin-only injectables during treatment.

Certain serious health conditions (suspected blocked or narrowed arteries, serious liver disease, severe high blood pressure, blood clots in deep veins of legs or lungs, stroke, breast cancer, or damage to arteries, vision, kidneys, or nervous system caused by diabetes). See Signs and Symptoms of Serious Health Conditions, p. 320.

- Do not give next injection.
- Give her a backup method to use until the condition is evaluated.
- Refer for diagnosis and care if not already under care.

Suspected pregnancy

- Assess for pregnancy.
- Stop injections if pregnancy is confirmed.
- There are no known risks to a fetus conceived while a woman is using injectables (see Question 11, p. 80).

Questions and Answers About Progestin-Only Injectables

1. **Can women who could get sexually transmitted infections (STIs) use progestin-only injectables?**

    Yes. Women at risk for STIs can use progestin-only injectables. The few studies available have found that women using DMPA were more likely to acquire chlamydia than women not using hormonal contraception. The reason for this difference is not known. There are few studies available on use of NET-EN and STIs. Like anyone else at risk for STIs, a user of progestin-only injectables who may be at risk for STIs should be advised to use condoms correctly every time she has sex. Consistent and correct condom use will reduce her risk of becoming infected if she is exposed to an STI.

2. **If a woman does not have monthly bleeding while using progestin-only injectables, does this mean that she is pregnant?**

    Probably not, especially if she is breastfeeding. Eventually most women using progestin-only injectables will not have monthly bleeding. If she has been getting her injections on time, she is probably not pregnant and can keep using injectables. If she is still worried after being reassured, she can be offered a pregnancy test, if available, or referred for one. If not having monthly bleeding bothers her, switching to another method may help.

3. **Can a woman who is breastfeeding safely use progestin-only injectables?**

    Yes. This is a good choice for a breastfeeding mother who wants a hormonal method. Progestin-only injectables are safe for both the mother and the baby starting as early as 6 weeks after childbirth. They do not affect milk production.

4. **How much weight do women gain when they use progestin-only injectables?**

    Women gain an average of 1–2 kg per year when using DMPA. Some of the weight increase may be the usual weight gain as people age. Some women, particularly overweight adolescents, have gained much more than 1–2 kg per year. At the same time, some users of progestin-only injectables lose weight or have no significant change in weight. Asian women in particular do not tend to gain weight when using DMPA.

5. **Do DMPA and NET-EN cause abortion?**

    No. Research on progestin-only injectables finds that they do not disrupt an existing pregnancy. They should not be used to try to cause an abortion. They will not do so.

6. **Do progestin-only injectables make a woman infertile?**

No. There may be a delay in regaining fertility after stopping progestin-only injectables, but in time the woman will be able to become pregnant as before, although fertility decreases as women get older. The bleeding pattern a woman had before she used progestin-only injectables generally returns several months after the last injection even if she had no monthly bleeding while using injectables. Some women may have to wait several months before their usual bleeding pattern returns.

7. **How long does it take to become pregnant after stopping DMPA or NET-EN?**

Women who stop using DMPA wait about 4 months longer on average to become pregnant than women who have used other methods. This means they become pregnant on average 10 months after their last injection. Women who stop using NET-EN wait about one month longer on average to become pregnant than women who have used other methods, or 6 months after their last injection. These are averages. A woman should not be worried if she has not become pregnant even as much as 12 months after stopping use. The length of time a woman has used injectables makes no difference to how quickly she becomes pregnant once she stops having injections. After stopping progestin-only injectables, a woman may ovulate before her monthly bleeding returns—and thus can become pregnant. If she wants to continue avoiding pregnancy, she should start another method before monthly bleeding returns.

8. **Does DMPA cause cancer?**

Many studies show that DMPA does not cause cancer. DMPA use helps protect against cancer of the lining of the uterus (endometrial cancer). Findings of the few studies on DMPA use and breast cancer are similar to findings with combined oral contraceptives: Women using DMPA were slightly more likely to be diagnosed with breast cancer while using DMPA or within 10 years after they stopped. It is unclear whether these findings are explained by earlier detection of existing breast cancers among DMPA users or by a biologic effect of DMPA on breast cancer.

A few studies on DMPA use and cervical cancer suggest that there may be a slightly increased risk of cervical cancer among women using DMPA for 5 years or more. Cervical cancer cannot develop because of DMPA alone, however. It is caused by persistent infection with human papillomavirus. Little information is available about NET-EN. It is expected to be as safe as DMPA and other contraceptive methods containing only a progestin, such as progestin-only pills and implants.

9. **Can a woman switch from one progestin-only injectable to another?**

Switching injectables is safe, and it does not decrease effectiveness. If switching is necessary due to shortages of supplies, the first injection of the new injectable should be given when the next injection of the old formulation would have been given. Clients need to be told that they are switching, the name of the new injectable, and its injection schedule.

10. **How does DMPA affect bone density?**

DMPA use decreases bone density. Research has not found that DMPA users of any age are likely to have more broken bones, however. When DMPA use stops, bone density increases again for women of reproductive age. Among adults who stop using DMPA, after 2 to 3 years their bone density appears to be similar to that of women who have not used DMPA. Among adolescents, it is not clear whether the loss in bone density prevents them from reaching their potential peak bone mass. No data are available on NET-EN and bone loss, but the effect is expected to be similar to the effect of DMPA.

11. **Do progestin-only injectables cause birth defects? Will the fetus be harmed if a woman accidentally uses progestin-only injectables while she is pregnant?**

No. Good evidence shows that progestin-only injectables will not cause birth defects and will not otherwise harm the fetus if a woman becomes pregnant while using progestin-only injectables or accidentally starts injectables when she is already pregnant.

12. **Do progestin-only injectables change women's mood or sex drive?**

Generally, no. Some women using injectables report these complaints. The great majority of injectables users do not report any such changes, however. It is difficult to tell whether such changes are due to progestin-only injectables or to other reasons. Providers can help a client with these problems (see Mood changes or changes in sex drive, p. 76). There is no evidence that progestin-only injectables affect women's sexual behavior.

13. **What if a woman returns for her next injection late?**

In 2008 WHO revised its guidance based on new research findings. The new guidance recommends giving a woman her next DMPA injection if she is up to 4 weeks late, without the need for further evidence that she is not pregnant. A woman can receive her next NET-EN injection if she is up to 2 weeks late. Some women return even later for their repeat injection, however. In such cases providers can use Further Options to Assess for Pregnancy, p. 370. Whether a woman is late for reinjection or not, her next injection of DMPA should be planned for 3 months later, or her next injection of NET-EN should be planned for 2 months later, as usual.

CHAPTER 5

Monthly Injectables

Key Points for Providers and Clients

- **Bleeding changes are common but not harmful.** Typically, lighter monthly bleeding, fewer days of bleeding, or irregular or infrequent bleeding.

- **Return on time.** Coming back every 4 weeks is important for greatest effectiveness.

- **Injection can be as much as 7 days early or late.** Client should come back even if later.

What Are Monthly Injectables?

- Monthly injectables contain 2 hormones—a progestin and an estrogen—like the natural hormones progesterone and estrogen in a woman's body. (Combined oral contraceptives also contain these 2 types of hormones.)

- Also called combined injectable contraceptives, CICs, the injection.

- Information in this chapter applies to medroxyprogesterone acetate (MPA)/estradiol cypionate and to norethisterone enanthate (NET-EN)/estradiol valerate. The information may also apply to older formulations, about which less is known.

- MPA/estradiol cypionate is marketed under the trade names Ciclofem, Ciclofemina, Cyclofem, Cyclo-Provera, Feminena, Lunella, Lunelle, Novafem, and others. NET-EN/estradiol valerate is marketed under the trade names Mesigyna and Norigynon.

- Work primarily by preventing the release of eggs from the ovaries (ovulation).

How Effective?

More effective

Effectiveness depends on returning on time: Risk of pregnancy is greatest when a woman is late for an injection or misses an injection.

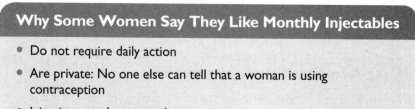

- As commonly used, about 3 pregnancies per 100 women using monthly injectables over the first year. This means that 97 of every 100 women using injectables will not become pregnant.

- When women have injections on time, less than 1 pregnancy per 100 women using monthly injectables over the first year (5 per 10,000 women).

Less effective

Return of fertility after injections are stopped: An average of about one month longer than with most other methods (see Question 11, p. 100).

Protection against sexually transmitted infections (STIs): None

---

Why Some Women Say They Like Monthly Injectables

- Do not require daily action
- Are private: No one else can tell that a woman is using contraception
- Injections can be stopped at any time
- Are good for spacing births

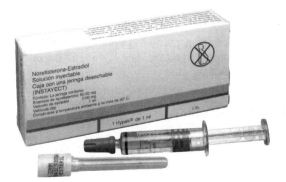

Side Effects, Health Benefits, and Health Risks

Side Effects (see Managing Any Problems, p. 95)

Some users report the following:

- Changes in bleeding patterns including:
  - Lighter bleeding and fewer days of bleeding
  - Irregular bleeding
  - Infrequent bleeding
  - Prolonged bleeding
  - No monthly bleeding
- Weight gain
- Headaches
- Dizziness
- Breast tenderness

Known Health Benefits and Health Risks

Long-term studies of monthly injectables are limited, but researchers expect that their health benefits and health risks are similar to those of combined oral contraceptives (see Combined Oral Contraceptives, Health Benefits and Health Risks, p. 3). There may be some differences in the effects on the liver, however (see Question 2, p. 98).

Correcting Misunderstandings (see also Questions and Answers, p. 98)

Monthly injectables:

- Can stop monthly bleeding, but this is not harmful. It is similar to not having monthly bleeding during pregnancy. Blood is not building up inside the woman.
- Are not in experimental phases of study. Government agencies have approved them.
- Do not make women infertile.
- Do not cause early menopause.
- Do not cause birth defects or multiple births.
- Do not cause itching.
- Do not change women's sexual behavior.

Who Can and Cannot Use Monthly Injectables

Safe and Suitable for Nearly All Women

Nearly all women can use monthly injectables safely and effectively, including women who:

- Have or have not had children
- Are not married
- Are of any age, including adolescents and women over 40 years old
- Have just had an abortion or miscarriage
- Smoke any number of cigarettes daily *and* are under 35 years old
- Smoke fewer than 15 cigarettes daily *and* are over 35 years old
- Have anemia now or had anemia in the past
- Have varicose veins
- Are infected with HIV, whether or not on antiretroviral therapy, unless that therapy includes ritonavir (see Monthly Injectables for Women With HIV, below)

Women can begin using monthly injectables:

- Without a pelvic examination
- Without any blood tests or other routine laboratory tests
- Without cervical cancer screening
- Without a breast examination
- Even when a woman is not having monthly bleeding at the time, if it is reasonably certain she is not pregnant (see Pregnancy Checklist, p. 372)

Monthly Injectables for Women With HIV

- Women can safely use monthly injectables even if they are infected with HIV, have AIDS, or are on antiretroviral (ARV) therapy unless their therapy includes ritonavir. Ritonavir may reduce the effectiveness of monthly injectables. (See Medical Eligibility Criteria, p. 330.)

- Urge these women to use condoms along with monthly injectables. Used consistently and correctly, condoms help prevent transmission of HIV and other STIs. Condoms also provide extra contraceptive protection for women on ARV therapy.

Monthly Injectables

Ask the client the questions below about known medical conditions. Examinations and tests are not necessary. If she answers "no" to all of the questions, then she can start monthly injectables if she wants. If she answers "yes" to a question, follow the instructions. In some cases she can still start monthly injectables.

1. **Are you breastfeeding a baby less than 6 months old?**

❏ NO ❏ YES

- If fully or nearly fully breastfeeding: She can start 6 months after giving birth or when breast milk is no longer the baby's main food—whichever comes first (see Fully or nearly fully breastfeeding, p. 89).

- If partially breastfeeding: She can start monthly injectables as soon as 6 weeks after giving birth (see Partially breastfeeding, p. 90).

2. **Have you had a baby in the last 3 weeks and you are not breastfeeding?**

❏ NO ❏ YES She can start monthly injectables as soon as 3 weeks after childbirth. (If there is an additional risk that she might develop a blood clot in a deep vein (deep vein thrombosis, or VTE), then she should not start monthly injectables at 3 weeks after childbirth, but can start at 6 weeks instead. These additional risk factors include previous VTE, thrombophilia, caesarean delivery, blood transfusion at delivery, postpartum hemorrhage, pre-eclampsia, obesity (≥ 30 kg/m^2), smoking, and being bedridden for a prolonged time.)

3. **Do you smoke 15 or more cigarettes a day?**

❏ NO ❏ YES If she is 35 years of age or older and smokes more than 15 cigarettes a day, do not provide monthly injectables. Urge her to stop smoking and help her choose another method.

4. **Do you have severe cirrhosis of the liver, a liver infection, or liver tumor? (Are her eyes or skin unusually yellow? [signs of jaundice])**

❏ NO ❏ YES If she reports serious active liver disease (jaundice, active hepatitis, severe cirrhosis, liver tumor), do not provide monthly injectables. Help her choose a method without hormones. (If she has mild cirrhosis or gall bladder disease, she can use monthly injectables.)

(Continued on next page)

5. Do you have high blood pressure?

❑ NO   ❑ YES If you cannot check blood pressure and she reports a history of high blood pressure, or if she is being treated for high blood pressure, do not provide monthly injectables. Refer her for a blood pressure check if possible or help her choose another method without estrogen.

Check her blood pressure if possible:

- If blood pressure is below 140/90 mm Hg, provide monthly injectables.

- If systolic blood pressure is 140 mm Hg or higher or diastolic blood pressure is 90 or higher, do not provide monthly injectables. Help her choose a method without estrogen, but not progestin-only injectables if systolic blood pressure is 160 or higher or diastolic pressure is 100 or higher.

(One blood pressure reading in the range of 140–159/90–99 mm Hg is not enough to diagnose high blood pressure. Provide a backup method* to use until she can return for another blood pressure check, or help her choose another method now if she prefers. If blood pressure at next check is below 140/90, she can use monthly injectables.)

6. Have you had diabetes for more than 20 years *or* damage to your arteries, vision, kidneys, or nervous system caused by diabetes?

❑ NO   ❑ YES Do not provide monthly injectables. Help her choose a method without estrogen but not progestin-only injectables.

7. Have you ever had a stroke, blood clot in your legs or lungs, heart attack, or other serious heart problems?

❑ NO   ❑ YES If she reports heart attack, heart disease due to blocked or narrowed arteries, or stroke, do not provide monthly injectables. Help her choose a method without estrogen but not progestin-only injectables. If she reports a current blood clot in the deep veins of the leg or in the lung (not superficial clots), help her choose a method without hormones.

---

* *Backup methods include abstinence, male and female condoms, spermicides, and withdrawal. Tell her that spermicides and withdrawal are the least effective contraceptive methods. If possible, give her condoms.*

8. **Do you have or have you ever had breast cancer?**

❏ NO   ❏ YES Do not provide monthly injectables. Help her choose a method without hormones.

9. **Do you sometimes see a bright area of lost vision in the eye before a very bad headache (migraine aura)? Do you get throbbing, severe head pain, often on one side of the head, that can last from a few hours to several days and can cause nausea or vomiting (migraine headaches)? Such headaches are often made worse by light, noise, or moving about.**

❏ NO   ❏ YES If she has migraine aura at any age, do not provide monthly injectables. If she has migraine headaches *without* aura *and* is age 35 or older, do not provide monthly injectables. Help these women choose a method without estrogen. If she is under 35 and has migraine headaches without aura, she can use monthly injectables (see Identifying Migraine Headaches and Auras, p. 368).

10. **Are you planning major surgery that will keep you from walking for one week or more?**

❏ NO   ❏ YES If so, she can start monthly injectables 2 weeks after the surgery. Until she can start monthly injectables, she should use a backup method.

11. **Do you have several conditions that could increase your chances of heart disease (coronary artery disease) or stroke, such as older age, smoking, high blood pressure, or diabetes?**

❏ NO   ❏ YES Do not provide monthly injectables. Help her choose a method without estrogen, but not progestin-only injectables.

12. **Are you taking lamotrigine or ritonavir?**

❏ NO   ❏ YES Do not provide monthly injectables. Monthly injectables can make lamotrigine less effective. Ritonavir can make monthly injectables less effective. Help her choose a method without estrogen.

Also, women should not use monthly injectables if they report having thrombogenic mutations or lupus with positive (or unknown) antiphospholipid antibodies. For complete classifications, see Medical Eligibility Criteria for Contraceptive Use, p. 324. Be sure to explain the health benefits and risks and the side effects of the method that the client will use. Also, point out any conditions that would make the method inadvisable, when relevant to the client.

Using Clinical Judgment in Special Cases

Usually, a woman with any of the conditions listed below should not use monthly injectables. In special circumstances, however, when other, more appropriate methods are not available or acceptable to her, a qualified provider who can carefully assess a specific woman's condition and situation may decide that she can use monthly inject- ables. The provider needs to consider the severity of her condition and, for most conditions, whether she will have access to follow-up.

- Not breastfeeding and less than 3 weeks since giving birth
- Not breastfeeding and between 3 and 6 weeks postpartum with additional risk that she might develop a blood clot in a deep vein (VTE)
- Primarily breastfeeding between 6 weeks and 6 months since giving birth
- Age 35 or older and smokes more than 15 cigarettes a day
- High blood pressure (systolic blood pressure between 140 and 159 mm Hg or diastolic blood pressure between 90 and 99 mm Hg)
- Controlled high blood pressure, where continuing evaluation is possible
- History of high blood pressure, where blood pressure cannot be taken (including pregnancy-related high blood pressure)
- Severe liver disease, infection, or tumor
- Age 35 or older and has migraine headaches without aura
- Younger than age 35 and has migraine headaches that have devel- oped or have gotten worse while using monthly injectables
- Had breast cancer more than 5 years ago, and it has not returned
- Diabetes for more than 20 years or damage to arteries, vision, kidneys, or nervous system caused by diabetes
- Multiple risk factors for arterial cardiovascular disease, such as older age, smoking, diabetes, and high blood pressure
- Taking lamotrigine. Monthly injectables may reduce the effective- ness of lamotrigine.
- Taking ritonavir or ritonavir-boosted protease inhibitors. A backup contraceptive method should also be used because these medica- tions reduce the effectiveness of monthly injectables.

Providing Monthly Injectables

When to Start

IMPORTANT: A woman can start injectables any time she wants if it is reasonably certain she is not pregnant. To be reasonably certain she is not pregnant, use the Pregnancy Checklist (see p. 372).

Woman's situation	When to start
Having menstrual cycles or switching from a nonhormonal method	**Any time of the month** • If she is starting within 7 days after the start of her monthly bleeding, no need for a backup method. • If it is more than 7 days after the start of her monthly bleeding, she can start injectables any time it is reasonably certain she is not pregnant. She will need a backup method* for the first 7 days after the injection. • If she is switching from an IUD, she can start injectables immediately (see Copper-Bearing IUD, Switching From an IUD to Another Method, p. 148).
Switching from a hormonal method	• Immediately, if she has been using the hormonal method consistently and correctly or if it is otherwise reasonably certain she is not pregnant. No need to wait for her next monthly bleeding. No need for a backup method. • If she is switching from another injectable, she can have the new injectable when the repeat injection would have been given. No need for a backup method.
Fully or nearly fully breastfeeding Less than 6 months after giving birth	• Delay her first injection until 6 months after giving birth or when breast milk is no longer the baby's main food—whichever comes first.

* *Backup methods include abstinence, male and female condoms, spermicides, and withdrawal. Tell her that spermicides and withdrawal are the least effective contraceptive methods. If possible, give her condoms.*

Woman's situation	When to start

Fully or nearly fully breastfeeding (continued)

More than 6 months after giving birth	• If her monthly bleeding has not returned, she can start injectables any time it is reasonably certain she is not pregnant. She will need a backup method for the first 7 days after the injection.
	• If her monthly bleeding has returned, she can start injectables as advised for women having menstrual cycles (see p. 89).

Partially breastfeeding

Less than 6 weeks after giving birth	• Delay her first injection until at least 6 weeks after giving birth.
More than 6 weeks after giving birth	• If her monthly bleeding has not returned, she can start injectables any time it is reasonably certain she is not pregnant.[†] She will need a backup method for the first 7 days after the injection.
	• If her monthly bleeding has returned, she can start injectables as advised for women having menstrual cycles (see p. 89).

Not breastfeeding

Less than 4 weeks after giving birth	• She can start injectables at any time on days 21–28 after giving birth. No need for a backup method. (If additional risk for VTE, wait until 6 weeks. See p. 85, Question 2.)
More than 4 weeks after giving birth	• If her monthly bleeding has not returned, she can start injectables any time it is reasonably certain she is not pregnant.[†] She will need a backup method for the first 7 days after the injection.
	• If her monthly bleeding has returned, she can start injectables as advised for women having menstrual cycles (see p. 89).

[†] *Where a visit 6 weeks after childbirth is routinely recommended and other opportunities to obtain contraception limited, some providers and programs may give the first injection at the 6-week visit, without further evidence that the woman is not pregnant, if her monthly bleeding has not yet returned.*

Woman's situation	When to start
No monthly bleeding (not related to childbirth or breastfeeding)	• She can start injectables any time it is reasonably certain she is not pregnant. She will need a backup method for the first 7 days after the injection.
After miscarriage or abortion	• Immediately. If she is starting within 7 days after first- or second-trimester miscarriage or abortion, no need for a backup method. • If it is more than 7 days after first- or second-trimester miscarriage or abortion, she can start injectables any time it is reasonably certain she is not pregnant. She will need a backup method for the first 7 days after the injection.
After taking emergency contraceptive pills (ECPs)	• She can start injectables on the same day as the ECPs. There is no need to wait for her next monthly bleeding to have the injection. She will need a backup method for the first 7 days after the injection.

Giving Advice on Side Effects

IMPORTANT: Thorough counseling about bleeding changes and other side effects must come before giving the injection. Counseling about bleeding changes may be the most important help a woman needs to keep using the method.

Describe the most common side effects	• Lighter bleeding and fewer days of bleeding, irregular bleeding, and infrequent bleeding. • Weight gain, headaches, dizziness, breast tenderness, and possibly other side effects.
Explain about these side effects	• Side effects are not signs of illness. • Usually become less or stop within the first few months after starting injections. • Common, but some women do not have them. • The client can come back for help if side effects bother her.

Giving the Injection

1. Obtain one dose of injectable, needle and syringe

- 25 mg MPA/estradiol cypionate or 50 mg NET-EN/estradiol valerate, intramuscular injection needle, and 2 ml or 5 ml syringe. (NET-EN/estradiol valerate is sometimes available in prefilled syringes.)

- For each injection use a disposable auto-disable syringe and needle from a new sealed package (within expiration date and not damaged), if available.

2. Wash

- Wash hands with soap and water, if possible.

- If injection site is dirty, wash it with soap and water.

- No need to wipe site with antiseptic.

3. Prepare vial

- MPA/estradiol cypionate: Gently shake the vial.

- NET-EN/estradiol valerate: Shaking the vial is not necessary.

- No need to wipe top of vial with antiseptic.

- If vial is cold, warm to skin temperature before giving the injection.

4. Fill syringe

- Pierce top of vial with sterile needle and fill syringe with proper dose. (Omit this step if syringe is preloaded with injectable formulation.)

5. Inject formula

- Insert sterile needle deep into the hip (ventrogluteal muscle), the upper arm (deltoid muscle), the buttocks (gluteal muscle, upper outer portion), or outer (anterior) thigh, whichever the woman prefers. Inject the contents of the syringe.

- Do not massage injection site.

6. Dispose of disposable syringes and needles safely

- Do not recap, bend, or break needles before disposal.

- Place in a puncture-proof sharps container.

  - Do not reuse disposable syringes and needles. They are meant to be destroyed after a single use. Because of their shape, they are very difficult to disinfect. Therefore, reuse might transmit diseases such as HIV and hepatitis.

    - If reusable syringe and needle are used, they must be sterilized again after each use (see Infection Prevention in the Clinic, p. 312).

Supporting the User

Give specific instructions

- Tell her not to massage the injection site.

- Tell the client the name of the injection and agree on a date for her next injection in about 4 weeks.

"Come Back Any Time": Reasons to Return Before the Next Injection

Assure every client that she is welcome to come back any time—for example, if she has problems, questions, or wants another method; she has a major change in health status; or she thinks she might be pregnant.

General health advice: Anyone who suddenly feels that something is seriously wrong with her health should immediately seek medical care from a nurse or doctor. Her contraceptive method is most likely not the cause of the condition, but she should tell the nurse or doctor what method she is using.

Planning the Next Injection

1. Agree on a date for her next injection in 4 weeks.

2. Ask her to try to come on time. She may come up to 7 days early or 7 days late and still get an injection.

3. She should come back no matter how late she is for her next injection. If more than 7 days late, she should abstain from sex or use condoms, spermicides, or withdrawal until she can get an injection. She can also consider emergency contraceptive pills if she is more than 7 days late and she has had unprotected sex in the past 5 days (see Emergency Contraceptive Pills, p. 45).

Helping Continuing Users

Repeat Injection Visits

1. Ask how the client is doing with the method and whether she is satisfied. Ask if she has any questions or anything to discuss.

2. Ask especially if she is concerned about bleeding changes. Give her any information or help that she needs (see Managing Any Problems, next page).

3. Give her the injection. Injection can be given up to 7 days early or late.

4. Plan for her next injection. Agree on a date for her next injection (in 4 weeks). Remind her that she should try to come on time, but she should come back no matter how late she is.

5. Every year or so, check her blood pressure if possible (see Medical Eligibility Criteria, Question 5, p. 86).

6. Ask a long-term client if she has had any new health problems. Address problems as appropriate. For new health problems that may require switching methods, see p. 97.

7. Ask a long-term client about major life changes that may affect her needs—particularly plans for having children and STI/HIV risk. Follow up as needed.

Managing Late Injections

- If the client is less than 7 days late for a repeat injection, she can receive her next injection. No need for tests, evaluation, or a backup method.

- A client who is more than 7 days late can receive her next injection if:

    - She has not had sex since 7 *days after* she should have had her last injection, or

    - She has used a backup method or has taken emergency contraceptive pills (ECPs) after any unprotected sex since 7 *days after* she should have had her last injection.

    She will need a backup method for the first 7 days after the injection.

- If the client is more than 7 days late and does not meet these criteria, additional steps can be taken to be reasonably certain she is not pregnant (see Further Options to Assess for Pregnancy, p. 370).

- Discuss why the client was late and solutions. If coming back on time is often a problem, discuss using a backup method when she is late for her next injection, taking ECPs, or choosing another method.

Managing Any Problems

Problems Reported as Side Effects

May or may not be due to the method.

- Problems with side effects affect women's satisfaction and use of injectables. They deserve the provider's attention. If the client reports side effects, listen to her concerns, give her advice, and, if appropriate, treat.

- Offer to help the client choose another method—now, if she wishes, or if problems cannot be overcome.

Irregular bleeding (bleeding at unexpected times that bothers the client)

- Reassure her that many women using monthly injectables experience irregular bleeding. It is not harmful and usually becomes less or stops after the first few months of use.

- For modest short-term relief, she can try 800 mg ibuprofen 3 times daily after meals for 5 days or other nonsteroidal anti-inflammatory drug (NSAID), beginning when irregular bleeding starts. NSAIDs provide some relief of irregular bleeding for implants, progestin-only injectables, and IUDs, and they may also help for monthly injectables.

- If irregular bleeding continues or starts after several months of normal or no monthly bleeding, or you suspect that something may be wrong for other reasons, consider underlying conditions unrelated to method use (see Unexplained vaginal bleeding, p. 97).

Heavy or prolonged bleeding (twice as much as usual or longer than 8 days)

- Reassure her that many women using monthly injectables experience heavy or prolonged bleeding. It is generally not harmful and usually becomes less or stops after a few months.

- For modest short-term relief, she can try 800 mg ibuprofen 3 times daily after meals for 5 days or other NSAID, beginning when heavy bleeding starts. NSAIDs provide some relief of heavy bleeding for implants, progestin-only injectables, and IUDs, and they may also help for monthly injectables.

- To help prevent anemia, suggest she take iron tablets and tell her it is important to eat foods containing iron, such as meat and poultry (especially beef and chicken liver), fish, green leafy vegetables, and legumes (beans, bean curd, lentils, and peas).

- If heavy or prolonged bleeding continues or starts after several months of normal or no monthly bleeding, or you suspect that something may be wrong for other reasons, consider underlying conditions unrelated to method use (see Unexplained vaginal bleeding, next page).

No monthly bleeding

- Reassure her that some women using monthly injectables stop having monthly bleeding, and this not harmful. There is no need to lose blood every month. It is similar to not having monthly bleeding during pregnancy. She is not infertile. Blood is not building up inside her. (Some women are happy to be free from monthly bleeding.)

Weight gain

- Review diet and counsel as needed.

Ordinary headaches (nonmigrainous)

- Suggest aspirin (325–650 mg), ibuprofen (200–400 mg), paracetamol (325–1000 mg), or other pain reliever.

- Any headaches that get worse or occur more often during use of injectables should be evaluated.

Breast tenderness

- Recommend that she wear a supportive bra (including during strenuous activity and sleep).

- Try hot or cold compresses.

- Suggest aspirin (325–650 mg), ibuprofen (200–400 mg), paracetamol (325–1000 mg), or other pain reliever.

- Consider locally available remedies.

Dizziness

- Consider locally available remedies.

New Problems That May Require Switching Methods

May or may not be due to the method.

Unexplained vaginal bleeding (that suggests a medical condition not related to the method)

- Refer or evaluate by history and pelvic examination. Diagnose and treat as appropriate.
- She can continue using monthly injectables while her condition is being evaluated.
- If bleeding is caused by sexually transmitted infection or pelvic inflammatory disease, she can continue using monthly injectables during treatment.

Migraine headaches (see Identifying Migraine Headaches and Auras, p. 368)

- Regardless of her age, a woman who develops migraine headaches, with or without aura, or whose migraine headaches become worse while using monthly injectables, should stop using injectables.
- Help her choose a method without estrogen.

Circumstances that will keep her from walking for one week or more

- If she is having major surgery, or her leg is in a cast, or for other reasons she will be unable to move about for several weeks, she should:
  - Tell her doctors that she is using monthly injectables.
  - Stop injections one month before scheduled surgery, if possible, and use a backup method during this period.
  - Restart monthly injectables 2 weeks after she can move about again.

Certain serious health conditions (suspected heart or liver disease, high blood pressure, blood clots in deep veins of legs or lungs, stroke, breast cancer, or damage to arteries, vision, kidneys, or nervous system caused by diabetes). See Signs and Symptoms of Serious Health Conditions, p. 320.

- Do not give the next injection.
- Give her a backup method to use until the condition is evaluated.
- Refer for diagnosis and care if not already under care.

Suspected pregnancy

- Assess for pregnancy.
- Stop injections if pregnancy is confirmed.
- There are no known risks to a fetus conceived while a woman is using injectables (see Question 3, p. 98).

Starting treatment with lamotrigine or ritonavir

- Combined hormonal methods, including monthly injectables, can make lamotrigine less effective. Unless she can use a different medication for seizures than lamotrigine, help her choose a method without estrogen.
- Ritonavir and ritonavir-boosted protease inhibitors may make monthly injectables less effective. She can use progestin-only injectables, implants, the LNG-IUD, or any nonhormonal method.

Questions and Answers About Monthly Injectables

1. **How are monthly injectables different from DMPA or NET-EN?**

   The major difference between monthly injectables and DMPA or NET-EN is that a monthly injectable contains an estrogen as well as a progestin, making it a combined method. In contrast, DMPA and NET-EN contain progestin only. Also, monthly injectables contain less progestin. These differences result in more regular bleeding and fewer bleeding disturbances than with DMPA or NET-EN. Monthly injectables require a monthly injection, whereas NET-EN is injected every 2 months and DMPA, every 3 months.

2. **Do monthly injectables function like combined oral contraceptives?**

   Largely, yes. Monthly injectables (also called combined injectable contraceptives) are similar to combined oral contraceptives (COCs). There are few long-term studies done on monthly injectables, but researchers assume that most of the findings about COCs also apply to monthly injectables. Monthly injectables, however, do not pass through the liver first because they are not taken by mouth like COCs. Short-term studies have shown that monthly injectables have less effect than COCs on blood pressure, blood clotting, the breakdown of fatty substances (lipid metabolism), and liver function. Long-term studies of the health risks and benefits of monthly injectables are underway.

3. **Do monthly injectables cause birth defects? Will the fetus be harmed if a woman accidentally uses monthly injectables while she is pregnant?**

   No. Good evidence from studies on other hormonal methods shows that hormonal contraception will not cause birth defects and will not otherwise harm the fetus if a woman becomes pregnant while using monthly injectables or accidentally starts injectables when she is already pregnant.

4. **Do monthly injectables cause abortion?**

   No. Research on combined contraceptives finds that they do not disrupt an existing pregnancy. They should not be used to try to cause an abortion. They will not do so.

5. **Should the dates for a woman's repeat injections be based on when monthly bleeding starts?**

   No. Some providers think that the next injection should only be given when the next monthly bleeding begins. Bleeding episodes should not guide the injection schedule, however. A woman should receive the injection every 4 weeks. The timing of injections should not be based on her monthly bleeding.

6. **Can monthly injectables be used to bring on monthly bleeding?**

   No. A woman may experience some vaginal bleeding (a "withdrawal bleed") as a result of an injection, but there is no evidence that giving a woman who has irregular bleeding a single injection of a monthly injectable will cause her monthly bleeding to begin properly about one month later. Also, giving a pregnant woman an injection will not cause an abortion.

7. **Can women who smoke use monthly injectables safely?**

   Women younger than age 35 who smoke any number of cigarettes and women 35 and older who smoke fewer than 15 cigarettes a day can safely use monthly injectables. (In contrast, women 35 and older who smoke any number of cigarettes should not use combined oral contraceptives.) Women 35 and older who smoke more than 15 cigarettes a day should choose a method without estrogen such as progestin-only injectables, if available. All women who smoke should be urged to stop smoking.

8. **Do monthly injectables change women's mood or sex drive?**

Generally, no. Some women using monthly injectables report these complaints. The great majority of injectables users do not report any such changes, however, and some report that both mood and sex drive improve. It is difficult to tell whether such changes are due to monthly injectables or to other reasons. There is no evidence that monthly injectables affect women's sexual behavior.

9. **Can women with varicose veins use monthly injectables?**

Yes. Monthly injectables are safe for women with varicose veins. Varicose veins are enlarged blood vessels close to the surface of the skin. They are not dangerous. They are not blood clots, nor are these veins the deep veins in the legs where a blood clot can be dangerous (deep vein thrombosis). A woman who has or has had deep vein thrombosis should not use monthly injectables.

10. **Do monthly injectables make a woman infertile?**

No. There may be a delay in regaining fertility after stopping monthly injectables, but in time the woman will be able to become pregnant as before, although fertility decreases as women get older. The bleeding pattern a woman had before she used monthly injectables generally returns a few months after the last injection. Some women may have to wait a few months before their usual bleeding pattern returns

11. **How long does it take to become pregnant after stopping monthly injectables?**

Women who stop using monthly injectables wait about one month longer on average to become pregnant than women who have used other methods. This means they become pregnant on average 5 months after their last injection. These are averages. A woman should not be worried if she has not become pregnant even as much as 12 months after stopping use. After stopping monthly injectables, a woman may ovulate before her monthly bleeding returns—and thus can become pregnant. If she wants to continue avoiding pregnancy, she should start another method before monthly bleeding returns.

12. **What if a woman returns for her next injection late?**

Current WHO guidance recommends giving a woman her next monthly injection if she is up to 7 days late, without the need for further evidence that she is not pregnant. Some women return even later for their repeat injection, however. Providers can use Further Options to Assess for Pregnancy (see p. 370) if a user of monthly injectables is more than 7 days late for her repeat injection.

Combined Patch

Key Points for Providers and Clients

- **Requires wearing a small adhesive patch.** Worn on the body every day and night. A new patch is put on each week, for 3 weeks, followed by a week with no patch.

- **Replace each patch on time for greatest effectiveness.**

- **Bleeding changes are common but not harmful.** Typically, irregular bleeding for the first few months and then lighter and more regular bleeding.

What Is the Combined Patch?

- A small, thin, square of flexible plastic worn on the body.

- Continuously releases 2 hormones—a progestin and an estrogen, like the natural hormones progesterone and estrogen in a woman's body—directly through the skin into the bloodstream.

- A new patch is worn every week for 3 weeks, then no patch for the fourth week. During this fourth week the woman will have monthly bleeding.

- Also called Ortho Evra and Evra.

- Works primarily by preventing the release of eggs from the ovaries (ovulation).

How Effective?

Effectiveness depends on the user: Risk of pregnancy is greatest when a woman is late to change the patch.

- The combined patch is new, and research on effectiveness is limited. Effectiveness rates in clinical trials of the patch suggest that it may be more effective than combined oral contraceptives, both as commonly used and with consistent and correct use (see Combined Oral Contraceptives, How Effective?, p. 1).

More
effective

↑

Less
effective

- Pregnancy rates may be slightly higher among women weighing 90 kg or more.

Return of fertility after patch use is stopped: No delay

Protection against sexually transmitted infections: None

Side Effects, Health Benefits, and Health Risks

Side Effects

Some users report the following:

- Skin irritation or rash where the patch is applied
- Changes in monthly bleeding:

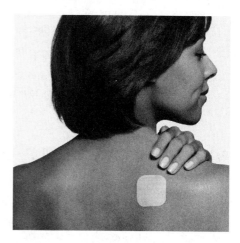

  - Lighter bleeding and fewer days of bleeding
  - Irregular bleeding
  - Prolonged bleeding
  - No monthly bleeding
- Headaches
- Nausea
- Vomiting
- Breast tenderness and pain
- Abdominal pain
- Flu symptoms/upper respiratory infection
- Irritation, redness, or inflammation of the vagina (vaginitis)

Known Health Benefits and Health Risks

Long-term studies of the patch are limited, but researchers expect that its health benefits and risks are like those of combined oral contraceptives (see Combined Oral Contraceptives, Health Benefits and Health Risks, p. 3).

Medical eligibility criteria (see p. 6), guidelines for when to start (see p. 10), and helping continuing users (see p. 16) are the same for the combined patch as for combined oral contraceptives.

Providing the Combined Patch

Explaining How to Use

Explain how to remove the patch from the pouch and remove backing	• Explain that she should tear the foil pouch along the edge. • She should then pull out the patch and peel away the backing without touching the sticky surface.
Show her where and how to apply the patch	• Explain that she can apply it on the upper outer arm, back, stomach, abdomen, or buttocks, wherever it is clean and dry, but not on the breasts. • She must press the sticky, medicated part against her skin for 10 seconds. She should run her finger along the edge to make sure it sticks. • The patch will stay on even during work, exercise, swimming, and bathing.
She must change the patch every week for 3 weeks in a row	• She should apply each new patch on the same day of each week—the "patch-change day." For example, if she puts on her first patch on a Sunday, all of her patches should be applied on a Sunday. • Explain that to avoid irritation, she should not apply the new patch to the same place on the skin where the previous patch was.
She should not wear a patch on the fourth week	• She will probably have monthly bleeding this week.
After the patch-free week, she should apply a new patch	• She should never go without wearing a patch for more than 7 days. Doing so risks pregnancy.

Supporting the User

Instructions for Late Removal or Replacement

Forgot to apply a new patch at the start of any patch cycle (during week one)?	• Apply a new patch as soon as possible. • Record this day of the week as the new patch-change day. • Use a backup method* for the first 7 days of patch use. • Also, if the new patch was applied 3 or more days late (patch was left off for 10 days or more in a row) and she had unprotected sex in the past 5 days, consider taking emergency contraceptive pills (see Emergency Contraceptive Pills, p. 45).

Forgot to change the patch in the middle of the patch cycle (during week 2 or 3)?	• If late by 1 or 2 days (up to 48 hours):
	  – Apply a new patch as soon as remembered
	  – Keep the same patch-change day
	  – No need for a backup method
	
	• If late by more than 2 days (more than 48 hours):
	  – Stop the current cycle and start a new 4-week cycle by applying a new patch immediately
	  – Record this day of the week as the new patch-change day
	  – Use a backup method for the first 7 days of patch use

Forgot to remove the patch at the end of the patch cycle (week 4)?	• Remove the patch. • Start the next cycle on the usual patch-change day. • No need for a backup method.

* Backup methods include abstinence, male and female condoms, spermicides, and withdrawal. Tell her that spermicides and withdrawal are the least effective contraceptive methods. If possible, give her condoms.

Only CHAPTER 7
the Essentials

Combined Vaginal Ring

Key Points for Providers and Clients

- **Requires keeping a flexible ring in the vagina.** It is kept in place all the time, every day and night for 3 weeks, followed by a week with no ring in place.

- **Start each new ring on time for greatest effectiveness.**

- **Bleeding changes are common but not harmful.** Typically, irregular bleeding for the first few months and then lighter and more regular bleeding.

What Is the Combined Vaginal Ring?

- A flexible ring placed in the vagina.

- Continuously releases 2 hormones—a progestin and an estrogen, like the natural hormones progesterone and estrogen in a woman's body—from inside the ring. Hormones are absorbed through the wall of the vagina directly into the bloodstream.

- The ring is kept in place for 3 weeks, then removed for the fourth week. During this fourth week the woman will have monthly bleeding.

- Also called NuvaRing.

- Works primarily by preventing the release of eggs from the ovaries (ovulation).

How Effective?

More effective

Effectiveness depends on the user: Risk of pregnancy is greatest when a woman is late to start a new ring.

- The combined vaginal ring is new, and research on effectiveness is limited. Effectiveness rates in clinical trials of the vaginal ring suggest that it may be more effective than combined oral contraceptives, both as commonly used and with consistent and correct use (see Combined Oral Contraceptives, How Effective?, p. 1).

Return of fertility after ring use is stopped: No delay

Protection against sexually transmitted infections: None

Less effective

Side Effects, Health Benefits, and Health Risks

Side Effects

Some users report the following:

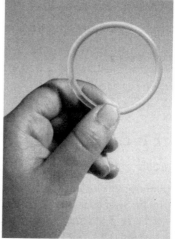

- Changes in monthly bleeding, including:
  - Lighter bleeding and fewer days of bleeding
  - Irregular bleeding
  - Infrequent bleeding
  - Prolonged bleeding
  - No monthly bleeding
- Headaches
- Irritation, redness, or inflammation of the vagina (vaginitis)
- White vaginal discharge

Known Health Benefits and Health Risks

Long-term studies of the vaginal ring are limited, but researchers expect that its health benefits and risks are like those of combined oral contraceptives (see Combined Oral Contraceptives, Health Benefits and Health Risks, p. 3).

> Medical eligibility criteria (see p. 6), guidelines for when to start (see p. 10), and helping continuing users (see p. 16) are the same for the combined ring as for combined oral contraceptives.

Providing the Combined Vaginal Ring

Explaining How to Use

Explain how to insert the ring

- She can choose the position most comfortable for her—for example, standing with one leg up, squatting, or lying down.

- She should press opposite sides of the ring together and gently push the folded ring entirely inside the vagina.

- The exact position is not important, but inserting it deeply helps it to stay in place, and she is less likely to feel it. The muscles of the vagina naturally keep the ring in place.

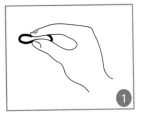
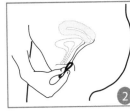
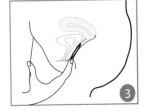

Explain that the ring must be left in place for 3 weeks

- She should keep the ring in place all the time, every day and night for 3 weeks.

- She can take the ring out at the end of the third week and dispose of it in a waste receptacle.

She should take out the ring for the fourth week

- To remove the ring, she should hook her index finger inside it, or squeeze the ring between her index and middle fingers, and pull it out.

- She will probably have monthly bleeding this week.

- If she forgets and leaves the ring in for as long as a fourth week, no special action is needed.

Ring should never be left out for more than 3 hours until the fourth week

- The ring can be removed for sex, cleaning, or other reasons, although removing it is not necessary.

- If the ring slips out, she should rinse it in clean water and immediately reinsert it.

Supporting the User

Instructions for Late Replacement or Removal

Left ring out for more than 3 hours during weeks 1 or 2?	• Put the ring back in as soon as possible. Use a backup method* for the next 7 days.
Left ring out for more than 3 hours during week 3?	• Stop the current cycle and discard the ring. • Insert a new ring immediately and keep it in place for 3 weeks, starting a new cycle. Use a backup method for the next 7 days. (Another option, if the ring was used continuously and correctly for the past 7 days: Leave the ring out and make the next 7 days the week with no ring. After those 7 days, insert a new ring, starting a new cycle, and keep it in place for 3 weeks. Use a backup method for the first 7 days with the new ring.)
Waited more than 7 days before inserting a new ring, or kept ring in longer than 4 weeks?	• Insert a new ring as soon as possible and begin a new 4-week cycle. Use a backup method for the first 7 days of ring use. • Also, if a new ring was inserted 3 or more days late (ring was left out for 10 days or more in a row) and unprotected sex took place in the past 5 days, consider taking emergency contraceptive pills (see Emergency Contraceptive Pills, p. 45).

---

* *Backup methods include abstinence, male and female condoms, spermicides, and withdrawal. Tell her that spermicides and withdrawal are the least effective contraceptive methods. If possible, give her condoms.*

CHAPTER 8

Implants

Key Points for Providers and Clients

- **Implants are small flexible rods or capsules** that are placed just under the skin of the upper arm.

- **Provide long-term pregnancy protection.** Very effective for 3 to 7 years, depending on the type of implant, immediately reversible.

- **Require specifically trained provider to insert and remove.** A woman cannot start or stop implants on her own.

- **Little required of the client once implants are in place.**

- **Bleeding changes are common but not harmful.** Typically, prolonged irregular bleeding over the first year, and then lighter, more regular bleeding or infrequent bleeding.

What Are Implants?

- Small plastic rods or capsules, each about the size of a matchstick, that release a progestin like the natural hormone progesterone in a woman's body.

- A specifically trained provider performs a minor surgical procedure to place the implants under the skin on the inside of a woman's upper arm.

- Do not contain estrogen, and so can be used throughout breastfeeding and by women who cannot use methods with estrogen.

- Many types of implants:

  - Jadelle: 2 rods, effective for 5 years
  - Implanon: 1 rod, effective for 3 years (studies are underway to see if it lasts 4 years)
  - Sino-Implant (II), also known as Femplant, Trust Implant, and Zarin: 2 rods, effective for 4 years (may be extended to 5 years)
  - Norplant: 6 capsules, labeled for 5 years of use (large studies have found it is effective for 7 years)

- Work primarily by:

  - Thickening cervical mucus (this blocks sperm from meeting an egg)
  - Disrupting the menstrual cycle, including preventing the release of eggs from the ovaries (ovulation)

How Effective?

More
effective

One of the most effective and long-lasting methods:

- Less than 1 pregnancy per 100 women using implants over the first year (5 per 10,000 women). This means that **9,995 of every 10,000 women using implants will not become pregnant.**

- A small risk of pregnancy remains beyond the first year of use and continues as long as the woman is using implants.

  - Over 5 years of Jadelle use: About 1 pregnancy per 100 women

  - Over 3 years of Implanon use: Less than 1 pregnancy per 100 women (1 per 1,000 women)

  - Over 7 years of Norplant use: About 2 pregnancies per 100 women

Less
effective

- Jadelle, Sino-Implant (II), and Norplant implants start to lose effectiveness sooner for heavier women:

  - For women weighing 80 kg or more, Jadelle, Sino-Implant (II), and Norplant become less effective after 4 years of use.

  - For women weighing 70–79 kg, Norplant becomes less effective after 5 years of use.

  - These users may want to replace their implants sooner (see p. 130, Q&A 9).

Return of fertility after implants are removed: No delay

Protection against sexually transmitted infections (STIs): None

Why Some Women Say They Like Implants

- Do not require the user to do anything once they are inserted
- Prevent pregnancy very effectively
- Are long-lasting
- Do not interfere with sex

Side Effects, Health Benefits, Health Risks, and Complications

Side Effects (see Managing Any Problems, p. 124)

Some users report the following:

- Changes in bleeding patterns including:

First several months:

- Lighter bleeding and fewer days of bleeding
- Irregular bleeding
- Infrequent bleeding
- No monthly bleeding

After about one year:

- Lighter bleeding and fewer days of bleeding
- Irregular bleeding
- Infrequent bleeding

Implanon users are more likely to have infrequent or no monthly bleeding than irregular bleeding.

- Headaches
- Abdominal pain
- Acne (can improve or worsen)
- Weight change
- Breast tenderness
- Dizziness
- Mood changes
- Nausea

Other possible physical changes:

- Enlarged ovarian follicles

Known Health Benefits

Help protect against:

- Risks of pregnancy
- Symptomatic pelvic inflammatory disease

May help protect against:

- Iron-deficiency anemia

Known Health Risks

None

Complications

Uncommon:

- Infection at insertion site (most infections occur within the first 2 months after insertion)
- Difficult removal (rare if properly inserted and the provider is skilled at removal)

Rare:

- Expulsion of implant (expulsions most often occur within the first 4 months after insertion)

Correcting Misunderstandings (see also Questions and Answers, p. 128)

Implants:

- Stop working once they are removed. Their hormones do not remain in a woman's body.
- Can stop monthly bleeding, but this is not harmful. It is similar to not having monthly bleeding during pregnancy. Blood is not building up inside the woman.
- Do not make women infertile.
- Do not move to other parts of the body.
- Substantially reduce the risk of ectopic pregnancy.

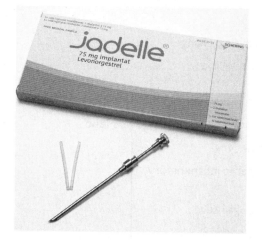

Who Can and Cannot Use Implants

Safe and Suitable for Nearly All Women

Nearly all women can use implants safely and effectively, including women who:

- Have or have not had children
- Are not married
- Are of any age, including adolescents and women over 40 years old
- Have just had an abortion, miscarriage, or ectopic pregnancy
- Smoke cigarettes, regardless of woman's age or number of cigarettes smoked
- Are breastfeeding (starting as soon as 6 weeks after childbirth; however, see p. 129, Q&A 8)
- Have anemia now or in the past
- Have varicose veins
- Are infected with HIV, whether or not on antiretroviral therapy (see Implants for Women With HIV, p. 115)

Women can begin using implants:

- Without a pelvic examination
- Without any blood tests or other routine laboratory tests
- Without cervical cancer screening
- Without a breast examination
- Even when a woman is not having monthly bleeding at the time, if it is reasonably certain she is not pregnant (see Pregnancy Checklist, p. 372)

Implants

Ask the client the questions below about known medical conditions. Examinations and tests are not necessary. If she answers "no" to all of the questions, then she can have implants inserted if she wants. If she answers "yes" to a question, follow the instructions. In some cases she can still start using implants.

1. **Are you breastfeeding a baby less than 6 weeks old?**

   ❏ NO   ❏ YES She can start using implants as soon as 6 weeks after childbirth (see Fully or nearly fully breastfeeding or Partially breastfeeding, p. 117).

2. **Do you have severe cirrhosis of the liver, a liver infection, or liver tumor? (Are her eyes or skin unusually yellow? [signs of jaundice])**

   ❏ NO   ❏ YES If she reports serious active liver disease (jaundice, severe cirrhosis, liver tumor), do not provide implants. Help her choose a method without hormones.

3. **Do you have a serious problem now with a blood clot in your legs or lungs?**

   ❏ NO   ❏ YES If she reports a current blood clot (not superficial clots), and she is not on anticoagulant therapy, do not provide implants. Help her choose a method without hormones.

4. **Do you have vaginal bleeding that is unusual for you?**

   ❏ NO   ❏ YES If she has unexplained vaginal bleeding that suggests pregnancy or an underlying medical condition, implants could make diagnosis and monitoring of any treatment more difficult. Help her choose a method to use while being evaluated and treated (not progestin-only injectables, or a copper-bearing or hormonal IUD). After treatment, re-evaluate for use of implants.

5. **Do you have or have you ever had breast cancer?**

   ❏ NO   ❏ YES Do not provide implants. Help her choose a method without hormones.

Be sure to explain the health benefits and risks and the side effects of the method that the client will use. Also, point out any conditions that would make the method inadvisable, when relevant to the client.

Using Clinical Judgment in Special Cases

Usually, a woman with any of the conditions listed below should not use implants. In special circumstances, however, when other, more appropriate methods are not available or acceptable to her, a qualified provider who can carefully assess a specific woman's condition and situation may decide that she can use implants. The provider needs to consider the severity of her condition and, for most conditions, whether she will have access to follow-up.

- Breastfeeding and less than 6 weeks since giving birth (considering the risks of another pregnancy and that a woman may have limited further access to implants)
- Acute blood clot in deep veins of legs or lungs
- Unexplained vaginal bleeding before evaluation for possible serious underlying condition
- Had breast cancer more than 5 years ago, and it has not returned
- Severe liver disease, infection, or tumor
- Systemic lupus erythematosus with positive (or unknown) antiphospholipid antibodies

Implants for Women With HIV

- Women who are infected with HIV, have AIDS, or are on antiretroviral (ARV) therapy can safely use implants.
- Urge these women to use condoms along with implants. Used consistently and correctly, condoms help prevent transmission of HIV and other STIs.

Providing Implants

When to Start

IMPORTANT: A woman can start using implants any time she wants if it is reasonably certain she is not pregnant. To be reasonably certain she is not pregnant, use the Pregnancy Checklist (see p. 372).

Woman's situation	When to start
Having menstrual cycles or switching from a nonhormonal method	**Any time of the month** • If she is starting within 7 days after the start of her monthly bleeding (5 days for Implanon), no need for a backup method. • If it is more than 7 days after the start of her monthly bleeding (more than 5 days for Implanon), she can have implants inserted any time it is reasonably certain she is not pregnant. She will need a backup method* for the first 7 days after insertion. • If she is switching from an IUD, she can have implants inserted immediately (see Copper-Bearing IUD, Switching From an IUD to Another Method, p. 148).
Switching from a hormonal method	• Immediately, if she has been using the hormonal method consistently and correctly or if it is otherwise reasonably certain she is not pregnant. No need to wait for her next monthly bleeding. No need for a backup method. • If she is switching from injectables, she can have implants inserted when the repeat injection would have been given. No need for a backup method.

---

* Backup methods include abstinence, male and female condoms, spermicides, and withdrawal. Tell her that spermicides and withdrawal are the least effective contraceptive methods. If possible, give her condoms.

Woman's situation	When to start
Fully or nearly fully breastfeeding	
Less than 6 months after giving birth	• If she gave birth less than 6 weeks ago, delay insertion until at least 6 weeks after giving birth. (See p. 129, Q&A 8.)
	• If her monthly bleeding has not returned, she can have implants inserted any time between 6 weeks and 6 months. No need for a backup method.
	• If her monthly bleeding has returned, she can have implants inserted as advised for women having menstrual cycles (see previous page).
More than 6 months after giving birth	• If her monthly bleeding has not returned, she can have implants inserted any time it is reasonably certain she is not pregnant. She will need a backup method for the first 7 days after insertion.
	• If her monthly bleeding has returned, she can have implants inserted as advised for women having menstrual cycles (see previous page).
Partially breastfeeding	
Less than 6 weeks after giving birth	• Delay insertion until at least 6 weeks after giving birth. (See p. 129, Q&A 8.)
More than 6 weeks after giving birth	• If her monthly bleeding has not returned, she can have implants inserted any time it is reasonably certain she is not pregnant.[†] She will need a backup method for the first 7 days after insertion.
	• If her monthly bleeding has returned, she can have implants inserted as advised for women having menstrual cycles (see previous page).
Not breastfeeding	
Less than 4 weeks after giving birth	• She can have implants inserted at any time. No need for a backup method.

[†] *Where a visit 6 weeks after childbirth is routinely recommended and other opportunities to obtain contraception limited, some providers and programs may insert implants at the 6-week visit, without further evidence that the woman is not pregnant, if her monthly bleeding has not yet returned.*

Woman's situation	When to start
Not breastfeeding (continued)	
More than 4 weeks after giving birth	• If her monthly bleeding has not returned, she can have implants inserted any time it is reasonably certain she is not pregnant.[†] She will need a backup method for the first 7 days after insertion.
	• If her monthly bleeding has returned, she can have implants inserted as advised for women having menstrual cycles (see p. 116).
No monthly bleeding (not related to childbirth or breastfeeding)	• She can have implants inserted any time it is reasonably certain she is not pregnant. She will need a backup method for the first 7 days after insertion.
After miscarriage or abortion	• Immediately. If implants are inserted within 7 days after first- or second-trimester miscarriage or abortion, no need for a backup method.
	• If it is more than 7 days after first- or second-trimester miscarriage or abortion, she can have implants inserted any time it is reasonably certain she is not pregnant. She will need a backup method for the first 7 days after insertion.
After taking emergency contraceptive pills (ECPs)	• Implants can be inserted within 7 days after the start of her next monthly bleeding (within 5 days for Implanon) or any other time it is reasonably certain she is not pregnant. Give her a backup method, or oral contraceptives to start the day after she finishes taking the ECPs, to use until the implants are inserted.

[†] *Where a visit 6 weeks after childbirth is routinely recommended and other opportunities to obtain contraception limited, some providers and programs may insert implants at the 6-week visit, without further evidence that the woman is not pregnant, if her monthly bleeding has not yet returned.*

Giving Advice on Side Effects

IMPORTANT: Thorough counseling about bleeding changes and other side effects must come before inserting implants. Counseling about bleeding changes may be the most important help a woman needs to keep using the method.

Describe the most common side effects	• Changes in her bleeding pattern:
	
	  – Irregular bleeding that lasts more than 8 days at a time over the first year.
	
	  – Regular, infrequent, or no bleeding at all later.
	
	• Headaches, abdominal pain, breast tenderness, and possibly other side effects.

Explain about these side effects	• Side effects are not signs of illness. • Most side effects usually become less or stop within the first year. • Common, but some women do not have them. • Client can come back for help if side effects bother her.

Inserting Implants

Explaining the Insertion Procedure for Jadelle and Norplant

A woman who has chosen implants needs to know what will happen during insertion. The following description can help explain the procedure to her. Learning to insert and remove implants requires training and practice under direct supervision. Therefore, this description is a summary and not detailed instructions.

Inserting implants usually takes only a few minutes but can sometimes take longer, depending on the skill of the provider. Related complications are rare and also depend on the skill of the provider. (Implanon is inserted with a specially made applicator similar to a syringe. It does not require an incision.)

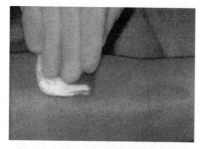

1. The provider uses proper infection-prevention procedures.

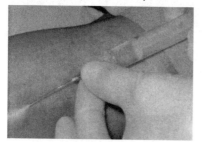

2. The woman receives an injection of local anesthetic under the skin of her arm to prevent pain while the implants are being inserted. This injection may sting. She stays fully awake throughout the procedure.

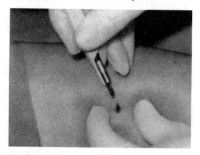

3. The provider makes a small incision in the skin on the inside of the upper arm.

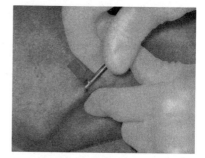

4. The provider inserts the implants just under the skin. The woman may feel some pressure or tugging.

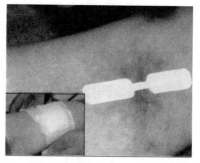

5. After all implants are inserted, the provider closes the incision with an adhesive bandage. Stitches are not needed. The incision is covered with a dry cloth and the arm is wrapped with gauze.

Removing Implants

IMPORTANT: Providers must not refuse or delay when a woman asks to have her implants removed, whatever her reason, whether it is personal or medical. All staff must understand and agree that she must not be pressured or forced to continue using implants.

Explaining the Removal Procedure

A woman needs to know what will happen during removal. The following description can help explain the procedure to her. The same removal procedure is used for all types of implants.

1. The provider uses proper infection-prevention procedures.

2. The woman receives an injection of local anesthetic under the skin of her arm to prevent pain during implant removal. This injection may sting. She stays fully awake throughout the procedure.

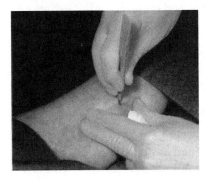 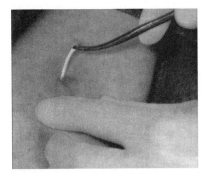

3. The health care provider makes a small incision in the skin on the inside of the upper arm, near the site of insertion.

4. The provider uses an instrument to pull out each implant. A woman may feel tugging, slight pain, or soreness during the procedure and for a few days after.

5. The provider closes the incision with an adhesive bandage. Stitches are not needed. An elastic bandage may be placed over the adhesive bandage to apply gentle pressure for 2 or 3 days and keep down swelling.

If a woman wants new implants, they are placed above or below the site of the previous implants or in the other arm.

Supporting the User

Giving Specific Instructions

Keep arm dry	• She should keep the insertion area dry for 4 days. She can take off the elastic bandage or gauze after 2 days and the adhesive bandage after 5 days.
Expect soreness, bruising	• After the anesthetic wears off, her arm may be sore for a few days. She also may have swelling and bruising at the insertion site. This is common and will go away without treatment.

Length of pregnancy protection	• Discuss how to remember the date to return.
	 • Give each woman the following information in writing on a reminder card, like the one shown below, if possible, and explain:
	   – The type of implant she has
	   – Date of insertion
	   – Month and year when implants will need to be removed or replaced
	   – Where to go if she has problems or questions with her implants

Have implants removed before they start to lose effectiveness	• Return or see another provider before the implants start losing effectiveness (for removal or, if she wishes, replacement).

Implant Reminder Card

Client's name: _____

Type of implant: _____

Date inserted: _____

Remove or replace by: Month: _____ Year: _____

If you have any problems or questions, go to:

(name and location of facility)

"Come Back Any Time": Reasons to Return

Assure every client that she is welcome to come back any time—for example, if she has problems, questions, or wants another method; she has a major change in health status; or she thinks she might be pregnant. Also if:

- She has pain, heat, pus, or redness at the insertion site that becomes worse or does not go away, or she sees a rod coming out.

- She has gained a lot of weight. This may decrease the length of time her implants remain highly effective.

General health advice: Anyone who suddenly feels that something is seriously wrong with her health should immediately seek medical care from a nurse or doctor. Her contraceptive method is most likely not the cause of the condition, but she should tell the nurse or doctor what method she is using.

Helping Continuing Users

IMPORTANT: No routine return visit is required until it is time to remove the implants. The client should be clearly invited to return any time she wishes, however.

1. Ask how the client is doing with the method and whether she is satisfied. Ask if she has any questions or anything to discuss.

2. Ask especially if she is concerned about bleeding changes. Give her any information or help that she needs (see Managing Any Problems, p. 124).

3. Ask a long-term client if she has had any new health problems since her last visit. Address problems as appropriate. For new health problems that may require switching methods, see p. 127.

4. Ask a long-term client about major life changes that may affect her needs—particularly plans for having children and STI/HIV risk. Follow up as needed.

5. If possible, weigh the client who is using Jadelle or Norplant implants. If her weight has changed enough to affect the duration of her implants' effectiveness, update her reminder card, if she has one, or give her a new reminder card with the proper date (see Question 9, p. 130).

6. If she wants to keep using implants and no new medical condition prevents it, remind her how much longer her implants will protect her from pregnancy.

Managing Any Problems

Problems Reported as Side Effects or Complications

May or may not be due to the method.

- Problems with side effects and complications affect women's satisfaction and use of implants. They deserve the provider's attention. If the client reports any side effects or complications, listen to her concerns, give her advice, and, if appropriate, treat.

- Offer to help the client choose another method—now, if she wishes, or if problems cannot be overcome.

Irregular bleeding (bleeding at unexpected times that bothers the client)

- Reassure her that many women using implants experience irregular bleeding. It is not harmful and usually becomes less or stops after the first year of use.

- For modest short-term relief, she can take 800 mg ibuprofen or 500 mg mefenamic acid 3 times daily after meals for 5 days, beginning when irregular bleeding starts.

- If these drugs do not help her, she can try one of the following, beginning when irregular bleeding starts:

  - Combined oral contraceptives with the progestin levonorgestrel. Ask her to take one pill daily for 21 days.

  - 50 µg ethinyl estradiol daily for 21 days.

- If irregular bleeding continues or starts after several months of normal or no monthly bleeding, or you suspect that something may be wrong for other reasons, consider underlying conditions unrelated to method use (see Unexplained vaginal bleeding, p. 127).

No monthly bleeding

- Reassure her that some women stop having monthly bleeding when using implants, and this is not harmful. There is no need to lose blood every month. It is similar to not having monthly bleeding during pregnancy. She is not infertile. Blood is not building up inside her. (Some women are happy to be free from monthly bleeding.)

Heavy or prolonged bleeding (twice as much as usual or longer than 8 days)

- Reassure her that some women using implants experience heavy or prolonged bleeding. It is generally not harmful and usually becomes less or stops after a few months.

- For modest short-term relief, she can try any of the treatments for irregular bleeding, above, beginning when heavy bleeding starts. Combined oral contraceptives with 50 µg of ethinyl estradiol may work better than lower-dose pills.

- To help prevent anemia, suggest she take iron tablets and tell her it is important to eat foods containing iron, such as meat and poultry (especially beef and chicken liver), fish, green leafy vegetables, and legumes (beans, bean curd, lentils, and peas).

- If heavy or prolonged bleeding continues or starts after several months of normal or no monthly bleeding, or you suspect that something may be wrong for other reasons, consider underlying conditions unrelated to method use (see Unexplained vaginal bleeding, p. 127).

Ordinary headaches (nonmigrainous)

- Suggest aspirin (325–650 mg), ibuprofen (200–400 mg), paracetamol (325–1000 mg), or other pain reliever.

- Any headaches that get worse or occur more often during use of implants should be evaluated.

Mild abdominal pain

- Suggest aspirin (325–650 mg), ibuprofen (200–400 mg), paracetamol (325–1000 mg), or other pain reliever.

- Consider locally available remedies.

Acne

- If client wants to stop using implants because of acne, she can consider switching to COCs. Many women's acne improves with COC use.

- Consider locally available remedies.

Weight change

- Review diet and counsel as needed.

Breast tenderness

- Recommend that she wear a supportive bra (including during strenuous activity and sleep).

- Try hot or cold compresses.

- Suggest aspirin (325–650 mg), ibuprofen (200–400 mg), paracetamol (325–1000 mg), or other pain reliever.

- Consider locally available remedies.

Mood changes or changes in sex drive

- Ask about changes in her life that could affect her mood or sex drive, including changes in her relationship with her partner. Give her support as appropriate.

- Clients who have serious mood changes such as major depression should be referred for care.

- Consider locally available remedies.

Nausea or dizziness

- Consider locally available remedies.

Pain after insertion or removal

- For pain after insertion, check that the bandage or gauze on her arm is not too tight.

- Put a new bandage on the arm and advise her to avoid pressing on the site for a few days.

- Give her aspirin (325–650 mg), ibuprofen (200–400 mg), paracetamol (325–1000 mg), or other pain reliever.

Infection at the insertion site (redness, heat, pain, pus)

- Do not remove the implants.

- Clean the infected area with soap and water or antiseptic.

- Give oral antibiotics for 7 to 10 days.

- Ask the client to return after taking all antibiotics if the infection does not clear. If infection has not cleared, remove the implants or refer for removal.

- Expulsion or partial expulsion often follows infection. Ask the client to return if she notices an implant coming out.

Abscess (pocket of pus under the skin due to infection)

- Clean the area with antiseptic.

- Cut open (incise) and drain the abscess.

- Treat the wound.

- Give oral antibiotics for 7 to 10 days.

- Ask the client to return after taking all antibiotics if she has heat, redness, pain, or drainage of the wound. If infection is present when she returns, remove the implants or refer for removal.

Expulsion (when one or more implants begins to come out of the arm)

- Rare. Usually occurs within a few months of insertion or with infection.

- If no infection is present, replace the expelled rod or capsule through a new incision near the other rods or capsules, or refer for replacement.

Severe pain in lower abdomen

- Abdominal pain may be due to various problems, such as enlarged ovarian follicles or cysts.

  - A woman can continue to use implants during evaluation.

  - There is no need to treat enlarged ovarian follicles or cysts unless they grow abnormally large, twist, or burst. Reassure the client that they usually disappear on their own. To be sure the problem is resolving, see the client again in 6 weeks, if possible.

- With severe abdominal pain, be particularly alert for additional signs or symptoms of ectopic pregnancy, which is rare and not caused by implants, but it can be life-threatening (see p. 129, Question 7). In the early stages of ectopic pregnancy, symptoms may be absent or mild, but eventually they will become severe. A combination of these signs or symptoms should increase suspicion of ectopic pregnancy:
  - Unusual abdominal pain or tenderness
  - Abnormal vaginal bleeding or no monthly bleeding—especially if this is a change from her usual bleeding pattern
  - Light-headedness or dizziness
  - Fainting
- If ectopic pregnancy or other serious health condition is suspected, refer at once for immediate diagnosis and care. (See Female Sterilization, Managing Ectopic Pregnancy, p. 179, for more on ectopic pregnancies.)

New Problems That May Require Switching Methods

May or may not be due to method.

Unexplained vaginal bleeding (that suggests a medical condition not related to the method)

- Refer or evaluate by history and pelvic examination. Diagnose and treat as appropriate.
- If no cause of bleeding can be found, consider stopping implants to make diagnosis easier. Provide another method of her choice to use until the condition is evaluated and treated (not progestin-only injectables, or a copper-bearing or hormonal IUD).
- If bleeding is caused by sexually transmitted infection or pelvic inflammatory disease, she can continue using implants during treatment.

Migraine headaches (see Identifying Migraine Headaches and Auras, p. 368)

- If she has migraine headaches without aura, she can continue to use implants if she wishes.
- If she has migraine aura, remove the implants. Help her choose a method without hormones.

8

Implants

Certain serious health conditions (suspected blood clots in deep veins of legs or lungs, serious liver disease, or breast cancer). See Signs and Symptoms of Serious Health Conditions, p. 320.

- Remove the implants or refer for removal.
- Give her a backup method to use until her condition is evaluated.
- Refer for diagnosis and care if not already under care.

Heart disease due to blocked or narrowed arteries (ischemic heart disease) **or stroke**

- A woman who has one of these conditions can safely start implants. If, however, the condition develops while she is using implants:
  - Remove the implants or refer for removal.
  - Help her choose a method without hormones.
  - Refer for diagnosis and care if not already under care.

Suspected pregnancy

- Assess for pregnancy, including ectopic pregnancy.
- Remove the implants or refer for removal if she will carry the pregnancy to term.
- There are no known risks to a fetus conceived while a woman has implants in place (see Question 5, next page).

Questions and Answers About Implants

1. **Do users of implants require follow-up visits?**

   No. Routine periodic visits are not necessary for implant users. Annual visits may be helpful for other preventive care, but they are not required. Of course, women are welcome to return at any time with questions.

2. **Can implants be left permanently in a woman's arm?**

   Leaving the implants in place beyond their effective lifespan is generally not recommended if the woman continues to be at risk of pregnancy. The implants themselves are not dangerous, but as the hormone levels in the implants drop, they become less and less effective.

3. **Do implants cause cancer?**

   No. Studies have not shown increased risk of any cancer with use of implants.

4. **How long does is take to become pregnant after the implants are removed?**

Women who stop using implants can become pregnant as quickly as women who stop nonhormonal methods. Implants do not delay the return of a woman's fertility after they are removed. The bleeding pattern a woman had before she used implants generally returns after they are removed. Some women may have to wait a few months before their usual bleeding pattern returns.

5. **Do implants cause birth defects? Will the fetus be harmed if a woman accidentally becomes pregnant with implants in place?**

No. Good evidence shows that implants will not cause birth defects and will not otherwise harm the fetus if a woman becomes pregnant while using implants or accidentally has implants inserted when she is already pregnant.

6. **Can implants move around within a woman's body or come out of her arm?**

Implants do not move around in a woman's body. The implants remain where they are inserted until they are removed. Rarely, a rod may start to come out, most often in the first 4 months after insertion. This usually happens because they were not inserted well or because of an infection where they were inserted. In these cases, the woman will see the implants coming out. Some women may have a sudden change in bleeding pattern. If a woman notices a rod coming out, she should start using a backup method and return to the clinic at once.

7. **Do implants increase the risk of ectopic pregnancy?**

No. On the contrary, implants greatly reduce the risk of ectopic pregnancy. Ectopic pregnancies are extremely rare among implant users. The rate of ectopic pregnancy among women with implants is 6 per 100,000 women per year. The rate of ectopic pregnancy among women in the United States using no contraceptive method is 650 per 100,000 women per year.

On the very rare occasions that implants fail and pregnancy occurs, 10 to 17 of every 100 of these pregnancies are ectopic. Thus, the great majority of pregnancies after implants fail are not ectopic. Still, ectopic pregnancy can be life-threatening, so a provider should be aware that ectopic pregnancy is possible if implants fail.

8. **How soon can a breastfeeding woman start a progestin-only method—implants, progestin-only pills or injectables, or LNG-IUD?**

WHO guidance calls for waiting until at least 6 weeks after childbirth to start a progestin-only contraceptive (4 weeks for the LNG-IUD). In special cases a provider could make the clinical judgment that a woman can start a progestin-only method sooner (see p. 115).

A WHO expert consultation in 2008 endorsed WHO's current guidance, based on theoretical concerns about the effect on infant development of hormones in breast milk. These experts noted, however, that, where pregnancy risks are high and access to services is limited, progestin-only methods may be among the few available. Also, starting implants and IUDs requires providers with special training. These providers may be available only when a woman gives birth. The experts concluded, "Any decisions regarding choice of a contraceptive method should also consider these facts."

Also note: Guidance in some countries, based on their own expert panel reviews, allows breastfeeding women to start progestin-only methods at any time.[‡] This includes starting immediately postpartum, a long-standing practice in these countries.

9. **Should heavy women avoid implants?**

No. These women should know, however, that they need to have Jadelle or Norplant implants replaced sooner to maintain a high level of protection from pregnancy. In studies of Norplant implants pregnancy rates among women who weighed 70–79 kg were 2 per 100 women in the sixth year of use. Such women should have their implants replaced, if they wish, after 5 years. Among women who used Norplant or Jadelle implants and who weighed 80 kg or more, the pregnancy rate was 6 per 100 in the fifth year of use. These women should have their implants replaced after 4 years. Studies of Implanon have not found that weight decreases effectiveness within the lifespan approved for this type of implant.

10. **What should be done if an implant user has an ovarian cyst?**

The great majority of cysts are not true cysts but actually fluid-filled structures in the ovary (follicles) that continue to grow beyond the usual size in a normal menstrual cycle. They may cause some mild abdominal pain, but they only require treatment if they grow abnormally large, twist, or burst. These follicles usually go away without treatment (see Severe pain in lower abdomen, p. 126).

11. **Can a woman work soon after having implants inserted?**

Yes, a woman can do her usual work immediately after leaving the clinic as long as she does not bump the insertion site or get it wet.

12. **Must a woman have a pelvic examination before she can have implants inserted?**

No. Instead, asking the right questions can help the provider be reasonably certain she is not pregnant (see Pregnancy Checklist, p. 372). No condition that can be detected by a pelvic examination rules out use of implants.

[‡] See, for example, Faculty of Sexual and Reproductive Healthcare (FRSH). *UK Medical Eligibility Criteria.* London, FSRH, 2006. and Centers for Disease Control. U.S. medical eligibility criteria for contraceptive use, 2010. Morbidity and Mortality Weekly Report 59. May 28, 2010.

CHAPTER 9

Copper-Bearing Intrauterine Device

This chapter describes primarily the TCu-380A intrauterine device (for the Levonorgestrel Intrauterine Device, see p. 157).

Key Points for Providers and Clients

- **Long-term pregnancy protection.** Shown to be very effective for 12 years, immediately reversible.

- **Inserted into the uterus by a specifically trained provider.**

- **Little required of the client once the IUD is in place.**

- **Bleeding changes are common.** Typically, longer and heavier bleeding and more cramps or pain during monthly bleeding, especially in the first 3 to 6 months.

What Is the Intrauterine Device?

- The copper-bearing intrauterine device (IUD) is a small, flexible plastic frame with copper sleeves or wire around it. A specifically trained health care provider inserts it into a woman's uterus through her vagina and cervix.

- Almost all types of IUDs have one or two strings, or threads, tied to them. The strings hang through the cervix into the vagina.

- Works primarily by causing a chemical change that damages sperm and egg before they can meet.

How Effective?

One of the most effective and long-lasting methods:

- Less than 1 pregnancy per 100 women using an IUD over the first year (6 to 8 per 1,000 women). This means that 992 to 994 of every 1,000 women using IUDs will not become pregnant.

- A small risk of pregnancy remains beyond the first year of use and continues as long as the woman is using the IUD.

  - Over 10 years of IUD use: About 2 pregnancies per 100 women

More effective

Less effective

- Studies have found that the TCu-380A is effective for 12 years. The TCu-380A is labeled for up to 10 years of use, however. (Providers should follow program guidelines as to when the IUD should be removed.)

Return of fertility after IUD is removed: No delay

Protection against sexually transmitted infections (STIs): None

Side Effects, Health Benefits, Health Risks, and Complications

Side Effects (see Managing Any Problems, p. 149)

Some users report the following:

- Changes in bleeding patterns (especially in the first 3 to 6 months) including:
  - Prolonged and heavy monthly bleeding
  - Irregular bleeding
  - More cramps and pain during monthly bleeding

Known Health Benefits

Helps protect against:

- Risks of pregnancy

May help protect against:

- Cancer of the lining of the uterus (endometrial cancer)

Known Health Risks

Uncommon:

- May contribute to anemia if a woman already has low iron blood stores before insertion and the IUD causes heavier monthly bleeding

Rare:

- Pelvic inflammatory disease (PID) may occur if the woman has chlamydia or gonorrhea at the time of IUD insertion

Complications

Rare:

- Puncturing (perforation) of the wall of the uterus by the IUD or an instrument used for insertion. Usually heals without treatment.
- Miscarriage, preterm birth, or infection in the rare case that the woman becomes pregnant with the IUD in place.

Correcting Misunderstandings (see also Questions and Answers, p. 154)

Intrauterine devices:

- Rarely lead to PID.
- Do not increase the risk of contracting STIs, including HIV.
- Do not increase the risk of miscarriage when a woman becomes pregnant after the IUD is removed.
- Do not make women infertile.
- Do not cause birth defects.
- Do not cause cancer.
- Do not move to the heart or brain.
- Do not cause discomfort or pain for the woman during sex.
- Substantially reduce the risk of ectopic pregnancy.

Why Some Women Say They Like the IUD

- Prevents pregnancy very effectively
- Is long-lasting
- Has no further costs after the IUD is inserted
- Does not require the user to do anything once the IUD is inserted

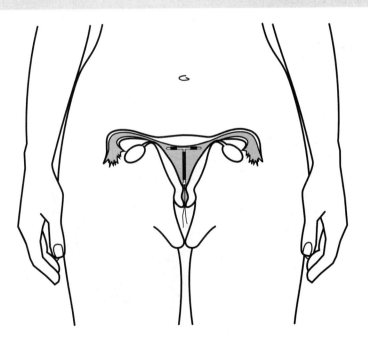

Who Can and Cannot Use the Copper-Bearing IUD

Safe and Suitable for Nearly All Women

Most women can use IUDs safely and effectively, including women who:

- Have or have not had children
- Are not married
- Are of any age, including adolescents and women over 40 years old
- Have just had an abortion or miscarriage (if no evidence of infection)
- Are breastfeeding
- Do hard physical work
- Have had ectopic pregnancy
- Have had pelvic inflammatory disease (PID)
- Have vaginal infections
- Have anemia
- Are infected with HIV or on antiretroviral therapy and doing well (see IUDs for Women With HIV, p. 138)

Women can begin using IUDs:

- Without STI testing
- Without an HIV test
- Without any blood tests or other routine laboratory tests
- Without cervical cancer screening
- Without a breast examination

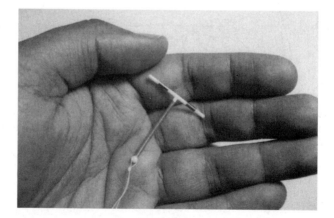

Copper-Bearing IUDs

Ask the client the questions below about known medical conditions. If she answers "no" to all of the questions, then she can have an IUD inserted if she wants. If she answers "yes" to a question, follow the instructions. In some cases she can still have an IUD inserted. These questions also apply to the levonorgestrel IUD (see p. 160).

1. **Did you give birth more than 48 hours ago but less than 4 weeks ago?**

❏ NO   ❏ YES Delay inserting an IUD until 4 or more weeks after childbirth (see Soon after childbirth, p. 140).

2. **Do you have an infection following childbirth or abortion?**

❏ NO   ❏ YES If she currently has infection of the reproductive organs during the first 6 weeks after childbirth (puerperal sepsis) or she just had an abortion-related infection in the uterus (septic abortion), do not insert the IUD. Treat or refer if she is not already receiving care. Help her choose another method or offer a backup method.* After treatment, re-evaluate for IUD use.

3. **Do you have vaginal bleeding that is unusual for you?**

❏ NO   ❏ YES If she has unexplained vaginal bleeding that suggests pregnancy or an underlying medical condition, use of an IUD could make diagnosis and monitoring of any treatment more difficult. Help her choose a method to use while being evaluated and treated (but not a hormonal IUD, progestin-only injectables, or implants). After treatment, re-evaluate for IUD use.

4. **Do you have any female conditions or problems (gynecologic or obstetric conditions or problems), such as genital cancer or pelvic tuberculosis? If so, what problems?**

❏ NO   ❏ YES Known current cervical, endometrial, or ovarian cancer; gestational trophoblast disease; pelvic tuberculosis: Do not insert an IUD. Treat or refer for care if she is not already receiving care. Help her choose another method. In case of pelvic tuberculosis, re-evaluate for IUD use after treatment.

(Continued on next page)

---

* Backup methods include abstinence, male and female condoms, spermicides, and withdrawal. Tell her that spermicides and withdrawal are the least effective contraceptive methods. If possible, give her condoms.

Copper-Bearing Intrauterine Device

9

5. Do you have AIDS?

❏ NO   ❏ YES Do not insert an IUD if she has AIDS unless she is clinically well on antiretroviral therapy. If she is infected with HIV but does not have AIDS, she can use an IUD. If a woman who has an IUD in place develops AIDS, she can keep the IUD (see IUDs for Women With HIV, p. 138).

6. Assess whether she is at very high individual risk for gonorrhea or chlamydia.

Women who have a very high individual likelihood of exposure to gonorrhea or chlamydia should not have an IUD inserted (see Assessing Women for Risk of Sexually Transmitted Infections, p. 138).

7. Assess whether the client might be pregnant.

Ask the client the questions in the pregnancy checklist (see p. 372). If she answers "yes" to any question, she can have an IUD inserted (see also When to Start, p. 140).

For complete classifications, see Medical Eligibility Criteria for Contraceptive Use, p. 324. Be sure to explain the health benefits and risks and the side effects of the method that the client will use. Also, point out any conditions that would make the method inadvisable, when relevant to the client.

Using Clinical Judgment in Special Cases

Usually, a woman with any of the conditions listed below should not have an IUD inserted. In special circumstances, however, when other, more appropriate methods are not available or acceptable to her, a qualified provider who can carefully assess a specific woman's condition and situation may decide that she can use an IUD. The provider needs to consider the severity of her condition and, for most conditions, whether she will have access to follow-up.

- Between 48 hours and 4 weeks since giving birth
- Noncancerous (benign) gestational trophoblast disease
- Current ovarian cancer
- Is at very high individual risk for gonorrhea or chlamydia at the time of insertion
- Has AIDS and is not on antiretroviral therapy and clinically well
- Has systemic lupus erythematosus with severe thrombocytopenia

Screening Questions for Pelvic Examination Before IUD Insertion

When performing the pelvic examination, asking yourself the questions below helps you check for signs of conditions that would rule out IUD insertion. If the answer to all of the questions is "no," then the client can have an IUD inserted. If the answer to any question is "yes," do not insert an IUD.

For questions 1 through 5, if the answer is "yes," refer for diagnosis and treatment as appropriate. Help her choose another method and counsel her about condom use if she faces any risk of sexually transmitted infections (STIs). Give her condoms, if possible. If STI or pelvic inflammatory disease (PID) is confirmed and she still wants an IUD, it may be inserted as soon as she finishes treatment, if she is not at risk for reinfection before insertion.

1. **Is there any type of ulcer on the vulva, vagina, or cervix?**

❑ NO ❑ YES Possible STI.

2. **Does the client feel pain in her lower abdomen when you move the cervix?**

❑ NO ❑ YES Possible PID.

3. **Is there tenderness in the uterus, ovaries, or fallopian tubes (adnexal tenderness)?**

❑ NO ❑ YES Possible PID.

4. **Is there a purulent cervical discharge?**

❑ NO ❑ YES Possible STI or PID.

5. **Does the cervix bleed easily when touched?**

❑ NO ❑ YES Possible STI or cervical cancer.

6. **Is there an anatomical abnormality of the uterine cavity that will prevent correct IUD insertion?**

❑ NO ❑ YES If an anatomical abnormality distorts the uterine cavity, proper IUD placement may not be possible. Help her choose another method.

7. **Were you unable to determine the size and/or position of the uterus?**

❑ NO ❑ YES Determining the size and position of the uterus before IUD insertion is essential to ensure high placement of the IUD and to minimize risk of perforation. If size and position cannot be determined, do not insert an IUD. Help her choose another method.

Intrauterine Devices for Women With HIV

- Women who are at risk of HIV or are infected with HIV can safely have the IUD inserted.

- Women who have AIDS, are on antiretroviral (ARV) therapy, and are clinically well can safely have the IUD inserted.

- Women who have AIDS but who are not on ARV therapy or who are not clinically well should *not* have the IUD inserted.

- If a woman develops AIDS while she has an IUD in place, it does not need to be removed.

- IUD users with AIDS should be monitored for pelvic inflammatory disease.

- Urge women to use condoms along with the IUD. Used consistently and correctly, condoms help prevent transmission of HIV and other STIs.

Assessing Women for Risk of Sexually Transmitted Infections

A woman who has gonorrhea or chlamydia now should not have an IUD inserted. Having these sexually transmitted infections (STIs) at insertion may increase the risk of pelvic inflammatory disease. These STIs may be difficult to diagnose clinically, however, and reliable laboratory tests are time-consuming, expensive, and often unavailable. Without clinical signs or symptoms and without laboratory testing, the only indication that a woman might already have an STI is whether her behavior or her situation places her at *very high individual risk* of infection. If this risk for the *individual* client is very high, she generally should not have an IUD inserted.[‡] (Local STI prevalence rates are not a basis for judging individual risk.)

There is no universal set of questions that will determine if a woman is at very high individual risk for gonorrhea and chlamydia. Instead of asking questions, providers can discuss with the client the personal behaviors and the situations in their community that are most likely to expose women to STIs.

Steps to take:

1. Tell the client that a woman who faces a very high individual risk of some STIs usually should not have an IUD inserted.

[‡] In contrast, if a *current* IUD user's situation changes and she finds herself at very high individual risk for gonorrhea or chlamydia, she can keep using her IUD.

2. Ask the woman to consider her own risk and to think about whether she might have an STI. A woman is often the best judge of her own risk.§ She does not have to tell the provider about her behavior or her partner's behavior. Providers can explain possibly risky situations that may place a woman at very high individual risk. The client can think about whether such situations occurred recently (in the past 3 months or so). If so, she may have an STI now and may want to choose a method other than the IUD.

Possibly risky situations include:

- A sexual partner has STI symptoms such as pus coming from his penis, pain or burning during urination, or an open sore in the genital area

- She or a sexual partner was diagnosed with an STI recently

- She has had more than one sexual partner recently

- She has a sexual partner who has had other partners recently

All of these situations pose less risk if a woman or her partner uses condoms consistently and correctly.

Also, a provider can mention other high-risk situations that exist locally.

3. Ask if she thinks she is a good candidate for an IUD or would like to consider other contraceptive methods. If, after considering her individual risk, she thinks she is a good candidate, and she is eligible, provide her with an IUD. If she wants to consider other methods or if you have strong reason to believe that the client is at very high individual risk of infection, help her choose another method.

Note: If she still wants the IUD while at very high individual risk of gonorrhea and chlamydia, and reliable testing is available, a woman who tests negative can have an IUD inserted. A woman who tests positive can have an IUD inserted as soon as she finishes treatment, if she is not at risk of reinfection by the time of insertion.

In special circumstances, if other, more appropriate methods are not available or not acceptable, a health care provider who can carefully assess a specific woman's condition and situation may decide that a woman at very high individual risk can have the IUD inserted even if STI testing is not available. (Depending on the circumstances, the provider may consider presumptively treating her with a full curative dose of antibiotics effective against both gonorrhea and chlamydia and inserting the IUD after she finishes treatment.) Whether or not she receives presumptive treatment, the provider should be sure that the client can return for the follow-up visit, will be carefully checked for infection, and will be treated immediately if needed. She should be asked to return at once if she develops a fever and either lower abdominal pain or abnormal vaginal discharge or both.

§ Any woman who thinks she might have an STI should seek care immediately.

Providing the Intrauterine Device

When to Start

IMPORTANT: In many cases a woman can start the IUD any time it is reasonably certain she is not pregnant. To be reasonably certain she is not pregnant, use the Pregnancy Checklist (see p. 372).

Woman's situation	When to start
Having menstrual cycles	**Any time of the month** • If she is starting within 12 days after the start of her monthly bleeding, no need for a backup method. • If it is more than 12 days after the start of her monthly bleeding, she can have the IUD inserted any time it is reasonably certain she is not pregnant. No need for a backup method.
Switching from another method	• Immediately, if she has been using the method consistently and correctly or if it is otherwise reasonably certain she is not pregnant. No need to wait for her next monthly bleeding. No need for a backup method. • If she is switching from injectables, she can have the IUD inserted when the next injection would have been given. No need for a backup method.
Soon after childbirth	• Any time within 48 hours after giving birth, including by caesarean delivery. (Provider needs specific training in postpartum insertion.) Fewest expulsions when done just after delivery of placenta (if possible). • If it is more than 48 hours after giving birth, delay until 4 weeks or more after giving birth.
Fully or nearly fully breastfeeding	
Less than 6 months after giving birth	• If her monthly bleeding has not returned, she can have the IUD inserted any time between 4 weeks and 6 months after giving birth. No need for a backup method. • If her monthly bleeding has returned, she can have the IUD inserted as advised for women having menstrual cycles (see above).

Woman's situation	When to start
Fully or nearly fully breastfeeding (continued)	
More than 6 months after giving birth	• If her monthly bleeding has not returned, she can have the IUD inserted any time it is reasonably certain she is not pregnant. No need for a backup method.
	• If her monthly bleeding has returned, she can have the IUD inserted as advised for women having menstrual cycles (see previous page).
Partially breastfeeding or not breastfeeding	
More than 4 weeks after giving birth	• If her monthly bleeding has not returned, she can have the IUD inserted *if it can be determined that she is not pregnant.* No need for a backup method.
	• If her monthly bleeding has returned, she can have the IUD inserted as advised for women having menstrual cycles (see previous page).
No monthly bleeding (not related to childbirth or breastfeeding)	• Any time *if it can be determined that she is not pregnant.* No need for a backup method.
After miscarriage or abortion	• Immediately, if the IUD is inserted within 12 days after first- or second-trimester abortion or miscarriage and if no infection is present. No need for a backup method.
	• If it is more than 12 days after first- or second-trimester miscarriage or abortion and no infection is present, she can have the IUD inserted any time it is reasonably certain she is not pregnant. No need for a backup method.
	• If infection is present, treat or refer and help the client choose another method. If she still wants the IUD, it can be inserted after the infection has completely cleared.
	• IUD insertion after second-trimester abortion or miscarriage requires specific training. If not specifically trained, delay insertion until at least 4 weeks after miscarriage or abortion.

Woman's situation	When to start
For emergency contraception	• Within 5 days after unprotected sex. • When the time of ovulation can be estimated, she can have an IUD inserted up to 5 days after ovulation. Sometimes this may be more than 5 days after unprotected sex.
After taking emergency contraceptive pills (ECPs)	• The IUD can be inserted on the same day that she takes the ECPs. No need for a backup method.

Preventing Infection at IUD Insertion

Proper insertion technique can help prevent many problems, such as infection, expulsion, and perforation.

• Follow proper infection-prevention procedures.

• Use high-level disinfected or sterile instruments. High-level disinfect by boiling, steaming, or soaking them in disinfectant chemicals.

• Use a new, presterilized IUD that is packaged with its inserter.

• The "no-touch" insertion technique is best. This includes not letting the loaded IUD or uterine sound touch any unsterile surfaces (for example, hands, speculum, vagina, table top). The no-touch technique involves:

– Loading the IUD into the inserter while the IUD is still in the sterile package, to avoid touching the IUD directly

– Cleaning the cervix thoroughly with antiseptic before IUD insertion

– Being careful not to touch the vaginal wall or speculum blades with the uterine sound or loaded IUD inserter

– Passing both the uterine sound and the loaded IUD inserter only once each through the cervical canal

Giving Advice on Side Effects

IMPORTANT: Thorough counseling about bleeding changes must come before IUD insertion. Counseling about bleeding changes may be the most important help a woman needs to keep using the method.

Describe the most common side effects	• Changes in her bleeding pattern:
	   – Prolonged and heavy monthly bleeding
	   – Irregular bleeding
	   – More cramps and pain during monthly bleeding

Explain about these side effects	• Bleeding changes are not signs of illness. • Usually become less after the first several months after insertion. • Client can come back for help if problems bother her.

Inserting the IUD

Talk with the client before the procedure	• Explain the insertion procedure (see p. 144). • Show her the speculum, tenaculum, and the IUD and inserter in the package. • Tell her that she will experience some discomfort or cramping during the procedure, and that this is to be expected. • Ask her to tell you any time that she feels discomfort or pain. • Ibuprofen (200–400 mg), paracetamol (325–1000 mg), or other pain reliever may be given 30 minutes before insertion to help reduce cramping and pain. Do not give aspirin, which slows blood clotting.
Talk with the client during the procedure	• Tell her what is happening, step by step, and reassure her. • Alert her before a step that may cause pain or might startle her. • Ask from time to time if she is feeling pain.

Explaining the Insertion Procedure

A woman who has chosen the IUD needs to know what will happen during insertion. The following description can help explain the procedure to her. Learning IUD insertion requires training and practice under direct supervision. Therefore, this description is a summary and not detailed instructions.

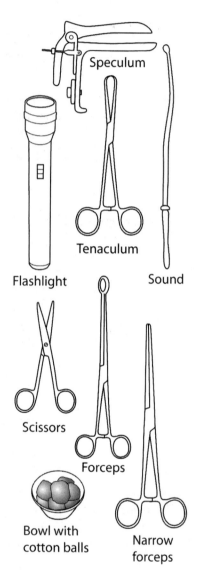

1. The provider conducts a pelvic examination to assess eligibility (see Screening Questions for Pelvic Examination Before IUD Insertion, p. 137). The provider first does the bimanual examination and then inserts a speculum into the vagina to inspect the cervix.

2. The provider cleans the cervix and vagina with appropriate antiseptic.

3. The provider slowly inserts the tenaculum through the speculum and closes the tenaculum just enough to gently hold the cervix and uterus steady.

4. The provider slowly and gently passes the uterine sound through the cervix to measure the depth and position of the uterus.

5. The provider loads the IUD into the inserter while both are still in the unopened sterile package.

6. The provider slowly and gently inserts the IUD and removes the inserter.

7. The provider cuts the strings on the IUD, leaving about 3 centimeters hanging out of the cervix.

8. After the insertion, the woman rests. She remains on the examination table until she feels ready to get dressed.

Speculum

Tenaculum

Flashlight

Sound

Scissors

Forceps

Bowl with cotton balls

Narrow forceps

Supporting the User

Giving Specific Instructions

Expect cramping and pain	• She can expect some cramping and pain for a few days after insertion.
	• Suggest ibuprofen (200–400 mg), paracetamol (325–1000 mg), or other pain reliever as needed.
	• Also, she can expect some bleeding or spotting immediately after insertion. This may continue for 3 to 6 months.
She can check the strings	• If she wants, she can check her IUD strings from time to time, especially in the first few months and after monthly bleeding, to confirm that her IUD is still in place (see Question 10, p. 156).
Length of pregnancy protection	• Discuss how to remember the date to return.
	• Give each woman the following information in writing on a reminder card, like the one shown below, if possible, and explain:
	– The type of IUD she has
	– Date of IUD insertion
	– Month and year when IUD will need to be removed or replaced
	– Where to go if she has problems or questions with her IUD

IUD Reminder Card

Client's name: _____

Type of IUD: _____

Date inserted: _____

Remove or replace by: Month [   ]   Year [   ]

If you have any problems or questions, go to:

(name and location of facility)

Follow-up visit	• A follow-up visit after her first monthly bleeding or 3 to 6 weeks after IUD insertion is recommended. No woman should be denied an IUD, however, because follow-up would be difficult or not possible.

"Come Back Any Time": Reasons to Return

Assure every client that she is welcome to come back any time—for example, if she has problems, questions, or wants another method; or she has a major change in health status. Also if:

- She thinks the IUD might be out of place. For example, she:
  - Feels the strings are missing.
  - Feels the hard plastic of an IUD that has partially come out.
- She has symptoms of pelvic inflammatory disease (increasing or severe pain in the lower abdomen, pain during sex, unusual vaginal discharge, fever, chills, nausea, and/or vomiting), especially in the first 20 days after insertion.
- She thinks she might be pregnant.

General health advice: Anyone who suddenly feels that something is seriously wrong with her health should immediately seek medical care from a nurse or doctor. Her contraceptive method is most likely not the cause of the condition, but she should tell the nurse or doctor what method she is using.

Helping Continuing Users

Post-Insertion Follow-Up Visit (3 to 6 Weeks)

1. Ask how the client is doing with the method and whether she is satisfied. Ask if she has any questions or anything to discuss.

2. Ask especially if she is concerned about bleeding changes. Give her any information or help that she needs (see Managing Any Problems, p. 149).

3. Ask her if she has:

   - Increasing or severe abdominal pain or pain during sex or urination
   - Unusual vaginal discharge
   - Fever or chills
   - Signs or symptoms of pregnancy (see p. 371 for common signs and symptoms)
   - Not been able to feel strings (if she has checked them)
   - Felt the hard plastic of an IUD that has partially come out

4. A routine pelvic examination at the follow-up visit is not required. It may be appropriate in some settings or for some clients, however. Conduct a pelvic examination particularly if the client's answers lead you to suspect:

- A sexually transmitted infection or pelvic inflammatory disease
- The IUD has partially or completely come out

Any Visit

1. Ask how the client is doing with the method and about bleeding changes (see Post-Insertion Follow-Up Visit, Items 1 and 2, previous page).

2. Ask a long-term client if she has had any new health problems. Address problems as appropriate. For new health problems that may require switching methods, see p. 153.

3. Ask a long-term client about major life changes that may affect her needs—particularly plans for having children and STI/HIV risk. Follow up as needed.

4. Remind her how much longer the IUD will protect her from pregnancy.

Removing the Intrauterine Device

IMPORTANT: Providers must not refuse or delay when a woman asks to have her IUD removed, whatever her reason, whether it is personal or medical. All staff must understand and agree that she must not be pressured or forced to continue using the IUD.

If a woman is finding side effects difficult to tolerate, first discuss the problems she is having (see Managing Any Problems, p. 149). See if she would rather try to manage the problem or to have the IUD removed immediately.

Removing an IUD is usually simple. It can be done any time of the month. Removal may be easier during monthly bleeding, when the cervix is naturally softened. In cases of uterine perforation or if removal is not easy, refer the woman to an experienced clinician who can use an appropriate removal technique.

Explaining the Removal Procedure

Before removing the IUD, explain what will happen during removal:

1. The provider inserts a speculum to see the cervix and IUD strings and carefully cleans the cervix and vagina with an antiseptic solution, such as iodine.

2. The provider asks the woman to take slow, deep breaths and to relax. The woman should say if she feels pain during the procedure.

3. Using narrow forceps, the provider pulls the IUD strings slowly and gently until the IUD comes completely out of the cervix.

Switching From an IUD to Another Method

These guidelines ensure that the client is protected from pregnancy without interruption when switching from a copper-bearing IUD or a hormonal IUD to another method. See also When to Start for each method.

Switching to	When to start
Combined oral contraceptives (COCs), progestin-only pills (POPs), progestin-only injectables, monthly injectables, combined patch, combined vaginal ring, or implants	• If starting during the first 7 days of monthly bleeding (first 5 days for COCs and POPs), start the hormonal method now and remove the IUD. No need for a backup method. • If starting after the first 7 days of monthly bleeding (after the first 5 days for COCs and POPs) and she has had sex since her last monthly bleeding, start the hormonal method now. It is recommended that the IUD be kept in place until her next monthly bleeding. • If starting after the first 7 days of monthly bleeding (after the first 5 days for COCs and POPs) and she has *not* had sex since her last monthly bleeding, the IUD can stay in place and be removed during her next monthly bleeding, or the IUD can be removed and she can use a backup method* for the next 7 days (2 days for POPs).
Male or female condoms, spermicides, diaphragms, cervical caps, or withdrawal	• Immediately the next time she has sex after the IUD is removed.
Fertility awareness methods	• Immediately after the IUD is removed.
Female sterilization	• If starting during the first 7 days of monthly bleeding, remove the IUD and perform the female sterilization procedure. No need for a backup method. • If starting after the first 7 days of monthly bleeding, perform the sterilization procedure. The IUD can be kept in place until her follow-up visit or her next monthly bleeding. If a follow-up visit is not possible, remove the IUD at the time of sterilization. No need for a backup method.

* Backup methods include abstinence, male and female condoms, spermicides, and withdrawal. Tell her that spermicides and withdrawal are the least effective contraceptive methods. If possible, give her condoms.

Switching to	When to start
Vasectomy	• Any time
	• The woman can keep the IUD for 3 months after her partner's vasectomy to keep preventing pregnancy until the vasectomy is fully effective.

Managing Any Problems

Problems Reported As Side Effects or Complications

May or may not be due to the method.

• Problems with side effects or complications affect women's satisfaction and use of IUDs. They deserve the provider's attention. If the client reports any side effects or complications, listen to her concerns, give her advice, and, if appropriate, treat.

• Offer to help her choose another method—now, if she wishes, or if problems cannot be overcome.

Heavy or prolonged bleeding (twice as much as usual or longer than 8 days)

• Reassure her that many women using IUDs experience heavy or prolonged bleeding. It is generally not harmful and usually becomes less or stops after the first several months of use.

• For modest short-term relief she can try (one at a time):

– Tranexamic acid (1500 mg) 3 times daily for 3 days, then 1000 mg once daily for 2 days, beginning when heavy bleeding starts.

– Nonsteroidal anti-inflammatory drugs (NSAIDs) such as ibuprofen (400 mg) or indomethacin (25 mg) 2 times daily after meals for 5 days, beginning when heavy bleeding starts. Other NSAIDs—except aspirin—also may provide some relief of heavy or prolonged bleeding.

• Provide iron tablets if possible and tell her it is important for her to eat foods containing iron (see Possible anemia, p. 150).

• If heavy or prolonged bleeding continues or starts after several months of normal bleeding or long after the IUD was inserted, or if you suspect that something may be wrong for other reasons, consider underlying conditions unrelated to method use (see Unexplained vaginal bleeding, p. 153).

Irregular bleeding (bleeding at unexpected times that bothers the client)

• Reassure her that many women using IUDs experience irregular bleeding. It is not harmful and usually becomes less or stops after the first several months of use.

- For modest short-term relief she can try NSAIDs such as ibuprofen (400 mg) or indomethacin (25 mg) 2 times daily after meals for 5 days, beginning when irregular bleeding starts.
- If irregular bleeding continues or starts after several months of normal bleeding, or you suspect that something may be wrong for other reasons, consider underlying conditions unrelated to method use (see Unexplained vaginal bleeding, p. 153).

Cramping and pain

- She can expect some cramping and pain for the first day or two after IUD insertion.
- Explain that cramping also is common in the first 3 to 6 months of IUD use, particularly during monthly bleeding. Generally, this is not harmful and usually decreases over time.
- Suggest aspirin (325–650 mg), ibuprofen (200–400 mg), paracetamol (325–1000 mg), or other pain reliever. If she also has heavy or prolonged bleeding, aspirin should not be used because it may increase bleeding.

If cramping continues and occurs outside of monthly bleeding:

- Evaluate for underlying health conditions and treat or refer.
- If no underlying condition is found and cramping is severe, discuss removing the IUD.
    - If the removed IUD looks distorted, or if difficulties during removal suggest that the IUD was out of proper position, explain to the client that she can have a new IUD that may cause less cramping.

Possible anemia

- The copper-bearing IUD may contribute to anemia if a woman already has low iron blood stores before insertion and the IUD causes heavier monthly bleeding.
- Pay special attention to IUD users with any of the following signs and symptoms:
    - Inside of eyelids or underneath fingernails looks pale, pale skin, fatigue or weakness, dizziness, irritability, headache, ringing in the ears, sore tongue, and brittle nails.
    - If blood testing is available, hemoglobin less than 9 g/dl or hematocrit less than 30.
- Provide iron tablets if possible.
- Tell her it is important to eat foods containing iron, such as meat and poultry (especially beef and chicken liver), fish, green leafy vegetables, and legumes (beans, bean curd, lentils, and peas).

Partner can feel IUD strings during sex

- Explain that this happens sometimes when strings are cut too short.

- If partner finds the strings bothersome, describe available options:

  - Strings can be cut even shorter so they are not coming out of the cervical canal. Her partner will not feel the strings, but the woman will no longer be able to check her IUD strings.

  - If the woman wants to be able to check her IUD strings, the IUD can be removed and a new one inserted. (To avoid discomfort, the strings should be cut so that 3 centimeters hang out of the cervix.)

Severe pain in lower abdomen (suspected pelvic inflammatory disease [PID])

- Some common signs and symptoms of PID often also occur with other abdominal conditions, such as ectopic pregnancy. If ectopic pregnancy is ruled out, assess for PID.

- If possible, do abdominal and pelvic examinations (see Signs and Symptoms of Serious Health Conditions, p. 320, for signs from the pelvic examination that would indicate PID).

- If a pelvic examination is not possible, and she has a combination of the following signs and symptoms in addition to lower abdominal pain, suspect PID:

  - Unusual vaginal discharge

  - Fever or chills

  - Pain during sex or urination

  - Bleeding after sex or between monthly bleeding

  - Nausea and vomiting

  - A tender pelvic mass

  - Pain when the abdomen is gently pressed (direct abdominal tenderness) or when gently pressed and then suddenly released (rebound abdominal tenderness)

- Treat PID or immediately refer for treatment:

  - Because of the serious consequences of PID, health care providers should treat all suspected cases, based on the signs and symptoms above. Treatment should be started as soon as possible. Treatment is more effective at preventing long-term complications when appropriate antibiotics are given immediately.

  - Treat for gonorrhea, chlamydia, and anaerobic bacterial infections. Counsel the client about condom use and, if possible, give her condoms.

  - There is no need to remove the IUD if she wants to continue using it. If she wants it removed, take it out after starting antibiotic treatment. (If the IUD is removed, see Switching from an IUD to Another Method, p. 148.)

9

Copper-Bearing Intrauterine Device

Severe pain in lower abdomen (suspected ectopic pregnancy)

- Many conditions can cause severe abdominal pain. Be particularly alert for additional signs or symptoms of ectopic pregnancy, which is rare and not caused by the IUD, but it can be life-threatening (see Question 11, p. 156).

- In the early stages of ectopic pregnancy, symptoms may be absent or mild, but eventually they will become severe. A combination of these signs or symptoms should increase suspicion of ectopic pregnancy:

  - Unusual abdominal pain or tenderness
  - Abnormal vaginal bleeding or no monthly bleeding—especially if this is a change from her usual bleeding pattern
  - Light-headedness or dizziness
  - Fainting

- If ectopic pregnancy or other serious health condition is suspected, refer at once for immediate diagnosis and care. (See Female Sterilization, Managing Ectopic Pregnancy, p. 179, for more on ectopic pregnancies.)

- If the client does not have these additional symptoms or signs, assess for pelvic inflammatory disease (see Severe pain in lower abdomen, p. 151).

Suspected uterine puncturing (perforation)

- If puncturing is suspected at the time of insertion or sounding of the uterus, stop the procedure immediately (and remove the IUD if inserted). Observe the client in the clinic carefully:

  - For the first hour, keep the woman at bed rest and check her vital signs (blood pressure, pulse, respiration, and temperature) every 5 to 10 minutes.

  - If the woman remains stable after one hour, check for signs of intra-abdominal bleeding, such as low hematocrit or hemoglobin, if possible, and her vital signs. Observe for several more hours. If she has no signs or symptoms, she can be sent home, but she should avoid sex for 2 weeks. Help her choose another method.

  - If she has a rapid pulse and falling blood pressure, or new pain or increasing pain around the uterus, refer her to a higher level of care.

  - If uterine perforation is suspected within 6 weeks after insertion or if it is suspected later and is causing symptoms, refer the client for evaluation to a clinician experienced at removing such IUDs (see Question 6, p. 155).

IUD partially comes out (partial expulsion)

- If the IUD partially comes out, remove the IUD. Discuss with the client whether she wants another IUD or a different method. If she wants another IUD, she can have one inserted at any time it is reasonably certain she is not pregnant. If the client does not want to continue using an IUD, help her choose another method.

- If the client reports that the IUD came out, discuss with her whether she wants another IUD or a different method. If she wants another IUD, she can have one inserted at any time it is reasonably certain she is not pregnant.

- If complete expulsion is suspected and the client does not know whether the IUD came out, refer for x-ray or ultrasound to assess whether the IUD might have moved to the abdominal cavity. Give her a backup method to use in the meantime.

Missing strings (suggesting possible pregnancy, uterine perforation, or expulsion)

- Ask the client:
  - Whether and when she saw the IUD come out
  - When she last felt the strings
  - When she had her last monthly bleeding
  - If she has any symptoms of pregnancy
  - If she has used a backup method since she noticed the strings were missing

- Always start with minor and safe procedures and be gentle. Check for the strings in the folds of the cervical canal with forceps. About half of missing IUD strings can be found in the cervical canal.

- If strings cannot be located in the cervical canal, either they have gone up into the uterus or the IUD has been expelled unnoticed. Rule out pregnancy before attempting more invasive procedures. Refer for evaluation. Give her a backup method to use in the meantime, in case the IUD came out.

New Problems That May Require Switching Methods

May or may not be due to the method.

Unexplained vaginal bleeding (that suggests a medical condition not related to the method)

- Refer or evaluate by history or pelvic examination. Diagnose and treat as appropriate.

- She can continue using the IUD while her condition is being evaluated.

- If bleeding is caused by sexually transmitted infection or pelvic inflammatory disease, she can continue using the IUD during treatment.

Suspected pregnancy

- Assess for pregnancy, including ectopic pregnancy.

- Explain that an IUD in the uterus during pregnancy increases the risk of preterm delivery or miscarriage, including infected (septic) miscarriage during the first or second trimester, which can be life-threatening.

Copper-Bearing Intrauterine Device

9

- If the woman does not want to continue the pregnancy, counsel her according to program guidelines.

- If she continues the pregnancy:

  - Advise her that it is best to remove the IUD.

  - Explain the risks of pregnancy with an IUD in place. Early removal of the IUD reduces these risks, although the removal procedure itself involves a small risk of miscarriage.

  - If she agrees to removal, gently remove the IUD or refer for removal.

  - Explain that she should return at once if she develops any signs of miscarriage or septic miscarriage (vaginal bleeding, cramping, pain, abnormal vaginal discharge, or fever).

  - If she chooses to keep the IUD, her pregnancy should be followed closely by a nurse or doctor. She should see a nurse or doctor at once if she develops any signs of septic miscarriage.

- If the IUD strings cannot be found in the cervical canal and the IUD cannot be safely retrieved, refer for ultrasound, if possible, to determine whether the IUD is still in the uterus. If it is, or if ultrasound is not available, her pregnancy should be followed closely. She should seek care at once if she develops any signs of septic miscarriage.

Questions and Answers About the Intrauterine Device

1. **Does the IUD cause pelvic inflammatory disease (PID)?**

   By itself, the IUD does not cause PID. Gonorrhea and chlamydia are the primary direct causes of PID. IUD *insertion* when a woman has gonorrhea or chlamydia may lead to PID, however. This does not happen often. When it does, it is most likely to occur in the first 20 days after IUD insertion. It has been estimated that, in a group of clients where STIs are common and screening questions identify half the STI cases, there might be 1 case of PID in every 666 IUD insertions (or less than 2 per 1,000) (see Assessing Women for Risk of Sexually Transmitted Infections, p. 138).

2. **Can young women and older women use IUDs?**

   Yes. There is no minimum or maximum age limit. An IUD should be removed after menopause has occurred—within 12 months after her last monthly bleeding (see Women Near Menopause, p. 272).

3. **If a current IUD user has a sexually transmitted infection (STI) or has become at very high individual risk of becoming infected with an STI, should her IUD be removed?**

No. If a woman develops a new STI after her IUD has been inserted, she is not especially at risk of developing PID because of the IUD. She can continue to use the IUD while she is being treated for the STI. Removing the IUD has no benefit and may leave her at risk of unwanted pregnancy. Counsel her on condom use and other strategies to avoid STIs in the future.

4. **Does the IUD make a woman infertile?**

No. A woman can become pregnant once the IUD is removed just as quickly as a woman who has never used an IUD, although fertility decreases as women get older. Good studies find no increased risk of infertility among women who have used IUDs, including young women and women with no children. Whether or not a woman has an IUD, however, if she develops PID and it is not treated, there is some chance that she will become infertile.

5. **Can a woman who has never had a baby use an IUD?**

Yes. A woman who has not had children generally can use an IUD, but she should understand that the IUD is more likely to come out because her uterus may be smaller than the uterus of a woman who has given birth.

6. **Can the IUD travel from the woman's uterus to other parts of her body, such as her heart or her brain?**

The IUD never travels to the heart, brain, or any other part of the body outside the abdomen. The IUD normally stays within the uterus like a seed within a shell. Rarely, the IUD may come through the wall of the uterus into the abdominal cavity. This is most often due to a mistake during insertion. If it is discovered within 6 weeks or so after insertion or if it is causing symptoms at any time, the IUD will need to be removed by laparoscopic or laparotomic surgery. Usually, however, the out-of-place IUD causes no problems and should be left where it is. The woman will need another contraceptive method.

7. **Should a woman have a "rest period" after using her IUD for several years or after the IUD reaches its recommended time for removal?**

No. This is not necessary, and it could be harmful. Removing the old IUD and immediately inserting a new IUD poses less risk of infection than 2 separate procedures. Also, a woman could become pregnant during a "rest period" before her new IUD is inserted.

8. **Should antibiotics be routinely given before IUD insertion?**

No, usually not. Most recent research done where STIs are not common suggests that PID risk is low with or without antibiotics. When appropriate questions to screen for STI risk are used and IUD insertion is done with proper infection-prevention procedures (including the no-touch insertion technique), there is little risk of infection. Antibiotics may be considered, however, in areas where STIs are common and STI screening is limited.

9. **Must an IUD be inserted only during a woman's monthly bleeding?**

No. For a woman having menstrual cycles, an IUD can be inserted at any time during her menstrual cycle if it is reasonably certain that the woman is not pregnant. Inserting the IUD during her monthly bleeding may be a good time because she is not likely to be pregnant, and insertion may be easier. It is not as easy to see signs of infection during monthly bleeding, however.

10. **Should a woman be denied an IUD because she does not want to check her IUD strings?**

No. A woman should not be denied an IUD because she is unwilling to check the strings. The importance of checking the IUD strings has been overemphasized. It is uncommon for an IUD to come out, and it is rare for it to come out without the woman noticing.

The IUD is most likely to come out during the first few months after IUD insertion, during monthly bleeding, among women who have had an IUD inserted soon after childbirth, a second-trimester abortion, or miscarriage, and among women who have never been pregnant. A woman can check her IUD strings if she wants reassurance that it is still in place. Or, if she does not want to check her strings, she can watch carefully in the first month or so and during monthly bleeding to see if the IUD has come out.

11. **Do IUDs increase the risk of ectopic pregnancy?**

No. On the contrary, IUDs greatly reduce the risk of ectopic pregnancy. Ectopic pregnancies are rare among IUD users. The rate of ectopic pregnancy among women with IUDs is 12 per 10,000 women per year. The rate of ectopic pregnancy among women in the United States using no contraceptive method is 65 per 10,000 women per year.

On the rare occasions that the IUD fails and pregnancy occurs, 6 to 8 of every 100 of these pregnancies are ectopic. Thus, the great majority of pregnancies after IUD failure are not ectopic. Still, ectopic pregnancy can be life-threatening, so a provider should be aware that ectopic pregnancy is possible if the IUD fails.

Levonorgestrel Intrauterine Device

Key Points for Providers and Clients

- **Long-term pregnancy protection.** Very effective for 5 years, immediately reversible.
- **Inserted into the uterus by a specifically trained provider.**
- **Little required of the client once the LNG-IUD is in place.**
- **Bleeding changes are common but not harmful.** Typically, lighter and fewer days of bleeding, or infrequent or irregular bleeding.

What Is the Levonorgestrel Intrauterine Device?

- The levonorgestrel intrauterine device (LNG-IUD) is a T-shaped plastic device that steadily releases small amounts of levonorgestrel each day. (Levonorgestrel is a progestin widely used in implants and oral contraceptive pills.)
- A specifically trained health care provider inserts it into a woman's uterus through her vagina and cervix.
- Also called the levonorgestrel-releasing intrauterine system, LNG-IUS, or hormonal IUD.
- Marketed under the brand name Mirena.
- Works primarily by suppressing the growth of the lining of uterus (endometrium).

How Effective?

One of the most effective and long-lasting methods:

More
effective

- Less than 1 pregnancy per 100 women using an LNG-IUD over the first year (2 per 1,000 women). This means that **998** of every 1,000 women using LNG-IUDs will not become pregnant.

- A small risk of pregnancy remains beyond the first year of use and continues as long as the woman is using the LNG-IUD.

    - Over 5 years of LNG-IUD use: Less than 1 pregnancy per 100 women (5 to 8 per 1,000 women).

- Approved for up to 5 years of use.

Less
effective

Return of fertility after LNG-IUD is removed: No delay

Protection against sexually transmitted infections (STIs): None

Side Effects, Health Benefits, Health Risks, and Complications

Side Effects

Some users report the following:

- Changes in bleeding patterns, including:
    - Lighter bleeding and fewer days of bleeding
    - Infrequent bleeding
    - Irregular bleeding
    - No monthly bleeding
    - Prolonged bleeding
- Acne
- Headaches
- Breast tenderness or pain
- Nausea
- Weight gain
- Dizziness
- Mood changes

Other possible physical changes:

- Ovarian cysts

Known Health Benefits

Helps protect against:

- Risks of pregnancy
- Iron-deficiency anemia

May help protect against:

- Pelvic inflammatory disease

Reduces:

- Menstrual cramps
- Symptoms of endometriosis
  (pelvic pain, irregular bleeding)

Known Health Risks

None

Complications

Rare:

- Puncturing (perforation) of the wall of the uterus by the LNG-IUD or an instrument used for insertion. Usually heals without treatment.

Very rare:

- Miscarriage, preterm birth, or infection in the very rare case that the woman becomes pregnant with the LNG-IUD in place.

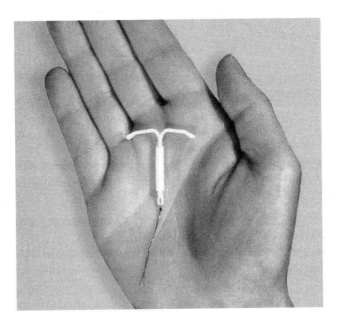

Who Can and Cannot Use Levonorgestrel IUDs

Safe and Suitable for Nearly All Women

Nearly all women can use the LNG-IUD safely and effectively.

Medical Eligibility Criteria for

Levonorgestrel IUDs

Ask the client the Medical Eligibility Criteria questions for Copper-Bearing IUDs (see p. 135). Also ask the questions below about known medical conditions. If she answers "no" to all of the questions here and for the copper-bearing IUD, then she can have an LNG-IUD inserted if she wants. If she answers "yes" to a question, follow the instructions. In some cases she can still have an LNG-IUD inserted.

1. Did you give birth less than 4 weeks ago?

❑ NO ❑ YES She can have the LNG-IUD inserted as soon as 4 weeks after childbirth (see When to Start, next page).

2. Do you now have a blood clot in the deep veins of your legs or lungs?

❑ NO ❑ YES If she reports current blood clot (except superficial clots), and she is not on anticoagulant therapy, help her choose a method without hormones.

3. Do you have severe cirrhosis of the liver, a liver infection, or liver tumor? (Are her eyes or skin unusually yellow? [signs of jaundice])

❑ NO ❑ YES If she reports serious active liver disease (jaundice, severe cirrhosis, liver tumor), do not provide the LNG-IUD. Help her choose a method without hormones.

4. Do you have or have you ever had breast cancer?

❑ NO ❑ YES Do not insert the LNG-IUD. Help her choose a method without hormones.

For complete classifications, see Medical Eligibility Criteria for Contraceptive Use, p. 324. Be sure to explain the health benefits and risks and the side effects of the method that the client will use. Also, point out any conditions that would make the method inadvisable, when relevant to the client.

Using Clinical Judgment in Special Cases

Usually, a woman with any of the conditions listed below should not use an LNG-IUD. In special circumstances, however, when other, more appropriate methods are not available or acceptable to her, a qualified provider who can carefully assess a specific woman's condition and situation may decide that she can use an LNG-IUD. The provider needs to consider the severity of her condition and, for most conditions, whether she will have access to follow-up.

- Breastfeeding and less than 4 weeks since giving birth (considering the risks of another pregnancy and that a woman may have limited further access to the LNG-IUD)
- Acute blood clot in deep veins of legs or lungs
- Had breast cancer more than 5 years ago, and it has not returned
- Severe liver disease, infection, or tumor
- Systemic lupus erythematosus with positive (or unknown) antiphospholipid antibodies

See also Copper-Bearing IUD, Using Clinical Judgment in Special Cases, p. 136.

Providing the Levonorgestrel Intrauterine Device

When to Start

IMPORTANT: In many cases a woman can start the LNG-IUD any time it is reasonably certain she is not pregnant. To be reasonably certain she is not pregnant, use the Pregnancy Checklist (see p. 372).

Woman's situation	When to start
Having menstrual cycles or switching from a nonhormonal method	**Any time of the month** • If she is starting within 7 days after the start of her monthly bleeding, no need for a backup method. • If it is more than 7 days after the start of her monthly bleeding, she can have the LNG-IUD inserted any time it is reasonably certain she is not pregnant. She will need a backup method* for the first 7 days after insertion.

---

* Backup methods include abstinence, male and female condoms, spermicides, and withdrawal. Tell her that spermicides and withdrawal are the least effective contraceptive methods. If possible, give her condoms.

Woman's situation	When to start
Switching from a hormonal method	• Immediately, if she has been using the method consistently and correctly or if it is otherwise reasonably certain she is not pregnant. No need to wait for her next monthly bleeding. No need for a backup method.
	• If she is switching from injectables, she can have the LNG-IUD inserted when the repeat injection would have been given. She will need a backup method for the first 7 days after insertion.
Soon after childbirth	• If not breastfeeding, any time within 48 hours after giving birth. (Requires a provider with specific training in postpartum insertion.) After 48 hours, delay until at least 4 weeks.
	• If breastfeeding, delay LNG-IUD insertion until 4 weeks after giving birth. (See p. 129, Q&A 8.)
Fully or nearly fully breastfeeding	
Less than 6 months after giving birth	• If she gave birth less than 4 weeks ago, delay insertion until at least 4 weeks after giving birth. (See p. 129, Q&A 8.)
	• If her monthly bleeding has not returned, she can have the LNG-IUD inserted any time between 4 weeks and 6 months. No need for a backup method.
	• If her monthly bleeding has returned, she can have the LNG-IUD inserted as advised for women having menstrual cycles (see p. 161).
More than 6 months since giving birth	• If her monthly bleeding has not returned, she can have the LNG-IUD inserted any time it is reasonably certain she is not pregnant. She will need a backup method for the first 7 days after insertion.
	• If her monthly bleeding has returned, she can have the LNG-IUD inserted as advised for women having menstrual cycles (see p. 161).
Partially breastfeeding or not breastfeeding	
Less than 4 weeks after giving birth	• Delay LNG-IUD insertion until at least 4 weeks after giving birth. (See p. 129, Q&A 8.)

Partially breastfeeding or not breastfeeding (continued)

More than 4 weeks after giving birth	• If her monthly bleeding has not returned, she can have the LNG-IUD inserted any time *if it can be determined that she is not pregnant.* She will need a backup method for the first 7 days after insertion.
	• If her monthly bleeding has returned, she can have the LNG-IUD inserted as advised for women having menstrual cycles (see p. 161).
No monthly bleeding (not related to childbirth or breastfeeding)	• Any time *if it can be determined that she is not pregnant.* She will need a backup method for the first 7 days after insertion.
After miscarriage or abortion	• Immediately, if the LNG-IUD is inserted within 7 days after first- or second-trimester abortion or miscarriage and if no infection is present. No need for a backup method.
	• If it is more than 7 days after first- or second-trimester miscarriage or abortion and no infection is present, she can have the LNG-IUD inserted any time it is reasonably certain she is not pregnant. She will need a backup method for the first 7 days after insertion.
	• If infection is present, treat or refer and help the client choose another method. If she still wants the LNG-IUD, it can be inserted after the infection has completely cleared.
	• LNG-IUD insertion after second-trimester abortion or miscarriage requires specific training. If not specifically trained, delay insertion until at least 4 weeks after miscarriage or abortion.
After taking emergency contraceptive pills (ECPs)	• The LNG-IUD can be inserted within 7 days after the start of her next monthly bleeding or any other time it is reasonably certain she is not pregnant. Give her a backup method, or oral contraceptives to start the day after she finishes taking the ECPs, to use until the LNG-IUD is inserted.

10

Levonorgestrel IUD

Giving Advice on Side Effects

IMPORTANT: Thorough counseling about bleeding changes must come before IUD insertion. Counseling about bleeding changes may be the most important help a woman needs to keep using the method.

Describe the most common side effects	• Changes in bleeding patterns: – No monthly bleeding, lighter bleeding, fewer days of bleeding, infrequent or irregular bleeding. • Acne, headaches, breast tenderness and pain, and possibly other side effects.
Explain about these side effects	• Bleeding changes usually are not signs of illness. • Usually become less after the first several months after insertion. • The client can come back for help if side effects bother her.

CHAPTER 11

Female Sterilization

Key Points for Providers and Clients

- **Permanent.** Intended to provide life-long, permanent, and very effective protection against pregnancy. Reversal is usually not possible.

- **Involves a physical examination and surgery.** The procedure is done by a specifically trained provider.

- **No long-term side effects.**

What Is Female Sterilization?

- Permanent contraception for women who will not want more children.

- The 2 surgical approaches most often used:

  - Minilaparotomy involves making a small incision in the abdomen. The fallopian tubes are brought to the incision to be cut or blocked.

  - Laparoscopy involves inserting a long thin tube with a lens in it into the abdomen through a small incision. This laparoscope enables the doctor to see and block or cut the fallopian tubes in the abdomen.

- Also called tubal sterilization, tubal ligation, voluntary surgical contraception, tubectomy, bi-tubal ligation, tying the tubes, minilap, and "the operation."

- Works because the fallopian tubes are blocked or cut. Eggs released from the ovaries cannot move down the tubes, and so they do not meet sperm.

More effective

How Effective?

One of the most effective methods but carries a small risk of failure:

- Less than 1 pregnancy per 100 women over the first year after having the sterilization procedure (5 per 1,000). This means that 995 of every 1,000 women relying on female sterilization will not become pregnant.

Less effective

- A small risk of pregnancy remains beyond the first year of use and until the woman reaches menopause.

  - Over 10 years of use: About 2 pregnancies per 100 women (18 to 19 per 1,000 women).

- Effectiveness varies slightly depending on how the tubes are blocked, but pregnancy rates are low with all techniques. One of the most effective techniques is cutting and tying the cut ends of the fallopian tubes after childbirth (postpartum tubal ligation).

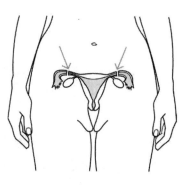

Fertility does not return because sterilization generally cannot be stopped or reversed. The procedure is intended to be permanent. Reversal surgery is difficult, expensive, and not available in most areas. When performed, reversal surgery often does not lead to pregnancy (see Question 7, p. 181).

Protection against sexually transmitted infections (STIs): None

Side Effects, Health Benefits, Health Risks, and Complications

Side Effects

None

Known Health Benefits

Helps protect against:

- Risks of pregnancy
- Pelvic inflammatory disease (PID)

May help protect against:

- Ovarian cancer

Known Health Risks

Uncommon to extremely rare:

- Complications of surgery and anesthesia (see below)

Complications of Surgery (see also Managing Any Problems, p. 178)

Uncommon to extremely rare:

- Female sterilization is a safe method of contraception. It requires surgery and anesthesia, however, which carry some risks such as infection or abscess of the wound. Serious complications are uncommon. Death, due to the procedure or anesthesia, is extremely rare.

The risk of complications with local anesthesia is significantly lower than with general anesthesia. Complications can be kept to a minimum if appropriate techniques are used and if the procedure is performed in an appropriate setting.

Female sterilization:

- Does not make women weak.
- Does not cause lasting pain in back, uterus, or abdomen.
- Does not remove a woman's uterus or lead to a need to have it removed.
- Does not cause hormonal imbalances.
- Does not cause heavier bleeding or irregular bleeding or otherwise change women's menstrual cycles.
- Does not cause any changes in weight, appetite, or appearance.
- Does not change women's sexual behavior or sex drive.
- Substantially reduces the risk of ectopic pregnancy.

Who Can Have Female Sterilization

Safe for All Women

With proper counseling and informed consent, any woman can have female sterilization safely, including women who:

- Have no children or few children
- Are not married
- Do not have husband's permission
- Are young
- Just gave birth (within the last 7 days)
- Are breastfeeding
- Are infected with HIV, whether or not on antiretroviral therapy (see Female Sterilization for Women With HIV, p. 171)

In some of these situations, especially careful counseling is important to make sure the woman will not regret her decision (see Because Sterilization Is Permanent, p. 174).

Women can have female sterilization:

- Without any blood tests or routine laboratory tests
- Without cervical cancer screening
- Even when a woman is not having monthly bleeding at the time, if it is reasonably certain she is not pregnant (see Pregnancy Checklist, p. 372)

11

- Has no side effects
- No need to worry about contraception again
- Is easy to use, nothing to do or remember

Medical Eligibility Criteria for
Female Sterilization

All women can have female sterilization. No medical conditions prevent a woman from using female sterilization. This checklist asks the client about known medical conditions that may limit when, where, or how the female sterilization procedure should be performed. Ask the client the questions below. If she answers "no" to all of the questions, then the female sterilization procedure can be performed in a routine setting without delay. If she answers "yes" to a question, follow the instructions, which recommend caution, delay, or special arrangements.

In the checklist below:

- *Caution* means the procedure can be performed in a routine setting but with extra preparation and precautions, depending on the condition.

- *Delay* means postpone female sterilization. These conditions must be treated and resolved before female sterilization can be performed. Give the client another method to use until the procedure can be performed.

- *Special* means special arrangements should be made to perform the procedure in a setting with an experienced surgeon and staff, equipment to provide general anesthesia, and other backup medical support. For these conditions, the capacity to decide on the most appropriate procedure and anesthesia regimen also is needed. Give the client another method to use until the procedure can be performed.

1. **Do you have any current or past female conditions or problems (gynecologic or obstetric conditions or problems), such as infection or cancer? If so, what problems?**

❏ NO ❏ YES If she has any of the following, use *caution:*

- Past pelvic inflammatory disease since last pregnancy
- Breast cancer
- Uterine fibroids
- Previous abdominal or pelvic surgery

▶ If she has any of the following, *delay* female sterilization:

- Current pregnancy
- 7–42 days postpartum
- Postpartum after a pregnancy with severe pre-eclampsia or eclampsia
- Serious postpartum or postabortion complications (such as infection, hemorrhage, or trauma) except uterine rupture or perforation (*special;* see below)
- A large collection of blood in the uterus
- Unexplained vaginal bleeding that suggests an underlying medical condition
- Pelvic inflammatory disease
- Purulent cervicitis, chlamydia, or gonorrhea
- Pelvic cancers (treatment may make her sterile in any case)
- Malignant trophoblast disease

▶ If she has any of the following, make *special* arrangements:

- AIDS (see Female Sterilization for Women With HIV, p. 171)
- Fixed uterus due to previous surgery or infection
- Endometriosis
- Hernia (abdominal wall or umbilical)
- Postpartum or postabortion uterine rupture or perforation

(Continued on next page)

11

Female Sterilization

2. **Do you have any cardiovascular conditions, such as heart problems, stroke, high blood pressure, or complications of diabetes? If so, what?**

❏ NO ❏ YES If she has any of the following, use *caution:*

- Controlled high blood pressure
- Mild high blood pressure (140/90 to 159/99 mm Hg)
- Past stroke or heart disease without complications

▶ If she has any of the following, *delay* female sterilization:

- Heart disease due to blocked or narrowed arteries
- Blood clots in deep veins of legs or lungs

▶ If she has any of the following, make *special* arrangements:

- Several conditions together that increase chances of heart disease or stroke, such as older age, smoking, high blood pressure, or diabetes
- Moderately high or severely high blood pressure (160/100 mm Hg or higher)
- Diabetes for more than 20 years *or* damage to arteries, vision, kidneys, or nervous system caused by diabetes
- Complicated valvular heart disease

3. **Do you have any lingering, long-term diseases or any other conditions? If so, what?**

❏ NO ❏ YES If she has any of the following, use *caution:*

- Epilepsy
- Diabetes without damage to arteries, vision, kidneys, or nervous system
- Hypothyroidism
- Mild cirrhosis of the liver, liver tumors (Are her eyes or skin unusually yellow?), or schistosomiasis with liver fibrosis
- Moderate iron-deficiency anemia (hemoglobin 7–10 g/dl)
- Sickle cell disease
- Inherited anemia (thalassemia)
- Kidney disease
- Diaphragmatic hernia
- Severe lack of nutrition (Is she extremely thin?)

- Obesity (Is she extremely overweight?)
- Elective abdominal surgery at time sterilization is desired
- Depression
- Young age
- Uncomplicated lupus

▶ If she has any of the following, *delay* female sterilization:

- Gallbladder disease with symptoms
- Active viral hepatitis
- Severe iron-deficiency anemia (hemoglobin less than 7 g/dl)
- Lung disease (bronchitis or pneumonia)
- Systemic infection or significant gastroenteritis
- Abdominal skin infection
- Undergoing abdominal surgery for emergency or infection, or major surgery with prolonged immobilization

▶ If she has any of the following, make *special* arrangements:

- Severe cirrhosis of the liver
- Hyperthyroidism
- Coagulation disorders (blood does not clot)
- Chronic lung disease (asthma, bronchitis, emphysema, lung infection)
- Pelvic tuberculosis
- Lupus with positive (or unknown) antiphospholipid antibodies, with severe thrombocytopenia, or on immunosuppressive treatment

Female Sterilization for Women With HIV

- Women who are infected with HIV, have AIDS, or are on antiretroviral (ARV) therapy can safely undergo female sterilization. Special arrangements are needed to perform female sterilization on a woman with AIDS.
- Urge these women to use condoms in addition to female sterilization. Used consistently and correctly, condoms help prevent transmission of HIV and other STIs.
- No one should be coerced or pressured into having female sterilization, and that includes women with HIV.

Providing Female Sterilization

When to Perform the Procedure

IMPORTANT: If there is no medical reason to delay, a woman can have the female sterilization procedure any time she wants if it is reasonably certain she is not pregnant. To be reasonably certain she is not pregnant, use the Pregnancy Checklist (see p. 372).

Woman's situation	When to perform
Having menstrual cycles or switching from another method	**Any time of the month** • Any time within 7 days after the start of her monthly bleeding. No need to use another method before the procedure. • If it is more than 7 days after the start of her monthly bleeding, she can have the procedure any time it is reasonably certain she is not pregnant. • If she is switching from oral contraceptives, she can continue taking pills until she has finished the pill pack to maintain her regular cycle. • If she is switching from an IUD, she can have the procedure immediately (see Copper-Bearing IUD, Switching From an IUD to Another Method, p. 148).
No monthly bleeding	• Any time it is reasonably certain she is not pregnant.
After childbirth	• Immediately or within 7 days after giving birth, if she has made a voluntary, informed choice in advance. • Any time 6 weeks or more after childbirth if it is reasonably certain she is not pregnant.
After miscarriage or abortion	• Within 48 hours after uncomplicated abortion, if she has made a voluntary, informed choice in advance.
After using emergency contraceptive pills (ECPs)	• The sterilization procedure can be done within 7 days after the start of her next monthly bleeding or any other time it is reasonably certain she is not pregnant. Give her a backup method or oral contraceptives to start the day after she finishes taking the ECPs, to use until she can have the procedure.

Ensuring Informed Choice

IMPORTANT: A friendly counselor who listens to a woman's concerns, answers her questions, and gives clear, practical information about the procedure—especially its permanence—will help a woman make an informed choice and be a successful and satisfied user, without later regret (see Because Sterilization Is Permanent, p. 174). Involving her partner in counseling can be helpful but is not required.

The 6 Points of Informed Consent

Counseling must cover all 6 points of informed consent. In some programs the client and the counselor also sign an informed consent form. To give informed consent to sterilization, the client must understand the following points:

1. Temporary contraceptives also are available to the client.

2. Voluntary sterilization is a surgical procedure.

3. There are certain risks of the procedure as well as benefits. (Both risks and benefits must be explained in a way that the client can understand.)

4. If successful, the procedure will prevent the client from ever having any more children.

5. The procedure is considered permanent and probably cannot be reversed.

6. The client can decide against the procedure at any time before it takes place (without losing rights to other medical, health, or other services or benefits).

A woman or man considering sterilization should think carefully: "Could I want more children in the future?" Health care providers can help the client think about this question and make an informed choice. If the answer is "Yes, I could want more children," another family planning method would be a better choice.

Asking questions can help. The provider might ask:

- "Do you want to have any more children in the future?"
- "If not, do you think you could change your mind later? What might change your mind? For example, suppose one of your children died?"
- "Suppose you lost your spouse, and you married again?"
- "Does your partner want more children in the future?"

Clients who cannot answer these questions may need encouragement to think further about their decisions about sterilization.

In general, people most likely to regret sterilization:

- Are young
- Have few or no children
- Have just lost a child
- Are not married
- Are having marital problems
- Have a partner who opposes sterilization

None of these characteristics rules out sterilization, but health care providers should make especially sure that people with these characteristics make informed, thoughtful choices.

Also, for a woman, just after delivery or abortion is a convenient and safe time for voluntary sterilization, but women sterilized at this time may be more likely to regret it later. Thorough counseling during pregnancy and a decision made before labor and delivery help to avoid regrets.

The Decision About Sterilization Belongs to the Client Alone

A man or woman may consult a partner and others about the decision to have sterilization and may consider their views, but the decision cannot be made for them by a partner, another family member, a health care provider, a community leader, or anyone else. Family planning providers have a duty to make sure that the decision for or against sterilization is made by the client and is not pressured or forced by anyone.

Performing the Sterilization Procedure

Explaining the Procedure

A woman who has chosen female sterilization needs to know what will happen during the procedure. The following description can help explain the procedure to her. Learning to perform female sterilization takes training and practice under direct supervision. Therefore, this description is a summary and not detailed instructions.

(The description below is for procedures done more than 6 weeks after childbirth. The procedure used up to 7 days after childbirth is slightly different.)

The Minilaparotomy Procedure

1. The provider uses proper infection-prevention procedures at all times (see Infection Prevention in the Clinic, p. 312).

2. The provider performs a physical examination and a pelvic examination. The pelvic examination is to assess the condition and mobility of the uterus.

3. The woman usually receives light sedation (with pills or into a vein) to relax her. She stays awake. Local anesthetic is injected above the pubic hair line.

4. The provider makes a small vertical incision (2–5 centimeters) in the anesthetized area. This usually causes little pain. (For women who have just given birth, the incision is made horizontally at the lower edge of the navel.)

5. The provider inserts a special instrument (uterine elevator) into the vagina, through the cervix, and into the uterus to raise each of the 2 fallopian tubes so they are closer to the incision. This may cause discomfort.

6. Each tube is tied and cut or else closed with a clip or ring.

7. The provider closes the incision with stitches and covers it with an adhesive bandage.

8. The woman receives instructions on what to do after she leaves the clinic or hospital (see Explaining Self-Care for Female Sterilization, p. 177). She usually can leave in a few hours.

The Laparoscopy Procedure

1. The provider uses proper infection-prevention procedures at all times (see Infection Prevention in the Clinic, p. 312).

2. The provider performs a physical examination and a pelvic examination. The pelvic examination is to assess condition and mobility of the uterus.

3. The woman usually receives light sedation (with pills or into a vein) to relax her. She stays awake. Local anesthetic is injected under her navel.

4. The provider places a special needle into the woman's abdomen and, through the needle, inflates (insufflates) the abdomen with gas or air. This raises the wall of the abdomen away from the pelvic organs.

5. The provider makes a small incision (about one centimeter) in the anesthetized area and inserts a laparoscope. A laparoscope is a long, thin tube containing lenses. Through the lenses the provider can see inside the body and find the 2 fallopian tubes.

6. The provider inserts an instrument through the laparoscope (or, sometimes, through a second incision) to close off the fallopian tubes.

7. Each tube is closed with a clip or a ring, or by electric current applied to block the tube (electrocoagulation).

8. The provider then removes the instrument and laparoscope. The gas or air is let out of the woman's abdomen. The provider closes the incision with stitches and covers it with an adhesive bandage.

9. The woman receives instructions on what to do after she leaves the clinic or hospital (see Explaining Self-Care for Female Sterilization, next page). She usually can leave in a few hours.

Local Anesthesia Is Best for Female Sterilization

Local anesthesia, used with or without mild sedation, is preferable to general anesthesia. Local anesthesia:

- Is safer than general, spinal, or epidural anesthesia

- Lets the woman leave the clinic or hospital sooner

- Allows faster recovery

- Makes it possible to perform female sterilization in more facilities

Sterilization under local anesthesia can be done when a member of the surgical team has been trained to provide sedation and the surgeon has been trained to provide local anesthesia. The surgical team should be trained to manage emergencies, and the facility should have the basic equipment and drugs to manage any emergencies.

Health care providers can explain to a woman ahead of time that being awake during the procedure is safer for her. During the procedure providers can talk with the woman and help to reassure her if needed.

Many different anesthetics and sedatives may be used. Dosage of anesthetic must be adjusted to body weight. Oversedation should be avoided because it can reduce the client's ability to stay conscious and could slow or stop her breathing.

In some cases, general anesthesia may be needed. See Medical Eligibility Criteria for Female Sterilization, p. 168, for medical conditions needing special arrangements, which may include general anesthesia.

Supporting the User

Explaining Self-Care for Female Sterilization

Before the procedure the woman should	• Use another contraceptive until the procedure. • Not eat anything for 8 hours before surgery. She can drink clear liquids until 2 hours before surgery. • Not take any medication for 24 hours before the surgery (unless she is told to do so). • Wear clean, loose-fitting clothing to the health facility if possible. • Not wear nail polish or jewelry. • If possible, bring a friend or relative to help her go home afterwards.

After the procedure the woman should	• Rest for 2 days and avoid vigorous work and heavy lifting for a week.
	
	  • Keep incision clean and dry for 1 to 2 days.
	
	  • Avoid rubbing the incision for 1 week.
	
	  • Not have sex for at least 1 week. If pain lasts more than 1 week, avoid sex until all pain is gone.

What to do about the most common problems	• She may have some abdominal pain and swelling after the procedure. It usually goes away within a few days. Suggest ibuprofen (200–400 mg), paracetamol (325–1000 mg), or other pain reliever. She should not take aspirin, which slows blood clotting. Stronger pain reliever is rarely needed. If she had laparascopy, she may have shoulder pain or feel bloated for a few days.
Plan the follow-up visit	• Following up within 7 days or at least within 2 weeks is strongly recommended. No woman should be denied sterilization, however, because follow-up would be difficult or not possible. • A health care provider checks the site of the incision, looks for any signs of infection, and removes any stitches. This can be done in the clinic, in the client's home (by a specifically trained paramedical worker, for example), or at any other health center.

"Come Back Any Time": Reasons to Return

Assure every client that she is welcome to come back any time—for example, if she has problems or questions, or she thinks she might be pregnant. (A few sterilizations fail and the woman becomes pregnant.) Also if:

- She has bleeding, pain, pus, heat, swelling, or redness of the wound that becomes worse or does not go away

- She develops high fever (greater than 38° C/101° F)

- She experiences fainting, persistent light-headedness, or extreme dizziness in the first 4 weeks and especially in the first week

General health advice: Anyone who suddenly feels that something is seriously wrong with her health should immediately seek medical care from a nurse or doctor. Her contraceptive method is most likely not the cause of the condition, but she should tell the nurse or doctor what method she is using.

Helping Users

Managing Any Problems

Problems Reported as Complications

- Problems affect women's satisfaction with female sterilization. They deserve the provider's attention. If the client reports complications of female sterilization, listen to her concerns and, if appropriate, treat.

Infection at the incision site (redness, heat, pain, pus)

- Clean the infected area with soap and water or antiseptic.

- Give oral antibiotics for 7 to 10 days.

- Ask the client to return after taking all antibiotics if the infection has not cleared.

Abscess (a pocket of pus under the skin caused by infection)

- Clean the area with antiseptic.

- Cut open (incise) and drain the abscess.

- Treat the wound.

- Give oral antibiotics for 7 to 10 days.

- Ask the client to return after taking all antibiotics if she has heat, redness, pain, or drainage of the wound.

- See Managing Ectopic Pregnancy, below.

Suspected pregnancy

- Assess for pregnancy, including ectopic pregnancy.

Managing Ectopic Pregnancy

- Ectopic pregnancy is any pregnancy that occurs outside the uterine cavity. Early diagnosis is important. Ectopic pregnancy is rare but could be life-threatening (see Question 11, p. 182).

- In the early stages of ectopic pregnancy, symptoms may be absent or mild, but eventually they will become severe. A combination of these signs or symptoms should increase suspicion of ectopic pregnancy:

  - Unusual abdominal pain or tenderness

  - Abnormal vaginal bleeding or no monthly bleeding—especially if this is a change from her usual bleeding pattern

  - Light-headedness or dizziness

  - Fainting

- *Ruptured ectopic pregnancy*: Sudden sharp or stabbing lower abdominal pain, sometimes on one side and sometimes throughout the body, suggests a ruptured ectopic pregnancy (when the fallopian tube breaks due to the pregnancy). Right shoulder pain may develop due to blood from a ruptured ectopic pregnancy pressing on the diaphragm. Usually, within a few hours the abdomen becomes rigid and the woman goes into shock.

- *Care*: Ectopic pregnancy is a life-threatening, emergency condition requiring immediate surgery. If ectopic pregnancy is suspected, perform a pelvic examination only if facilities for immediate surgery are available. Otherwise, immediately refer and/or transport the woman to a facility where definitive diagnosis and surgical care can be provided.

Questions and Answers About Female Sterilization

1. **Will sterilization change a woman's monthly bleeding or make monthly bleeding stop?**

   No. Most research finds no major changes in bleeding patterns after female sterilization. If a woman was using a hormonal method or IUD before sterilization, her bleeding pattern will return to the way it was before she used these methods. For example, women switching from combined oral contraceptives to female sterilization may notice heavier bleeding as their monthly bleeding returns to usual patterns. Note, however, that a woman's monthly bleeding usually becomes less regular as she approaches menopause.

2. **Will sterilization make a woman lose her sexual desire? Will it make her fat?**

   No. After sterilization a woman will look and feel the same as before. She can have sex the same as before. She may find that she enjoys sex more because she does not have to worry about getting pregnant. She will not gain weight because of the sterilization procedure.

3. **Should sterilization be offered only to women who have had a certain number of children, who have reached a certain age, or who are married?**

   No. There is no justification for denying sterilization to a woman just because of her age, the number of her living children, or her marital status. Health care providers must not impose rigid rules about age, number of children, age of last child, or marital status. Each woman must be allowed to decide for herself whether or not she will want more children and whether or not to have sterilization.

4. **Is it not easier for the woman and the health care provider to use general anesthesia? Why use local anesthesia?**

   Local anesthesia is safer. General anesthesia is more risky than the sterilization procedure itself. Correct use of local anesthesia removes the single greatest source of risk in female sterilization procedures—general anesthesia. Also, after general anesthesia, women usually feel nauseous. This does not happen as often after local anesthesia.

   When using local anesthesia with sedation, however, providers must take care not to overdose the woman with the sedative. They also must handle the woman gently and talk with her throughout the procedure. This helps her to stay calm. With many clients, sedatives can be avoided, especially with good counseling and a skilled provider.

5. **Does a woman who has had a sterilization procedure ever have to worry about getting pregnant again?**

Generally, no. Female sterilization is very effective at preventing pregnancy and is intended to be permanent. It is not 100% effective, however. Women who have been sterilized have a slight risk of becoming pregnant: About 5 of every 1,000 women become pregnant within a year after the procedure. The small risk of pregnancy remains beyond the first year and until the woman reaches menopause.

6. **Pregnancy after female sterilization is rare, but why does it happen at all?**

Most often it is because the woman was already pregnant at the time of sterilization. In some cases an opening in the fallopian tube develops. Pregnancy also can occur if the provider makes a cut in the wrong place instead of the fallopian tubes.

7. **Can sterilization be reversed if the woman decides she wants another child?**

Generally, no. Sterilization is intended to be permanent. People who may want more children should choose a different family planning method. Surgery to reverse sterilization is possible for only some women—those who have enough fallopian tube left. Even among these women, reversal often does not lead to pregnancy. The procedure is difficult and expensive, and providers who are able to perform such surgery are hard to find. When pregnancy does occur after reversal, the risk that the pregnancy will be ectopic is greater than usual. Thus, sterilization should be considered irreversible.

8. **Is it better for the woman to have female sterilization or the man to have a vasectomy?**

Each couple must decide for themselves which method is best for them. Both are very effective, safe, permanent methods for couples who know that they will not want more children. Ideally, a couple should consider both methods. If both are acceptable to the couple, vasectomy would be preferable because it is simpler, safer, easier, and less expensive than female sterilization.

9. **Will the female sterilization procedure hurt?**

Yes, a little. Women receive local anesthetic to stop pain, and, except in special cases, they remain awake. A woman can feel the health care provider moving her uterus and fallopian tubes. This can be uncomfortable. If a trained anesthetist or anesthesiologist and suitable equipment are available, general anesthesia may be chosen for women who are very frightened of pain. A woman may feel sore and weak for several days or even a few weeks after surgery, but she will soon regain her strength.

10. How can health care providers help a woman decide about female sterilization?

Provide clear, balanced information about female sterilization and other family planning methods, and help a woman think through her decision fully. Thoroughly discuss her feelings about having children and ending her fertility. For example, a provider can help a woman think how she would feel about possible life changes such as a change of partner or a child's death. Review The 6 Points of Informed Consent to be sure the woman understands the sterilization procedure (see p. 173).

11. Does female sterilization increase the risk of ectopic pregnancy?

No. On the contrary, female sterilization greatly reduces the risk of ectopic pregnancy. Ectopic pregnancies are very rare among women who have had a sterilization procedure. The rate of ectopic pregnancy among women after female sterilization is 6 per 10,000 women per year. The rate of ectopic pregnancy among women in the United States using no contraceptive method is 65 per 10,000 women per year.

On the rare occasions that sterilization fails and pregnancy occurs, 33 of every 100 (1 of every 3) of these pregnancies are ectopic. Thus, most pregnancies after sterilization failure are not ectopic. Still, ectopic pregnancy can be life-threatening, so a provider should be aware that ectopic pregnancy is possible if sterilization fails.

12. Where can female sterilization be performed?

If no pre-existing medical conditions require special arrangements:

- Minilaparotomy can be provided in maternity centers and basic health facilities where surgery can be done. These include both permanent and temporary facilities that can refer the woman to a higher level of care in case of emergency.

- Laparoscopy requires a better equipped center, where the procedure is performed regularly and an anesthetist is available.

13. What are transcervical methods of sterilization?

Transcervical methods involve new ways of reaching the fallopian tubes, through the vagina and uterus. A microcoil, Essure, is already available in some countries. Essure is a spring-like device that a specifically trained clinician using a viewing instrument (hysteroscope) inserts through the vagina into the uterus and then into each fallopian tube. Over the 3 months following the procedure, scar tissue grows into the device. The scar tissue permanently plugs the fallopian tubes so that sperm cannot pass through to fertilize an egg. Essure is unlikely to be introduced in low-resource settings soon, however, because of the high cost and complexity of the viewing instrument required for insertion.

CHAPTER 12

Vasectomy

Key Points for Providers and Clients

- **Permanent.** Intended to provide life-long, permanent, and very effective protection against pregnancy. Reversal is usually not possible.

- **Involves a safe, simple surgical procedure.**

- **3-month delay in taking effect.** The man or couple must use condoms or another contraceptive method for 3 months after the vasectomy.

- **Does not affect male sexual performance.**

What Is Vasectomy?

- Permanent contraception for men who will not want more children.

- Through a puncture or small incision in the scrotum, the provider locates each of the 2 tubes that carries sperm to the penis (vas deferens) and cuts or blocks it by cutting and tying it closed or by applying heat or electricity (cautery).

- Also called male sterilization and male surgical contraception.

- Works by closing off each vas deferens, keeping sperm out of semen. Semen is ejaculated, but it cannot cause pregnancy.

How Effective?

More
effective

One of the most effective methods but carries a small risk of failure:

- Where men cannot have their semen examined 3 months after the procedure to see if it still contains sperm, pregnancy rates are about 2 to 3 per 100 women over the first year after their partners have had a vasectomy. This means that 97 to 98 of every 100 women whose partners have had vasectomies will not become pregnant.

- Where men can have their semen examined after vasectomy, less than 1 pregnancy per 100 women over the first year after their partners have had vasectomies (2 per 1,000). This means that 998 of every 1,000 women whose partners have had vasectomies will not become pregnant.

Less
effective

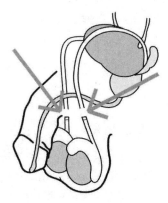

- Vasectomy is not fully effective for 3 months after the procedure.
  - Some pregnancies occur within the first year because the couple does not use condoms or another effective method consistently and correctly in the first 3 months, before the vasectomy is fully effective.
- A small risk of pregnancy remains beyond the first year after the vasectomy and until the man's partner reaches menopause.
  - Over 3 years of use: About 4 pregnancies per 100 women
- If the partner of a man who has had a vasectomy becomes pregnant, it may be because:
  - The couple did not always use another method during the first 3 months after the procedure
  - The provider made a mistake
  - The cut ends of the vas deferens grew back together

Fertility does not return because vasectomy generally cannot be stopped or reversed. The procedure is intended to be permanent. Reversal surgery is difficult, expensive, and not available in most areas. When performed, reversal surgery often does not lead to pregnancy (see Question 7, p. 196).

Protection against sexually transmitted infections (STIs): None

Why Some Men Say They Like Vasectomy

- Is safe, permanent, and convenient
- Has fewer side effects and complications than many methods for women
- The man takes responsibility for contraception—takes burden off the woman
- Increases enjoyment and frequency of sex

Side Effects, Health Benefits, Health Risks, and Complications

Side Effects, Known Health Benefits and Health Risks

None

Complications (see also Managing Any Problems, p. 194)

Uncommon to rare:

- Severe scrotal or testicular pain that lasts for months or years (see Question 2, p. 195).

Uncommon to very rare:

- Infection at the incision site or inside the incision (uncommon with conventional incision technique; very rare with no-scalpel technique; see Vasectomy Techniques, p. 190).

Rare:

- Bleeding under the skin that may cause swelling or bruising (hematoma).

Correcting Misunderstandings (see also Questions and Answers, p. 195)

Vasectomy:

- Does not remove the testicles. In vasectomy the tubes carrying sperm from the testicles are blocked. The testicles remain in place.
- Does not decrease sex drive.
- Does not affect sexual function. A man's erection is as hard, it lasts as long, and he ejaculates the same as before.
- Does not cause a man to grow fat or become weak, less masculine, or less productive.
- Does not cause any diseases later in life.
- Does not prevent transmission of sexually transmitted infections, including HIV.

Who Can Have a Vasectomy

Safe for All Men

With proper counseling and informed consent, any man can have a vasectomy safely, including men who:

- Have no children or few children
- Are not married
- Do not have wife's permission
- Are young
- Have sickle cell disease
- Are at high risk of infection with HIV or another STI
- Are infected with HIV, whether or not on antiretroviral therapy (see Vasectomy for Men with HIV, p. 188).

In some of these situations, especially careful counseling is important to make sure the man will not regret his decision (see Female Sterilization, Because Sterilization Is Permanent, p. 174).

Men can have a vasectomy:

- Without any blood tests or routine laboratory tests
- Without a blood pressure check
- Without a hemoglobin test
- Without a cholesterol or liver function check
- Even if the semen cannot be examined by microscope later to see if still contains sperm.

Vasectomy

All men can have vasectomy. No medical conditions prevent a man from using vasectomy. This checklist asks the client about known medical conditions that may limit when, where, or how the vasectomy procedure should be performed. Ask the client the questions below. If he answers "no" to all of the questions, then the vasectomy procedure can be performed in a routine setting without delay. If he answers "yes" to a question below, follow the instructions, which recommend caution, delay, or special arrangements.

In the checklist below:

- *Caution* means the procedure can be performed in a routine setting but with extra preparation and precautions, depending on the condition.

- *Delay* means postpone vasectomy. These conditions must be treated and resolved before vasectomy can be performed. Give the client another method to use until the procedure can be performed.

- *Special* means special arrangements should be made to perform the procedure in a setting with an experienced surgeon and staff, equipment to provide general anesthesia, and other backup medical support. For these conditions, the capacity to decide on the most appropriate procedure and anesthesia regimen also is needed. Give the client a backup method* to use until the procedure can be performed.

1. **Do you have any problems with your genitals, such as infections, swelling, injuries, or lumps on your penis or scrotum? If so, what problems?**

❏ NO ❏ YES If he has any of the following, use *caution:*

- Previous scrotal injury

- Swollen scrotum due to swollen veins or membranes in the spermatic cord or testes (large varicocele or hydrocele)

- Undescended testicle—one side only. (Vasectomy is performed only on the normal side. Then, if any sperm are present in a semen sample after 3 months, the other side must be done, too.)

(Continued on next page)

---

* Backup methods include abstinence, male and female condoms, spermicides, and withdrawal. Tell him that spermicides and withdrawal are the least effective contraceptive methods. If possible, give him condoms.

▶ If he has any of the following, *delay* vasectomy:

- Active sexually transmitted infection
- Swollen, tender (inflamed) tip of the penis, sperm ducts (epididymis), or testicles
- Scrotal skin infection or a mass in the scrotum

▶ If he has any of the following, make *special* arrangements:

- Hernia in the groin. (If able, the provider can perform the vasectomy at the same time as repairing the hernia. If this is not possible, the hernia should be repaired first.)
- Undescended testicles—both sides

2. Do you have any other conditions or infections? If so, what?

❏ NO   ❏ YES If he has the following, use *caution:*

- Diabetes
- Depression
- Young age
- Lupus with positive (or unknown) antiphospholipid antibodies or on immunosuppressive treatment

▶ If he has any of the following, *delay* vasectomy:

- Systemic infection or gastroenteritis
- Filariasis or elephantiasis

▶ If he has any of the following, make *special* arrangements:

- AIDS (see Vasectomy for Men With HIV, below)
- Blood fails to clot (coagulation disorders)
- Lupus with severe thrombocytopenia

Vasectomy for Men With HIV

- Men who are infected with HIV, have AIDS, or are on antiretroviral (ARV) therapy can safely have a vasectomy. Special arrangements are needed to perform vasectomy on a man with AIDS.

- Vasectomy does not prevent transmission of HIV.

- Urge these men to use condoms in addition to vasectomy. Used consistently and correctly, condoms help prevent transmission of HIV and other STIs.

- No one should be coerced or pressured into getting a vasectomy, and that includes men with HIV.

Providing Vasectomy

When to Perform the Procedure

- Any time a man requests it (if there is no medical reason to delay).

Ensuring Informed Choice

IMPORTANT: A friendly counselor who listens to a man's concerns, answers his questions, and gives clear, practical information about the procedure—especially its permanence—will help a man make an informed choice and be a successful and satisfied user, without later regret (see Female Sterilization, Because Sterilization Is Permanent, p. 174). Involving his partner in counseling can be helpful but is not required.

The 6 Points of Informed Consent

Counseling must cover all 6 points of informed consent. In some programs the client and the counselor sign an informed consent form. To give informed consent to vasectomy, the client must understand the following points:

1. Temporary contraceptives also are available to the client.

2. Voluntary vasectomy is a surgical procedure.

3. There are certain risks of the procedure as well as benefits. (Both risks and benefits must be explained in a way that the client can understand.)

4. If successful, the procedure will prevent the client from ever having any more children.

5. The procedure is considered permanent and probably cannot be reversed.

6. The client can decide against the procedure at any time before it takes place (without losing rights to other medical, health, or other services or benefits).

Vasectomy Techniques

Reaching the Vas: No-Scalpel Vasectomy

No-scalpel vasectomy is the recommended technique for reaching each of the 2 tubes in the scrotum (vas deferens) that carries sperm to the penis. It is becoming the standard around the world.

Differences from conventional procedure using incisions:

- Uses one small puncture instead of 1 or 2 incisions in the scrotum.
- No stitches required to close the skin.
- Special anesthesia technique needs only one needle puncture instead of 2 or more.

Advantages:

- Less pain and bruising and quicker recovery.
- Fewer infections and less collection of blood in the tissue (hematoma).
- Total time for the vasectomy has been shorter when skilled providers use the no-scalpel approach.

Both no-scalpel and conventional incision procedures are quick, safe, and effective.

Blocking the Vas

For most vasectomies ligation and excision is used. This entails cutting and removing a short piece of each tube and then tying both remaining cut ends of the vas. This procedure has a low failure rate. Applying heat or electricity to the ends of each vas (cauterizing) has an even lower failure rate than ligation and excision. The chances that vasectomy will fail can be reduced further by enclosing a cut end of the vas, after the ends have been tied or cauterized, in the thin layer of tissue that surrounds the vas (fascial interposition). If training and equipment are available, cautery and/or fascial interposition are recommended. Blocking the vas with clips is not recommended because of higher pregnancy rates.

Performing the Vasectomy Procedure

Explaining the Procedure

A man who has chosen a vasectomy needs to know what will happen during the procedure. The following description can help explain the procedure to him. Learning to perform a vasectomy takes training and practice under direct supervision. Therefore, this description is a summary and not detailed instructions.

1. The provider uses proper infection-prevention procedures at all times (see Infection Prevention in the Clinic, p. 312).

2. The man receives an injection of local anesthetic in his scrotum to prevent pain. He stays awake throughout the procedure.

3. The provider feels the skin of the scrotum to find each vas deferens— the 2 tubes in the scrotum that carry sperm.

4. The provider makes a puncture or incision in the skin:

   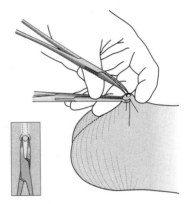

   - Using the no-scalpel vasectomy technique, the provider grasps the tube with specially designed forceps and makes a tiny puncture in the skin at the midline of the scrotum with a special sharp surgical instrument.

   - Using the conventional procedure, the provider makes 1 or 2 small incisions in the skin with a scalpel.

5. The provider lifts out a small loop of each vas from the puncture or incision. Most providers then cut each tube and tie one or both cut ends closed with thread. Some close off the tubes with heat or electricity. They may also enclose one end of the vas in the thin layer of tissue that surrounds the vas (see Vasectomy Techniques, previous page).

6. The puncture is covered with an adhesive bandage, or the incision may be closed with stitches.

7. The man receives instructions on what to do after he leaves the clinic or hospital (see Explaining Self-Care for Vasectomy, p. 192). The man may feel faint briefly after the procedure. He should stand first with help, and he should rest for 15 to 30 minutes. He usually can leave within an hour.

Supporting the User

Explaining Self-Care for Vasectomy

Before the procedure the man should	• Wear clean, loose-fitting clothing to the health facility.
After the procedure the man should	• Rest for 2 days if possible.
	• If possible, put cold compresses on the scrotum for the first 4 hours, which may decrease pain and bleeding. He will have some discomfort, swelling, and bruising. These should go away within 2 to 3 days.
	• Wear snug underwear or pants for 2 to 3 days to help support the scrotum. This will lessen swelling, bleeding, and pain.
	• Keep the puncture/incision site clean and dry for 2 to 3 days. He can use a towel to wipe his body clean but should not soak in water.
	• Not have sex for at least 2 to 3 days.
	• Use condoms or another effective family planning method for 3 months after the procedure. (The previously recommended alternative, to wait for 20 ejaculations, has proved less reliable than waiting 3 months and is no longer recommended.)
What to do about the most common problems	• Discomfort in scrotum usually lasts 2 to 3 days. Suggest ibuprofen (200–400 mg), paracetamol (325–1000 mg), or other pain reliever. He should not take aspirin, which slows blood clotting.
Plan the follow-up visit	• Ask him to return in 3 months for semen analysis, if available (see Question 4, p. 196).
	• No man should be denied a vasectomy, however because follow-up would be difficult or not possible.

"Come Back Any Time": Reasons to Return

Assure every client that he is welcome to come back any time—for example, if he has problems or questions, or his partner thinks she might be pregnant. (A few vasectomies fail and the men's partners become pregnant.) Also if:

- He has bleeding, pain, pus, heat, swelling, or redness in the genital area that becomes worse or does not go away.

General health advice: Anyone who suddenly feels that something is seriously wrong with his health should immediately seek medical care from a nurse or doctor. His contraceptive method is most likely not the cause of the condition, but he should tell the nurse or doctor what method he is using.

Helping Users

Managing Any Problems

Problems Reported as Complications

- Problems affect men's satisfaction with vasectomy. They deserve the provider's attention. If the client reports complications of vasectomy, listen to his concerns and, if appropriate, treat.

Bleeding or blood clots after the procedure

- Reassure him that minor bleeding and small uninfected blood clots usually go away without treatment within a couple of weeks.
- Large blood clots may need to be surgically drained.
- Infected blood clots require antibiotics and hospitalization.

Infection at the puncture or incision site (redness, heat, pain, pus)

- Clean the infected area with soap and water or antiseptic.
- Give oral antibiotics for 7 to 10 days.
- Ask the client to return after taking all antibiotics if the infection has not cleared.

Abscess (a pocket of pus under the skin caused by infection)

- Clean the area with antiseptic.
- Cut open (incise) and drain the abscess.
- Treat the wound.
- Give oral antibiotics for 7 to 10 days.
- Ask the client to return after taking all antibiotics if he has heat, redness, pain, or drainage of the wound.

Pain lasting for months

- Suggest elevating the scrotum with snug underwear or pants or an athletic supporter.
- Suggest soaking in warm water.
- Suggest aspirin (325–650 mg), ibuprofen (200–400 mg), paracetamol (325–1000 mg), or other pain reliever.
- Provide antibiotics if infection is suspected.
- If pain persists and cannot be tolerated, refer for further care (see Question 2, next page).

Questions and Answers About Vasectomy

1. **Will vasectomy make a man lose his sexual ability? Will it make him weak or fat?**

    No. After vasectomy, a man will look and feel the same as before. He can have sex the same as before. His erections will be as hard and last as long as before, and ejaculations of semen will be the same. He can work as hard as before, and he will not gain weight because of the vasectomy.

2. **Will there be any long-lasting pain from vasectomy?**

    Some men report having chronic pain or discomfort in the scrotum or testicles that can last from 1 to 5 years or more after a vasectomy. In the largest studies, involving several thousand men, less than 1% reported pain in the scrotum or testicles that had to be treated with surgery. In smaller studies, of about 200 men, as many as 6% reported severe pain in the scrotum or testicles more than 3 years after the vasectomy. In a similar group of men who did not have vasectomies, however, 2% reported similar pain. Few men with severe pain say that they regret having the vasectomy. The cause of the pain is unknown. It may result from pressure caused by the build-up of sperm that has leaked from an improperly sealed or tied vas deferens, or from nerve damage. Treatment includes elevating the scrotum and taking pain relievers. An anesthetic can be injected into the spermatic cord to numb the nerves to the testicles. Some providers report that surgery to remove the painful site or reversing the vasectomy relieves the pain. Severe, long-lasting pain following vasectomy is uncommon, but all men considering a vasectomy should be told about this risk.

3. **Does a man need to use another contraceptive method after a vasectomy?**

    Yes, for the first 3 months. If his partner has been using a contraceptive method, she can continue to use it during this time. Not using another method for the first 3 months is the main cause of pregnancies among couples relying on vasectomy.

4. Is it possible to check if a vasectomy is working?

Yes. A provider can examine a semen sample under a microscope to see if it still contains sperm. If the provider sees no moving (motile) sperm, the vasectomy is working. A semen examination is recommended at any time after 3 months following the procedure, but is not essential.

If there is less than one nonmotile sperm per 10 high-power fields (less than 100,000 sperm per milliliter) in the fresh sample, then the man can rely on his vasectomy and stop using a backup method for contraception. If his semen contains more moving sperm, the man should continue to use a backup method and return to the clinic monthly for a semen analysis. If his semen continues to have moving sperm, he may need to have a repeat vasectomy.

5. What if a man's partner gets pregnant?

Every man having a vasectomy should know that vasectomies sometimes fail and his partner could become pregnant as a result. He should not make the assumption that his partner was unfaithful if she becomes pregnant. If a man's partner becomes pregnant during the first 3 months after his vasectomy, remind the man that for the first 3 months they needed to use another contraceptive method. If possible, offer a semen analysis and, if sperm are found, a repeat vasectomy.

6. Will the vasectomy stop working after a time?

Generally, no. Vasectomy is intended to be permanent. In rare cases, however, the tubes that carry sperm grow back together and the man will require a repeat vasectomy.

7. Can a man have his vasectomy reversed if he decides that he wants another child?

Generally, no. Vasectomy is intended to be permanent. People who may want more children should choose a different family planning method. Surgery to reverse vasectomy is possible for only some men and reversal often does not lead to pregnancy. The procedure is difficult and expensive, and providers who are able to perform such surgery are hard to find. Thus, vasectomy should be considered irreversible.

8. **Is it better for the man to have a vasectomy or for the woman to have female sterilization?**

   Each couple must decide for themselves which method is best for them. Both are very effective, safe, permanent methods for couples who know that they will not want more children. Ideally, a couple should consider both methods. If both are acceptable to the couple, vasectomy would be preferable because it is simpler, safer, easier, and less expensive than female sterilization.

9. **How can health care providers help a man decide about vasectomy?**

   Provide clear, balanced information about vasectomy and other family planning methods, and help a man think through his decision fully. Thoroughly discuss his feelings about having children and ending his fertility. For example, a provider can help a man think how he would feel about possible life changes such as a change of partner or a child's death. Review The 6 Points of Informed Consent to be sure the man understands the vasectomy procedure (see p. 189).

10. **Should vasectomy be offered only to men who have reached a certain age or have a certain number of children?**

   No. There is no justification for denying vasectomy to a man just because of his age, the number of his living children, or his marital status. Health care providers must not impose rigid rules about age, number of children, age of last child, or marital status. Each man must be allowed to decide for himself whether or not he will want more children and whether or not to have vasectomy.

11. **Does vasectomy increase a man's risk of cancer or heart disease later in life?**

No. Evidence from large, well-designed studies shows that vasectomy does not increase risks of cancer of the testicles (testicular cancer) or cancer of the prostate (prostate cancer) or heart disease.

12. **Can a man who has a vasectomy transmit or become infected with sexually transmitted infections (STIs), including HIV?**

Yes. Vasectomies do not protect against STIs, including HIV. All men at risk of STIs, including HIV, whether or not they have had vasectomies, need to use condoms to protect themselves and their partners from infection.

13. **Where can vasectomies be performed?**

If no pre-existing medical conditions require special arrangements, vasectomy can be performed in almost any health facility, including health care centers, family planning clinics, and the treatment rooms of private doctors. Where other vasectomy services are not available, mobile teams can perform vasectomies and any follow-up examinations in basic health facilities and specially equipped vehicles, so long as basic medications, supplies, instruments, and equipment can be made available.

CHAPTER 13

Male Condoms

This chapter describes male latex condoms. Female condoms, which usually are plastic and inserted into a woman's vagina, are available in some areas (see Female Condoms, p. 211, and Comparing Condoms, p. 360).

Key Points for Providers and Clients

- **Male condoms help protect against sexually transmitted infections, including HIV.** Condoms are the only contraceptive method that can protect against both pregnancy and sexually transmitted infections.

- **Require correct use with every act of sex for greatest effectiveness.**

- **Require both male and female partner's cooperation.** Talking about condom use before sex can improve the chances one will be used.

- **May dull the sensation of sex for some men.** Discussion between partners sometimes can help overcome the objection.

13

Male Condoms

What Are Male Condoms?

- Sheaths, or coverings, that fit over a man's erect penis.
- Also called rubbers, "raincoats," "umbrellas," skins, and prophylactics; known by many different brand names.
- Most are made of thin latex rubber.
- Work by forming a barrier that keeps sperm out of the vagina, preventing pregnancy. Also keep infections in semen, on the penis, or in the vagina from infecting the other partner.

How Effective?

Effectiveness depends on the user: Risk of pregnancy or sexually transmitted infection (STI) is greatest when condoms are not used with every act of sex. Very few pregnancies or infections occur due to incorrect use, slips, or breaks.

Protection against pregnancy:

More effective

- As commonly used, about 15 pregnancies per 100 women whose partners use male condoms over the first year. This means that 85 of every 100 women whose partners use male condoms will not become pregnant.

- When used correctly with every act of sex, about 2 pregnancies per 100 women whose partners use male condoms over the first year.

Return of fertility after use of condoms is stopped: No delay

Protection against HIV and other STIs:

Less effective

- Male condoms significantly reduce the risk of becoming infected with HIV when used correctly with every act of sex.

- When used consistently and correctly, condom use prevents 80% to 95% of HIV transmission that would have occurred without condoms (see Question 2, p. 208).

- Condoms reduce the risk of becoming infected with many STIs when used consistently and correctly.

  - Protect best against STIs spread by discharge, such as HIV, gonorrhea, and chlamydia.

  - Also protect against STIs spread by skin-to-skin contact, such as herpes and human papillomavirus.

Side Effects, Health Benefits, and Health Risks

Side Effects

None

Known Health Benefits

Help protect against:

- Risks of pregnancy
- STIs, including HIV

May help protect against:

- Conditions caused by STIs:
  - Recurring pelvic inflammatory disease and chronic pelvic pain
  - Cervical cancer
  - Infertility (male and female)

Known Health Risks

Extremely rare:

- Severe allergic reaction (among people with latex allergy)

Why Some Men and Women Say They Like Condoms

- Have no hormonal side effects
- Can be used as a temporary or backup method
- Can be used without seeing a health care provider
- Are sold in many places and generally easy to obtain
- Help protect against both pregnancy and STIs, including HIV

Bringing Up Condom Use

Some women find it hard to discuss their desire to use condoms with their partners. Others have difficulty persuading their partners to use condoms every time they have sex. Men give different reasons for not using condoms. Some do not like the way condoms can dull the  sensation of sex. Sometimes men's reasons are based on rumors or misunderstanding. Having the facts can help a woman respond to her partner's objections (see Correcting Misunderstandings, p. 202).

Talking First Can Help. Woman who talk to their partners about using condoms before they begin to have sex can improve the chances that condoms are used. Women can try the approaches they think are best, depending on the partner and the circumstances. Some points that have been persuasive in different situations include:

- Emphasizing use of condoms for pregnancy prevention rather than STI protection.
- Appealing to concern for each other—for example: "Many people in the community have HIV infection, so we need to be careful."
- Taking an uncompromising stance—for example: "I cannot have sex with you unless you use a condom."
- Suggesting to try a female condom, if available. Some men prefer them to male condoms.
- For pregnant women, discussing the risks that STIs pose to the health of the baby and stressing how condoms can help protect the baby.

Also, a woman can suggest that her partner or the couple together come to the clinic for counseling on the importance of condom use.

Correcting Misunderstandings (see also Questions and Answers, p. 208)

Male condoms:

- Do not make men sterile, impotent, or weak.
- Do not decrease men's sex drive.
- Cannot get lost in the woman's body.
- Do not have holes that HIV can pass through.
- Are not laced with HIV.
- Do not cause illness in a woman because they prevent semen or sperm from entering her body.
- Do not cause illness in men because sperm "backs up."
- Are used by married couples. They are not only for use outside marriage.

Who Can and Cannot Use Male Condoms

Medical Eligibility Criteria for

Male Condoms

All men and women can safely use male condoms except those with:

- Severe allergic reaction to latex rubber

For more information on latex allergy, see Mild irritation in or around the vagina or penis or mild allergic reaction to condom, p. 207; Severe allergic reaction to condom, p. 207; and Question 11, p. 210.

Providing Male Condoms

When to Start

- Any time the client wants.

Explaining How to Use

IMPORTANT: Whenever possible, show clients how to put on a condom. Use a model of a penis, if available, or other item, like a banana, to demonstrate.

Explain the 5 Basic Steps of Using a Male Condom

Basic Steps	Important Details
1. Use a new condom for each act of sex	• Check the condom package. Do not use if torn or damaged. Avoid using a condom past the expiration date—do so only if a newer condom is not available. • Tear open the package carefully. Do not use fingernails, teeth, or anything that can damage the condom.
2. Before any physical contact, place the condom on the tip of the erect penis with the rolled side out	• For the most protection, put the condom on before the penis makes any genital, oral, or anal contact.
3. Unroll the condom all the way to the base of the erect penis	• The condom should unroll easily. Forcing it on could cause it to break during use. • If the condom does not unroll easily, it may be on backwards, damaged, or too old. Throw it away and use a new condom. • If the condom is on backwards and another one is not available, turn it over and unroll it onto the penis.
4. Immediately after ejaculation, hold the rim of the condom in place and withdraw the penis while it is still erect	• Withdraw the penis. • Slide the condom off, avoiding spilling semen. • If having sex again or switching from one sex act to another, use a new condom.
5. Dispose of the used condom safely	• Wrap the condom in its package and put in the rubbish or latrine. Do not put the condom into a flush toilet, as it can cause problems with plumbing.

13

Male Condoms

Supporting the User

Ensure client understands correct use	• Ask the client to explain the 5 basic steps of using a condom by putting it on a model or other object and then taking it off. When counseling, use the graphic on p. 363, Correctly Using a Male Condom.
Ask clients how many condoms they will need until they can return	• Give plenty of condoms and, if available, a water- or silicone-based lubricant. Oil-based lubricants should not be used with latex condoms. See box below. • Tell clients where they can buy condoms, if needed.
Explain why using a condom with every act of sex is important	• Just one unprotected act of sex can lead to pregnancy or STI—or both. • If a condom is not used for one act of sex, try to use one the next time. A mistake once or twice does not mean that it is pointless to use condoms in the future.
Explain about emergency contraceptive pills (ECPs)	• Explain ECP use in case of errors in condom use—including not using a condom—to help prevent pregnancy (see Emergency Contraceptive Pills, p. 45). Give ECPs, if available.
Discuss ways to talk about using condoms	• Discuss skills and techniques for negotiating condom use with partners (see Bringing Up Condom Use, p. 201).

Lubricants for Latex Condoms

Lubrication helps avoid condom breakage. There are 3 ways to provide lubrication—natural vaginal secretions, adding a lubricant, or using condoms packaged with lubricant on them.

Sometimes lubricants made of glycerine or silicone, which are safe to use with latex condoms, are available. Clean water and saliva also can be used for lubrication. Lubricants should be applied on the outside of the condom, in the vagina, or in the anus. Lubricants should not be put on the penis, as this can make the condom slip off. A drop or two of lubricant on the inside of the condom before it is unrolled can help increase the sensation of sex for some men. Too much lubricant inside, however, can make the condom slip off.

Do not use products made with oil as lubricants for latex condoms. They can damage latex. Materials that should *not* be used include: any oils (cooking, baby, coconut, mineral), petroleum jelly, lotions, cold creams, butter, cocoa butter, and margarine.

What Condom Users Should Not Do

Some practices can increase the risk that the condom will break and should be avoided.

- Do not unroll the condom first and then try to put it on the penis
- Do not use lubricants with an oil base because they damage latex
- Do not use a condom if the color is uneven or changed
- Do not use a condom that feels brittle, dried out, or very sticky
- Do not reuse condoms
- Do not have dry sex

Also, do not use the same condom when switching between different penetrative sex acts, such as from anal to vaginal sex. This can transfer bacteria that can cause infection.

"Come Back Any Time": Reasons to Return

Assure every client that she or he is welcome to come back any time—for example, if he or she has problems, questions, or wants another method or she thinks she might be pregnant. Also if:

- Client has difficulty using condoms correctly or every time he or she has sex.
- Client has signs or symptoms of severe allergic reaction to latex condom (see Severe allergic reaction to condom, p. 207).
- Woman recently had unprotected sex and wants to avoid pregnancy. She may be able to use ECPs (see Emergency Contraceptive Pills, p. 45).

Helping Continuing Users

1. Ask clients how they are doing with the method and whether they are satisfied. Ask if they have any questions or anything to discuss.

2. Ask especially if they are having any trouble using condoms correctly and every time they have sex. Give clients any information or help that they need (see Managing Any Problems, p. 206).

3. Give clients more condoms and encourage them to come back for more before their supply runs out. Remind them where else they can obtain condoms.

4. Ask a long-term client about major life changes that may affect her or his needs—particularly plans for having children and STI/HIV risk. Follow up as needed.

Managing Any Problems

Problems With Use

May or may not be due to the method.

- Problems with condoms affect clients' satisfaction and use of the method. They deserve the provider's attention. If the client reports any problems, listen to the client's concerns and give advice.

- Offer to help the client choose another method—now, if he or she wishes, or if problems cannot be overcome—unless condoms are needed for protection from STIs, including HIV.

Condom breaks, slips off the penis, or is not used

- ECPs can help prevent pregnancy in such cases (see Emergency Contraceptive Pills, p. 45). If a man notices a break or slip, he should tell his partner so that she can use ECPs if she wants.

- Little can be done to reduce the risk of STIs if a condom breaks, slips, or is not used (see Question 7, p. 209). If the client has signs or symptoms of STIs after having unprotected sex, assess or refer.

- If a client reports breaks or slips:

  – Ask clients to show how they are opening the condom package and putting the condom on, using a model or other item. Correct any errors.

  – Ask if any lubricants are being used. The wrong lubricant or too little lubricant can increase breakage (see Lubricants for Latex Condoms, p. 204). Too much lubricant can cause the condom to slip off.

  – Ask when the man withdraws his penis. Waiting too long to withdraw, when the erection begins to subside, can increase the chance of slips.

Difficulty putting on the condom

- Ask clients to show how they put the condom on, using a model or other item. Correct any errors.

Difficulty persuading partner to use condoms or not able to use a condom every time

- Discuss ways to talk about condoms with partner (see Bringing Up Condom Use, p. 201) and also dual protection rationales (see Choosing a Dual Protection Strategy, p. 280).

- Consider combining condoms with:

  – Another effective contraceptive method for better pregnancy protection.

  – If no risk of STIs, a fertility awareness method, and using condoms only during the fertile time (see Fertility Awareness Methods, p. 239).

- Especially if the client or partner is at risk for STIs, encourage continued condom use while working out problems. If neither partner has an infection, a mutually faithful sexual relationship provides STI protection without requiring condom use but does not protect against pregnancy.

Mild irritation in or around the vagina or penis or mild allergic reaction to condom (itching, redness, rash, and/or swelling of genitals, groin, or thighs during or after condom use)

- Suggest trying another brand of condoms. A person may be more sensitive to one brand of condoms than to others.
- Suggest putting lubricant or water on the condom to reduce rubbing that may cause irritation.
- If symptoms persist, assess or refer for possible vaginal infection or STI as appropriate.
  - If there is no infection and irritation continues or recurs, the client may have an allergy to latex.
  - If not at risk of STIs, including HIV, help the client choose another method.
  - If the client or partner is at risk for STIs, suggest using female condoms or plastic male condoms, if available. If not available, urge continued use of latex condoms. Tell the client to stop using latex condoms if symptoms become severe (see Severe allergic reaction to condom, below).
  - If neither partner has an infection, a mutually faithful sexual relationship provides STI protection without requiring condom use but does not protect against pregnancy.

New Problems That May Require Switching Methods

May or may not be due to the method.

Female partner is using miconazole or econazole (for treatment of vaginal infections)

- A woman should not rely on latex condoms during vaginal use of miconazole or econazole. They can damage latex. (Oral treatment will not harm condoms.)
- She should use female condoms or plastic male condoms, another contraceptive method, or abstain from sex until treatment is completed.

Severe allergic reaction to condom (hives or rash over much of body, dizziness, difficulty breathing, or loss of consciousness during or after condom use). See Signs and Symptoms of Serious Health Conditions, p. 320.

- Tell the client to stop using latex condoms.
- Refer for care, if necessary. Severe allergic reaction to latex could lead to life-threatening anaphylactic shock. Help the client choose another method.
- If the client or partner cannot avoid risk of STIs, suggest they use female condoms or plastic male condoms, if available. If neither partner has an infection, a mutually faithful sexual relationship provides STI protection without requiring condom use but does not protect against pregnancy.

13

Male Condoms

Questions and Answers About Male Condoms

1. **Are condoms effective at preventing pregnancy?**

   Yes, male condoms are effective, but only if used correctly with every act of sex. When used consistently and correctly, only 2 of every 100 women whose partners use condoms become pregnant over the first year of use. Many people, however, do not use condoms every time they have sex or do not use them correctly. This reduces protection from pregnancy.

2. **How well do condoms help protect against HIV infection?**

   On average, condoms are 80% to 95% effective in protecting people from HIV infection when used correctly with every act of sex. This means that condom use prevents 80% to 95% of HIV transmissions that would have occurred without condoms. (It does *not* mean that 5% to 20% of condom users will become infected with HIV.) For example, among 10,000 uninfected women whose partners have HIV, if each couple has vaginal sex just once and has no additional risk factors for infection, on average:

   - If all 10,000 did not use condoms, about 10 women would likely become infected with HIV.

   - If all 10,000 used condoms correctly, 1 or 2 women would likely become infected with HIV.

   The chances that a person who is exposed to HIV will become infected can vary greatly. These chances depend on the partner's stage of HIV infection (early and late stages are more infectious), whether the person exposed has other STIs (increases susceptibility), male circumcision status (uncircumcised men are more likely to become infected with HIV), and pregnancy (women who are pregnant may be at higher risk of infection), among other factors. On average, women face twice the risk of infection, if exposed, that men do.

3. **Does using a condom only some of the time offer any protection from STIs, including HIV?**

   For best protection, a condom should be used with every act of sex. In some cases, however, occasional use can be protective. For example, if a person has a regular, faithful partner and has one act of sex outside of the relationship, using a condom for that one act can be very protective. For people who are exposed to STIs, including HIV frequently, however, using a condom only some of the time will offer limited protection.

4. **Will using condoms reduce the risk of STI transmission during anal sex?**

Yes. STIs can be passed from one person to another during any sex act that inserts the penis into any part of another person's body (penetration). Some sex acts are riskier than others. For example, the risk of becoming infected with HIV is 5 times higher with unprotected receptive anal sex than with unprotected receptive vaginal sex. When using a latex condom for anal sex, a water- or silicone-based lubricant is essential to help keep the condom from breaking.

5. **Are plastic (synthetic) condoms effective for preventing STIs, including HIV?**

Yes. Plastic condoms are expected to provide the same protection as latex condoms, but they have not been studied as thoroughly. The United States Food and Drug Administration recommends that condoms made of plastic be used for protection from STIs, including HIV, only if a person cannot use latex condoms. Condoms made of animal skin such as lambskin (also called natural skin condoms) are not effective for preventing STIs, including HIV, however.

6. **Do condoms often break or slip off during sex?**

No. On average, about 2% of condoms break or slip off completely during sex, primarily because they are used incorrectly. Used properly, condoms seldom break. In some studies with higher breakage rates, often a few users experienced most of the breakage in the entire study. Other studies also suggest that, while most people use condoms correctly, there are a few who consistently misuse condoms, which leads to breaks or slips. Thus, it is important to teach people the right way to open, put on, and take off condoms (see Correctly Using a Male Condom, p. 363) and also to avoid practices that increase the risk of breakage (see What Condom Users Should Not Do, p. 205).

7. **What can men and women do to reduce the risk of pregnancy and STIs if a condom slips or breaks during sex?**

If a condom slips or breaks, taking emergency contraceptive pills can reduce the risk that a woman will become pregnant (see Emergency Contraceptive Pills, p. 45). Little can be done to reduce the risk of STIs, however, except for HIV. Washing the penis does not help. Vaginal douching is not very effective in preventing pregnancy, and it increases a woman's risk of acquiring STIs, including HIV, and pelvic inflammatory disease. If exposure to HIV is certain, treatment with antiretroviral medications (post-exposure prophylaxis), where available, can help reduce HIV transmission. If exposure to other STIs is certain, a provider can treat presumptively for those STIs—that is, treat the client as if he or she were infected.

13

Male Condoms

8. **Can a man put 2 or 3 condoms on at once for more protection?**

There is little evidence about the benefits of using 2 or more condoms. It is generally not recommended because of concerns that friction between the condoms could increase the chance of breakage. In one study, however, users reported less breakage when 2 condoms were used at once, compared with using 1 condom.

9. **Will condoms make a man unable to have an erection (impotent)?**

No, not for most men. Impotence has many causes. Some causes are physical, some are emotional. Condoms themselves do not cause impotence. A few men may have problems keeping an erection when using condoms, however. Other men—especially older men—may have difficulty keeping an erection because condoms can dull the sensation of having sex. Using more lubrication may help increase sensation for men using condoms.

10. **Aren't condoms used mainly in casual relationships or by people who have sex for money?**

No. While many casual partners rely on condoms for STI protection, married couples all over the world use condoms for pregnancy protection, too. In Japan, for example, 42% of married couples use condoms—more than any other family planning method.

11. **Is allergy to latex common?**

No. Allergy to latex is uncommon in the general population, and reports of mild allergic reactions to condoms are very rare. Severe allergic reactions to condoms are extremely rare.

People who have an allergic reaction to rubber gloves or balloons may have a similar reaction to latex condoms. A mild reaction involves redness, itching, rash, or swelling of the skin that comes in contact with latex rubber. A severe reaction involves hives or rash over much of the body, dizziness, difficulty breathing, or loss of consciousness after coming in contact with latex. Both men and women can be allergic to latex and latex condoms.

CHAPTER 14

Female Condoms

This chapter describes plastic (synthetic) female condoms.

Key Points for Providers and Clients

- **Female condoms help protect against sexually transmitted infections, including HIV.** Condoms are the only contraceptive method that can protect against both pregnancy and sexually transmitted infections.

- **Require correct use with every act of sex for greatest effectiveness.**

- **A woman can initiate female condom use,** but the method requires her partner's cooperation.

- **May require some practice.** Inserting and removing the female condom from the vagina becomes easier with experience.

What Are Female Condoms?

- Sheaths, or linings, that fit loosely inside a woman's vagina, made of thin, transparent, soft plastic film.
  - Have flexible rings at both ends
  - One ring at the closed end helps to insert the condom
  - The ring at the open end holds part of the condom outside the vagina
- Different brand names include Care, Dominique, FC Female Condom, Femidom, Femy, Myfemy, Protectiv', Reality, and Woman's Condom.
- Lubricated with a silicone-based lubricant on the inside and outside.
- Rubber female condoms are available in some countries. Different brand names include: L'amour, Reddy Female Condom, V Amour, and VA w.o.w. Condom Feminine, which are made of latex, and the FC 2 Female Condom, made of nitrile.
- Work by forming a barrier that keeps sperm out of the vagina, preventing pregnancy. Also keep infections in semen, on the penis, or in the vagina from infecting the other partner.

How Effective?

Effectiveness depends on the user: Risk of pregnancy or sexually transmitted infection (STI) is greatest when female condoms are not used with every act of sex. Few pregnancies or infections occur due to incorrect use, slips, or breaks.

Protection against pregnancy:

More effective

- As commonly used, about 21 pregnancies per 100 women using female condoms over the first year. This means that 79 of every 100 women using female condoms will not become pregnant.

- When used correctly with every act of sex, about 5 pregnancies per 100 women using female condoms over the first year.

Return of fertility after use of female condom is stopped: No delay

Protection against HIV and other STIs:

- Female condoms reduce the risk of infection with STIs, including HIV, when used correctly with every act of sex.

Less effective

Why Some Women Say They Like Female Condoms

- Women can initiate their use
- Have a soft, moist texture that feels more natural than male latex condoms during sex
- Help protect against both pregnancy and STIs, including HIV
- Outer ring provides added sexual stimulation for some women
- Can be used without seeing a health care provider

Why Some Men Say They Like Female Condoms

- Can be inserted ahead of time so do not interrupt sex
- Are not tight or constricting like male condoms
- Do not dull the sensation of sex like male condoms
- Do not have to be removed immediately after ejaculation

Side Effects, Health Benefits, and Health Risks

Side Effects

None

Known Health Benefits	*Known Health Risks*
Help protect against:	None
• Risks of pregnancy	
• STIs, including HIV	

Correcting Misunderstandings (see also Questions and Answers, p. 219)

Female condoms:

- Cannot get lost in the woman's body.
- Are not difficult to use, but correct use needs to be learned.
- Do not have holes that HIV can pass through.
- Are used by married couples. They are not only for use outside marriage.
- Do not cause illness in a woman because they prevent semen or sperm from entering her body.

Who Can Use Female Condoms

> **Medical Eligibility Criteria for**
> # Female Condoms
>
> *All women can use plastic female condoms.* No medical conditions prevent the use of this method.
>
> (For information on eligibility criteria for latex female condoms, see Medical Eligibility Criteria for Male Condoms, p. 202. For information on managing clients with latex allergy, see Male Condoms, Mild irritation in or around the vagina and penis or mild allergic reaction to condom, p. 207; and Severe allergic reaction to condom, p. 207.)

Providing Female Condoms

When to Start

- Any time the client wants.

Explaining How to Use

IMPORTANT: Whenever possible, show the client how to insert the female condom. Use a model or picture, if available, or your hands to demonstrate. You can create an opening similar to a vagina with one hand and show how to insert the female condom with the other hand.

Explain the 5 Basic Steps of Using a Female Condom

Basic Steps	Important Details
1. Use a new female condom for each act of sex	• Check the condom package. Do not use if torn or damaged. Avoid using a condom past the expiration date—do so only if newer condoms are not available. • If possible, wash your hands with mild soap and clean water before inserting the condom.
2. Before any physical contact, insert the condom into the vagina	• Can be inserted up to 8 hours before sex. For the most protection, insert the condom before the penis comes in contact with the vagina. • Choose a position that is comfortable for insertion—squat, raise one leg, sit, or lie down. • Rub the sides of the female condom together to spread the lubricant evenly. • Grasp the ring at the closed end, and squeeze it so it becomes long and narrow. • With the other hand, separate the outer lips (labia) and locate the opening of the vagina. • Gently push the inner ring into the vagina as far up as it will go. Insert a finger into the condom to push it into place. About 2 to 3 centimeters of the condom and the outer ring remain outside the vagina.

Basic Steps	Important Details

3. Ensure that the penis enters the condom and stays inside the condom

- The man or woman should carefully guide the tip of his penis inside the condom—not between the condom and the wall of the vagina. If his penis goes outside the condom, withdraw and try again.

- If the condom is accidentally pulled out of the vagina or pushed into it during sex, put the condom back in place.

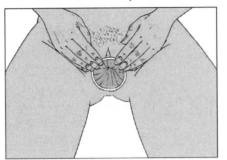

4. After the man withdraws his penis, hold the outer ring of the condom, twist to seal in fluids, and gently pull it out of the vagina

- The female condom does not need to be removed immediately after sex.

- Remove the condom before standing up, to avoid spilling semen.

- If the couple has sex again, they should use a new condom.

- Reuse of female condoms is not recommended (see Question 5, p. 220).

5. Dispose of the used condom safely

- Wrap the condom in its package and put it in the rubbish or latrine. Do not put the condom into a flush toilet, as it can cause problems with plumbing.

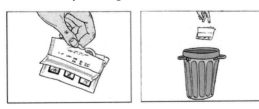

Supporting the User

Ensure client understands correct use	• Ask the client to explain the 5 basic steps of using the female condom while handling one. • If a model is available, the client can practice inserting the condom in the model and then taking it out.
Ask the client how many condoms she thinks she will need until she can return	• Give plenty of condoms and, if available, lubricant. • Tell the client where she can buy female condoms, if needed.
Explain why using a condom with every act of sex is important	• Just one unprotected act of sex can lead to pregnancy or STI—or both. • If a condom is not used for one act of sex, try to use one the next time. A mistake once or twice does not mean that it is pointless to use condoms in the future.
Explain about emergency contraceptive pills (ECPs)	• Explain ECP use in case of errors in condom use—including not using a condom—to help prevent pregnancy (see Emergency Contraceptive Pills, p. 45). Give ECPs if available.
Discuss ways to talk about using condoms	• Discuss skills and techniques for negotiating condom use with partners (see Bringing Up Condom Use, p. 201).

Lubricants for Female Condoms

Plastic female condoms come lubricated with a silicone-based lubricant. Unlike most male condoms, which are made of latex, plastic condoms can be used with any type of lubricant—whether made with water, silicone, or oil.

Some female condoms come with additional lubricant in the package. Some clinics may be able to provide clients with more lubricant. If a client needs additional lubrication, she can also use clean water, saliva, any oil or lotion, or a lubricant made of glycerine or silicone.

Tips for New Users

- Suggest to a new user that she practice putting in and taking out the condom before the next time she has sex. Reassure her that correct use becomes easier with practice. A woman may need to use the female condom several times before she is comfortable with it.

- Suggest she try different positions to see which way insertion is easiest for her.

- The female condom is slippery. Some women find insertion easier if they put it in slowly, especially the first few times.

- If a client is switching from another method to the female condom, suggest that she continue with the previous method until she can use the female condom with confidence.

"Come Back Any Time": Reasons to Return

Assure every client that she is welcome to come back any time—for example, if she has problems, questions, or wants another method; she has any major change in health status; or she thinks she might be pregnant. Also if:

- She has difficulty using female condoms correctly or every time she has sex.

- She recently had unprotected sex and wants to avoid pregnancy. She may be able to use ECPs (see Emergency Contraceptive Pills, p. 45).

Helping Continuing Users

1. Ask how the client is doing with the method and whether she is satisfied. Ask if she has any questions or anything to discuss.

2. Ask especially if she has any trouble using female condoms correctly and every time she has sex. Give her any information or help that she needs (see Managing Any Problems, p. 218).

3. Give her more female condoms and encourage her to come back for more before her supply runs out. Remind her where else she can obtain female condoms.

4. Ask a long-term client about major life changes that may affect her needs—particularly plans for having children and STI/HIV risk. Follow up as needed.

Managing Any Problems

Problems With Use

May or may not be due to the method.

- Problems with condoms affect clients' satisfaction and use of the method. They deserve the provider's attention. If the client reports any problems, listen to her concerns and give advice.

- Offer to help the client choose another method—now, if she wishes, or if problems cannot be overcome—unless condoms are needed for protection from STIs, including HIV.

Difficulty inserting the female condom

- Ask the client how she inserts a female condom. If a model is available, ask her to demonstrate and let her practice with the model. If not, ask her to demonstrate using her hands. Correct any errors.

Inner ring uncomfortable or painful

- Suggest that she reinsert or reposition the condom so that the inner ring is tucked back behind the pubic bone and out of the way.

Condom squeaks or makes noise during sex

- Suggest adding more lubricant to the inside of the condom or onto the penis.

Condom slips, is not used, or is used incorrectly

- ECPs can help prevent pregnancy (see Emergency Contraceptive Pills, p. 45).

- Little can be done to reduce the risk of STIs if a condom breaks, slips, or is not used (see Male Condoms, Question 7, p. 209). If the client has signs or symptoms of STIs after having unprotected sex, assess or refer.

- If a client reports slips, she may be inserting the female condom incorrectly. Ask her to show how she is inserting the condom, using a model or demonstrating with her hands. Correct any errors.

Difficulty persuading partner to use condoms or not able to use a condom every time

- Discuss ways to talk with her partner about the importance of condom use for protection from pregnancy and STIs. (See Male Condoms, Difficulty persuading partner to use condoms or not able to use a condom every time, p. 206.)

- Usually goes away on its own without treatment.

- Suggest adding lubricant to the inside of the condom or onto the penis to reduce rubbing that may cause irritation.

- If symptoms persist, assess and treat for possible vaginal infection or STI, as appropriate.

  – If there is no infection, help the client choose another method unless the client is at risk for STIs, including HIV

  – For clients at risk of STIs, including HIV, suggest using male condoms. If using male condoms is not possible, urge continued use of female condoms despite discomfort.

  – If neither partner has an infection, a mutually faithful sexual relationship provides STI protection without requiring condom use but does not protect against pregnancy.

Suspected pregnancy

- Assess for pregnancy.

- A woman can safely use female condoms during pregnancy for continued STI protection.

14

Female Condoms

Questions and Answers About Female Condoms

1. **Is the female condom difficult to use?**

   No, but it does require practice and patience. See Tips for New Users, p. 217.

2. **Can female condoms effectively prevent both pregnancy and STIs, including HIV?**

   Yes. Female condoms offer dual protection, against both pregnancy and STIs, including HIV, if used consistently and correctly. Many people, however, do not use condoms every time they have sex, or do not use them correctly. This reduces protection from both pregnancy and STIs.

3. **Can a female condom and a male condom be used at the same time?**

   No. Male and female condoms should not be used together. This can cause friction that may lead to slipping or tearing of the condoms.

4. **What is the best way to make sure the penis goes into the condom and not outside the condom?**

    To avoid incorrect use, the man should carefully guide his penis and place the tip inside the outer ring of the condom. If the penis goes between the wall of the vagina and the condom, the man should withdraw and try again.

5. **Can the female condom be used more than once?**

    Reuse of the female condom is not recommended. Reuse of currently available female condoms has not been tested.

6. **Can the female condom be used while a woman is having her monthly bleeding?**

    Women can use the female condom during their monthly bleeding. The female condom cannot be used at the same time as a tampon, however. The tampon must be removed before inserting a female condom.

7. **Isn't the female condom too big to be comfortable?**

    No. Female condoms are the same length as male condoms, but wider. They are very flexible and fit to the shape of the vagina. Female condoms have been carefully designed and tested to fit any woman, whatever the size of her vagina, and any man, whatever the size of his penis.

8. **Can a female condom get lost inside a woman's body?**

    No. The female condom remains in a woman's vagina until she takes it out. It cannot go past a woman's cervix and into the womb (uterus) because it is too large for that.

9. **Can the female condom be used in different sexual positions?**

    Yes. The female condom can be used in any sexual position.

CHAPTER 15

Spermicides and Diaphragms

Spermicides

Key Points for Providers and Clients

- Spermicides are placed deep in the vagina shortly before sex.
- Require correct use with every act of sex for greatest effectiveness.
- One of the least effective contraceptive methods.
- Can be used as a primary method or as a backup method.

What Are Spermicides?

- Sperm-killing substances inserted deep in the vagina, near the cervix, before sex.
  - Nonoxynol-9 is most widely used.
  - Others include benzalkonium chloride, chlorhexidine, menfegol, octoxynol-9, and sodium docusate.
- Available in foaming tablets, melting or foaming suppositories, cans of pressurized foam, melting film, jelly, and cream.
  - Jellies, creams, and foam from cans can be used alone, with a diaphragm, or with condoms.
  - Films, suppositories, foaming tablets, or foaming suppositories can be used alone or with condoms.
- Work by causing the membrane of sperm cells to break, killing them or slowing their movement. This keeps sperm from meeting an egg.

How Effective?

More effective

Effectiveness depends on the user: Risk of pregnancy is greatest when spermicides are not used with every act of sex.

- One of the least effective family planning methods.

- As commonly used, about 29 pregnancies per 100 women using spermicides over the first year. This means that 71 of every 100 women using spermicides will not become pregnant.

- When used correctly with every act of sex, about 18 pregnancies per 100 women using spermicides over the first year.

Return of fertility after spermicides are stopped: No delay

Less effective

Protection against sexually transmitted infections (STIs): None. Frequent use of nonoxynol-9 may increase risk of HIV infection (see Question 3, p. 235).

Side Effects, Health Benefits, and Health Risks

Side Effects (see Managing Any Problems, p. 233)

Some users report the following:

- Irritation in or around the vagina or penis

Other possible physical changes:

- Vaginal lesions

Known Health Benefits

Help protect against:

- Risks of pregnancy

Known Health Risks

Uncommon:

- Urinary tract infection, especially when using spermicides 2 or more times a day

Rare:

- Frequent use of nonoxynol-9 may increase risk of HIV infection (see Question 3, p. 235)

Correcting Misunderstandings (see also Questions and Answers, p. 235)

Spermicides:

- Do not reduce vaginal secretions or make women bleed during sex.
- Do not cause cervical cancer or birth defects.
- Do not protect against STIs.
- Do not change men's or women's sex drive or reduce sexual pleasure for most men.
- Do not stop women's monthly bleeding.

Why Some Women Say They Like Spermicides

- Are controlled by the woman
- Have no hormonal side effects
- Increase vaginal lubrication
- Can be used without seeing a health care provider
- Can be inserted ahead of time and so do not interrupt sex

Who Can and Cannot Use Spermicides

Safe and Suitable for Nearly All Women

Medical Eligibility Criteria for

Spermicides

All women can safely use spermicides except those who:

- Are at high risk for HIV infection
- Have HIV infection
- Have AIDS

Providing Spermicides

When to Start

- Any time the client wants.

Explaining How to Use Spermicides

Give spermicide	• Give as much spermicide as possible—even as much as a year's supply, if available.
Explain how to insert spermicide into the vagina	1. Check the expiration date and avoid using spermicides past their expiration date. 2. Wash hands with mild soap and clean water, if possible. 3. Foam or cream: Shake cans of foam hard. Squeeze spermicide from the can or tube into a plastic applicator. Insert the applicator deep into the vagina, near the cervix, and push the plunger. 4. Tablets, suppositories, jellies: Insert the spermicide deep into the vagina, near the cervix, with an applicator or with fingers. Film: Fold film in half and insert with fingers that are dry (or else the film will stick to the fingers and not the cervix).
Explain when to insert spermicide into the vagina	• Foam or cream: Any time less than one hour before sex. • Tablets, suppositories, jellies, film: Between 10 minutes and one hour before sex, depending on type.
Explain about multiple acts of sex	• Insert additional spermicide before each act of vaginal sex.
Do not wash the vagina (douche) **after sex**	• Douching is not recommended because it will wash away the spermicide and also increase the risk of sexually transmitted infections. • If you must douche, wait for at least 6 hours after sex before doing so.

Supporting the Spermicide User

Ensure client understands correct use	• Ask the client to repeat how and when to insert her spermicide.
Describe the most common side effects	• Itching and irritation in or around the vagina or penis.
Explain about emergency contraceptive pills (ECPs)	• Explain ECP use in case the spermicide is not used at all or is not used properly (see Emergency Contraceptive Pills, p. 45). Give her ECPs, if available.

Diaphragms

Key Points for Providers and Clients

- **The diaphragm is placed deep in the vagina before sex.** It covers the cervix. Spermicide provides additional contraceptive protection.

- **A pelvic examination is needed before starting use.** The provider must select a diaphragm that fits properly.

- **Require correct use with every act of sex for greatest effectiveness.**

What Is the Diaphragm?

- A soft latex cup that covers the cervix. Plastic and silicone diaphragms may also be available.

- The rim contains a firm, flexible spring that keeps the diaphragm in place.

- Used with spermicidal cream, jelly, or foam to improve effectiveness.

- Comes in different sizes and requires fitting by a specifically trained provider. A one-size-fits-all diaphragm may become available. It would not require seeing a provider for fitting.

- Works by blocking sperm from entering the cervix; spermicide kills or disables sperm. Both keep sperm from meeting an egg.

15

Spermicides and Diaphragms

How Effective?

Effectiveness depends on the user: Risk of pregnancy is greatest when the diaphragm with spermicide is not used with every act of sex.

- As commonly used, about 16 pregnancies per 100 women using the diaphragm with spermicide over the first year. This means that 84 of every 100 women using the diaphragm will not become pregnant.

- When used correctly with every act of sex, about 6 pregnancies per 100 women using the diaphragm with spermicide over the first year.

Return of fertility after use of the diaphragm is stopped: No delay

Protection against STIs: May provide some protection against certain STIs but should not be relied on for STI prevention (see Question 8, p. 236).

Side Effects, Health Benefits, and Health Risks

Side Effects (see Managing Any Problems, p. 233)

Some users report the following:

- Irritation in or around the vagina or penis

Other possible physical changes:

- Vaginal lesions

Known Health Benefits

Help protect against:
- Risks of pregnancy

May help protect against:
- Certain STIs (chlamydia, gonorrhea, pelvic inflammatory disease, trichomoniasis)

- Cervical precancer and cancer

Known Health Risks

Common to uncommon:
- Urinary tract infection

Uncommon:
- Bacterial vaginosis
- Candidiasis

Rare:
- Frequent use of nonoxynol-9 may increase risk of HIV infection (see Question 3, p. 235)

Extremely rare:
- Toxic shock syndrome

Correcting Misunderstandings (see also Questions and Answers, p. 235)

Diaphragms:

- Do not affect the feeling of sex. A few men report feeling the diaphragm during sex, but most do not.
- Cannot pass through the cervix. They cannot go into the uterus or otherwise get lost in the woman's body.
- Do not cause cervical cancer.

> ## Why Some Women Say They Like the Diaphragm
>
> - Is controlled by the woman
> - Has no hormonal side effects
> - Can be inserted ahead of time and so does not interrupt sex

Who Can and Cannot Use Diaphragms

Safe and Suitable for Nearly All Women

Nearly all women can use the diaphragm safely and effectively.

Medical Eligibility Criteria for

Diaphragms

Ask the client the questions below about known medical conditions. Examinations and tests are not necessary. If she answers "no" to all of the questions, then she can start using the diaphragm if she wants. If she answers "yes" to a question, follow the instructions. In some cases she can still start using the diaphragm. These questions also apply to the cervical cap (see p. 238).

1. Have you recently had a baby or second-trimester spontaneous or induced abortion? If so, when?

❑ NO ❑ YES The diaphragm should not be fitted until 6 weeks after childbirth or second-trimester abortion, when the uterus and cervix have returned to normal size. Give her a backup method* to use until then.

(Continued on next page)

* Backup methods include abstinence, male and female condoms, spermicides, and withdrawal. Tell her that spermicides and withdrawal are the least effective contraceptive methods. If possible, give her condoms.

15

Spermicides and Diaphragms

2. **Are you allergic to latex rubber?**

❑ NO ❑ **YES** She should not use a latex diaphragm. She can use a diaphragm made of plastic.

3. **Do you have HIV infection or AIDS? Do you think you are at high risk of HIV infection? (Discuss what places a woman at high risk for HIV [see Sexually Transmitted Infections, Including HIV, Who Is At Risk?, p. 276]. For example, her partner has HIV.)**

❑ NO ❑ **YES** Do not provide a diaphragm. For HIV protection, recommend using condoms alone or with another method.

For complete classifications, see Medical Eligibility Criteria for Contraceptive Use, p. 333. Be sure to explain the health benefits and risks and the side effects of the method that the client will use. Also, point out any conditions that would make the method inadvisable, when relevant to the client.

Using Clinical Judgment in Special Cases of Diaphragm Use

Usually, a woman with any of the conditions listed below should not use the diaphragm. In special circumstances, however, when other, more appropriate methods are not available or acceptable to her, a qualified provider who can carefully assess a specific woman's condition and situation may decide that she can use the diaphragm with spermicide. The provider needs to consider the severity of her condition and, for most conditions, whether she will have access to follow-up.

- History of toxic shock syndrome
- Allergy to latex, especially if the allergic reaction is mild (see Mild irritation in or around the vagina or penis or mild allergic reaction to condom, p. 207)
- HIV infection or AIDS

Providing Diaphragms

When to Start

Woman's situation	When to start
Any time	**At any time** • If she has had a full-term delivery or second-trimester spontaneous or induced abortion less than 6 weeks ago, give her a backup method* to use, if needed, until 6 weeks have passed.
Special advice for women switching from another method	• Suggest that she try the diaphragm for a time while still using her other method. This way she can safely gain confidence that she can use the diaphragm correctly.

Explaining the Fitting Procedure

Learning to fit women for a diaphragm requires training and practice. Therefore, this is a summary and not detailed instructions.

1. The provider uses proper infection-prevention procedures (see Infection Prevention in the Clinic, p. 312).

2. The woman lies down as for a pelvic examination.

3. The provider checks for conditions that may make it impossible to use the diaphragm, such as uterine prolapse.

4. The provider inserts the index and middle fingers into the vagina to determine the correct diaphragm size.

5. The provider inserts a special fitting diaphragm into the client's vagina so that it covers the cervix. The provider then checks the location of the cervix and makes sure that the diaphragm fits properly and does not come out easily.

6. The provider gives the woman a properly fitting diaphragm and plenty of spermicide to use with it, and teaches her to use it properly (see Explaining How to Use a Diaphragm, p. 230).

With a properly fitted diaphragm in place, the client should not be able to feel anything inside her vagina, even when she walks or during sex.

___
* Backup methods include abstinence, male and female condoms, spermicides, and withdrawal. Tell her that spermicides and withdrawal are the least effective contraceptive methods. If possible, give her condoms.

Explaining How to Use the Diaphragm

IMPORTANT: Whenever possible, show the woman the location of the pubic bone and cervix with a model or a picture. Explain that the diaphragm is inserted behind the pubic bone and covers the cervix.

Explain the 5 Basic Steps to Using a Diaphragm

Basic Steps	Important Details
1. Squeeze a spoonful of spermicidal cream, jelly, or foam into the diaphragm and around the rim	• Wash hands with mild soap and clean water, if possible. • Check the diaphragm for holes, cracks, or tears by holding it up to the light. • Check the expiration date of the spermicide and avoid using any beyond its expiration date. • Insert the diaphragm less than 6 hours before having sex.
2. Press the rim together; push into the vagina as far as it goes	• Choose a position that is comfortable for insertion—squatting, raising one leg, sitting, or lying down.
3. Feel diaphragm to make sure it covers the cervix	• Through the dome of the diaphragm, the cervix feels like the tip of the nose. • If the diaphragm feels uncomfortable, take it out and insert it again.

Basic Steps	Important Details
4. Keep in place for at least 6 hours after sex	• Keep the diaphragm in place at least 6 hours after having sex but no longer than 24 hours.
	• *Leaving the diaphragm in place for more than one day may increase the risk of toxic shock syndrome.* It can also cause a bad odor and vaginal discharge. (Odor and discharge go away on their own after the diaphragm is removed.)
	• For multiple acts of sex, make sure that the diaphragm is in the correct position and also insert additional spermicide in front of the diaphragm before each act of sex.
5. To remove, slide a finger under the rim of the diaphragm to pull it down and out	• Wash hands with mild soap and clean water, if possible.
	• Insert a finger into the vagina until the rim of the diaphragm is felt.
	• Gently slide a finger under the rim and pull the diaphragm down and out. Use care not to tear the diaphragm with a fingernail.
	• Wash the diaphragm with mild soap and clean water and dry it after each use.

Supporting the Diaphragm User

Ensure client understands correct use	• Ask the client to repeat how and when to insert and remove the diaphragm.
Explain that use becomes easier with time	• The more practice she has with inserting and removing the diaphragm, the easier it will get.
Describe the most common side effects	• Itching and irritation in or around the vagina or penis.
Explain about emergency contraceptive pills (ECPs)	• Explain ECP use in case the diaphragm moves out of place or is not used properly (see Emergency Contraceptive Pills, p. 45). Give her ECPs, if available.
Explain about replacement	• When a diaphragm gets thin, develops holes, or becomes stiff, it should not be used and needs to be replaced. She should obtain a new diaphragm about every 2 years.

Spermicides and Diaphragms

Tips for Users of Spermicides or the Diaphragm With Spermicide

- Spermicides should be stored in a cool, dry place, if possible, out of the sun. Suppositories may melt in hot weather. If kept dry, foaming tablets are not as likely to melt in hot weather.

- The diaphragm should be stored in a cool, dry place, if possible.

- She needs a new diaphragm fitted if she has had a baby or a second-trimester miscarriage or abortion.

"Come Back Any Time": Reasons to Return

Assure every client that she is welcome to come back any time—for example, if she has problems, questions, or wants another method; she has any major change in health status; or she thinks she might be pregnant.

General health advice: Anyone who suddenly feels that something is seriously wrong with her health should immediately seek medical care from a nurse or doctor. Her contraceptive method is most likely not the cause of the condition, but she should tell the nurse or doctor what method she is using.

Helping Continuing Users

1. Ask how the client is doing with the method and whether she is satisfied. Ask if she has any questions or anything to discuss.

2. Ask especially if she has any problems using the method correctly and every time she has sex. Give her any information or help she needs (see Managing Any Problems, next page).

3. Give her more supplies and encourage her to come back for more before she runs out. Remind her where else she can obtain more spermicides if needed.

4. Ask a long-term client if she has had any new health problems since her last visit. Address problems as appropriate. For new health problems that may require switching methods, see p. 234.

5. Ask a long-term client about major life changes that may affect her needs—particularly plans for having children and STI/HIV risk. Follow up as needed.

Managing Any Problems

Problems Reported as Side Effects or Problems With Use

May or may not be due to the method.

- Side effects or problems with spermicides or diaphragms affect women's satisfaction and use of the method. They deserve the provider's attention. If the client reports side effects or problems, listen to her concerns, give her advice, and, if appropriate, treat.

- Offer to help the client choose another method—now, if she wishes, or if problems cannot be overcome.

Difficulty inserting or removing diaphragm

- Give advice on insertion and removal. Ask her to insert and remove the diaphragm in the clinic. Check its placement after she inserts it. Correct any errors.

Discomfort or pain with diaphragm use

- A diaphragm that is too large can cause discomfort. Check if it fits well.
  - Fit her with a smaller diaphragm if it is too large.
  - If fit appears proper and different kinds of diaphragms are available, try a different diaphragm.

- Ask her to insert and remove the diaphragm in the clinic. Check the diaphragm's placement after she inserts it. Give further advice as needed.

- Check for vaginal lesions:
  - If vaginal lesions or sores exist, suggest she use another method temporarily (condoms or oral contraceptives) and give her supplies.
  - Assess for vaginal infection or sexually transmitted infection (STI). Treat or refer for treatment as appropriate.
  - Lesions will go away on their own if she switches to another method.

Irritation in or around the vagina or penis (she or her partner has itching, rash, or irritation that lasts for a day or more)

- Check for vaginal infection or STI and treat or refer for treatment as appropriate.

- If no infection, suggest trying a different type or brand of spermicides.

Urinary tract infection (burning or pain with urination, frequent urination in small amounts, blood in the urine, back pain)

- Treat with cotrimoxazole 240 mg orally once a day for 3 days, or trimethoprim 100 mg orally once a day for 3 days, or nitrofurantoin 50 mg orally twice a day for 3 days.

- If infection recurs, consider refitting the client with a smaller diaphragm.

Bacterial vaginosis (abnormal white or grey vaginal discharge with unpleasant odor; may also have burning during urination and/or itching around the vagina)

- Treat with metronidazole 2 g orally in a single dose or metronidazole 400–500 mg orally twice daily for 7 days.

Candidiasis (abnormal white vaginal discharge that can be watery or thick and chunky; may also have burning during urination and/or redness and itching around the vagina)

- Treat with fluconazole 150 mg orally in a single dose, miconazole 200 mg vaginal suppository, once a day for 3 days, or clotrimazole 100 mg vaginal tablets, twice a day for 3 days.

- Miconazole suppositories are oil-based and can weaken a latex diaphragm. Women using miconazole vaginally should not use latex diaphragms or condoms during treatment. They can use a plastic female or male condom or another method until all medication is taken. (Oral treatment will not harm latex.)

Suspected pregnancy

- Assess for pregnancy.

- There are no known risks to a fetus conceived while using spermicides.

New Problems That May Require Switching Methods

May or may not be due to the method.

Recurring urinary tract infections or vaginal infections (such as bacterial vaginosis or candidiasis)

- Consider refitting the client with a smaller diaphragm.

Latex allergy (redness, itching, rash, and/or swelling of genitals, groin, or thighs [mild reaction]; or hives or rash over much of the body, dizziness, difficulty breathing, loss of consciousness [severe reaction])

- Tell the client to stop using a latex diaphragm. Give her a plastic diaphragm, if available, or help her choose another method, but not latex condoms.

Toxic shock syndrome (sudden high fever, body rash, vomiting, diarrhea, dizziness, sore throat, and muscle aches). See Signs and Symptoms of Serious Health Conditions, p. 320.

- Treat or refer for immediate diagnosis and care. Toxic shock syndrome can be life-threatening.

- Tell the client to stop using the diaphragm. Help her choose another method but not the cervical cap.

Questions and Answers About Spermicides and Diaphragms

1. **Do spermicides cause birth defects? Will the fetus be harmed if a woman accidentally uses spermicides while she is pregnant?**

    No. Good evidence shows that spermicides will not cause birth defects or otherwise harm the fetus if a woman becomes pregnant while using spermicides or accidentally uses spermicides when she is already pregnant.

2. **Do spermicides cause cancer?**

    No, spermicides do not cause cancer.

3. **Do spermicides increase the risk of becoming infected with HIV?**

    Women who use nonoxynol-9 several times a day may face an increased risk of becoming infected with HIV. Spermicides can cause vaginal irritation, which may cause small lesions to form on the lining of the vagina or on the external genitals. These lesions may make it easier for a woman to become infected with HIV. Studies that suggest spermicide use increases HIV risk have involved women who used spermicides several times a day. Women who have multiple daily acts of sex should use another contraceptive method. A study among women using nonoxynol-9 an average of 3 times a week, however, found no increased risk of HIV infection for spermicide users compared with women not using spermicides. New spermicides that are less irritating may become available.

4. **Is the diaphragm uncomfortable for the woman?**

    No, not if it is fitted and inserted correctly. The woman and her partner usually cannot feel the diaphragm during sex. The provider selects the properly sized diaphragm for each woman so that it fits her and does not hurt. If it is uncomfortable, she should come back to have the fit checked and to make sure that she is inserting and removing the diaphragm properly.

5. **If a woman uses the diaphragm without spermicides, will it still prevent pregnancy?**

    There is not enough evidence to be certain. A few studies find that diaphragm users have higher pregnancy rates when they do not use a spermicide with it. Thus, using a diaphragm without spermicide is not recommended.

6. **Could a woman leave a diaphragm in all day?**

Yes, although doing so is usually not recommended. A woman could leave a diaphragm in all day if she cannot put it in shortly before having sex. She should not leave the diaphragm in for more than 24 hours, however. This can increase the risk of toxic shock syndrome.

7. **Can a woman use lubricants with a diaphragm?**

Yes, but only water- or silicone-based lubricants if the diaphragm is made of latex. Products made with oil cannot be used as lubricants because they damage latex. Materials that should not be used with latex diaphragms include any oils (cooking, baby, coconut, mineral), petroleum jelly, lotions, cold creams, butter, cocoa butter, and margarine. Oil-based lubricants will not harm a plastic diaphragm. Spermicides usually provide enough lubrication for diaphragm users.

8. **Do diaphragms help protect women from STIs, including HIV?**

Research suggests that the diaphragm may help protect somewhat against infections of the cervix such as gonorrhea and chlamydia. Some studies have also found that it also may help protect against pelvic inflammatory disease and trichomoniasis. Studies are underway to assess protection from HIV. Currently, only male and female condoms are recommended for protection from HIV and other STIs.

9. **What is the vaginal sponge, and how effective is it?**

The vaginal sponge is made of plastic and contains spermicides. It is moistened with water and inserted into the vagina so that it rests against the cervix. Each sponge can be used only once. It is not widely available.

Effectiveness depends on the user: Risk of pregnancy is greatest when a woman does not use the sponge with every act of sex.

Women who have given birth:

- One of the least effective methods, as commonly used.
- As commonly used, about 32 pregnancies per 100 women using the sponge over the first year.
- When used correctly with every act of sex, about 20 pregnancies per 100 women over the first year.

More effective among women who have not given birth:

- As commonly used, about 16 pregnancies per 100 women using the sponge over the first year.
- When used correctly with every act of sex, about 9 pregnancies per 100 women over the first year.

Cervical Caps

Key Points for Providers and Clients

- **The cervical cap is placed deep in the vagina before sex.** It covers the cervix.

- **Require correct use with every act of sex for greatest effectiveness.**

- **Used together with spermicide to improve effectiveness.**

What Is the Cervical Cap?

- A soft, deep, latex or plastic rubber cup that snugly covers the cervix.

- Comes in different sizes; requires fitting by a specifically trained provider.

- Different brand names include FemCap and Leah's Shield.

How Effective?

Effectiveness depends on the user: Risk of pregnancy is greatest when the cervical cap with spermicide is not used with every act of sex.

Women who have given birth:

- One of the least effective methods, as commonly used.

- As commonly used, about 32 pregnancies per 100 women using the cervical cap with spermicide over the first year. This means that 68 of every 100 women using the cervical cap will not become pregnant.

- When used correctly with every act of sex, about 20 pregnancies per 100 women using the cervical cap over the first year.

More effective among women who have not given birth:

- As commonly used, about 16 pregnancies per 100 women using the cervical cap with spermicide over the first year. This means that 84 of every 100 women using the cervical cap will not become pregnant.

- When used correctly with every act of sex, about 9 pregnancies per 100 women using the cervical cap over the first year.

Return of fertility after use of cervical cap is stopped: No delay

Protection against sexually transmitted infections: None

More effective

Never given birth

Have given birth

Less effective

16

Cervical Cap

Side Effects, Health Benefits, and Health Risks

Same as for diaphragms (see Diaphragms, Side Effects, Health Benefits, and Health Risks, p. 226).

Providing Cervical Caps

Providing the cervical cap is similar to providing (see p. 229) and helping diaphragm users (see p. 232). Differences include:

Inserting

- Fill one-third of the cap with spermicidal cream, jelly, or foam.
- Press the rim of the cap around the cervix until it is completely covered, pressing gently on the dome to apply suction and seal the cap.
- Insert the cervical cap any time up to 42 hours before having sex.

Removing

- Leave the cervical cap in for at least 6 hours after her partner's last ejaculation, but not more than 48 hours from the time it was put in.
- Leaving the cap in place for more than 48 hours may increase the risk of toxic shock syndrome and can cause a bad odor and vaginal discharge.
- Tip the cap rim sideways to break the seal against the cervix, then gently pull the cap down and out of the vagina.

CHAPTER 17

Fertility Awareness Methods

Key Points for Providers and Clients

- **Fertility awareness methods require partners' cooperation.** Couple must be committed to abstaining or using another method on fertile days.

- **Must stay aware of body changes or keep track of days, according to rules of the specific method.**

- **No side effects or health risks.**

What Are Fertility Awareness Methods?

- "Fertility awareness" means that a woman knows how to tell when the fertile time of her menstrual cycle starts and ends. (The fertile time is when she can become pregnant.)

- Sometimes called periodic abstinence or natural family planning.

- A woman can use several ways, alone or in combination, to tell when her fertile time begins and ends.

- *Calendar-based methods* involve keeping track of days of the menstrual cycle to identify the start and end of the fertile time.

  - Examples: Standard Days Method and calendar rhythm method.

- *Symptoms-based methods* depend on observing signs of fertility.

  - Cervical secretions: When a woman sees or feels cervical secretions, she may be fertile. She may feel just a little vaginal wetness.

  - Basal body temperature (BBT): A woman's resting body temperature goes up slightly after the release of an egg (ovulation), when she could become pregnant. Her temperature stays higher until the beginning of her next monthly bleeding.

  - Examples: TwoDay Method, BBT method, ovulation method (also known as Billings method or cervical mucus method), and the symptothermal method.

- Work primarily by helping a woman know when she could become pregnant. The couple prevents pregnancy by avoiding unprotected vaginal sex during these fertile days—usually by abstaining or by using condoms or a diaphragm. Some couples use spermicides or withdrawal, but these are among the least effective methods.

How Effective?

More
effective

Effectiveness depends on the user: Risk of pregnancy is greatest when couples have sex on the fertile days without using another method.

- As commonly used, in the first year about 25 pregnancies per 100 women using periodic abstinence. (How these women identified their fertile time is not known. Pregnancy rates for most of the specific fertility awareness methods as commonly used are not available.) This means that 75 of every 100 women relying on periodic abstinence will not become pregnant. Some newer fertility awareness methods may be easier to use and, thus, more effective (see Question 3, p. 254).

Less
effective

- Pregnancy rates with consistent and correct use vary for different types of fertility awareness methods (see table, below).

- In general, abstaining during fertile times is more effective than using another method during fertile times.

Pregnancy Rates With Consistent and Correct Use and Abstinence on Fertile Days

Method	Pregnancies per 100 Women Over the First Year
Calendar-based methods	
Standard Days Method	5
Calendar rhythm method	9
Symptoms-based methods	
TwoDay Method	4
Basal body temperature (BBT) method	1
Ovulation method	3
Symptothermal method	2

Return of fertility after fertility awareness methods are stopped: No delay

Protection against sexually transmitted infections (STIs): None

Side Effects, Health Benefits, and Health Risks

Side Effects

None

Known Health Benefits	*Known Health Risks*
Help protect against:	None
• Risks of pregnancy	

Why Some Women Say They Like Fertility Awareness Methods

- Have no side effects
- Do not require procedures and usually do not require supplies
- Help women learn about their bodies and fertility
- Allow some couples to adhere to their religious or cultural norms about contraception
- Can be used to identify fertile days by both women who want to become pregnant and women who want to avoid pregnancy

Correcting Misunderstandings (see also Questions and Answers, p. 253)

Fertility awareness methods:

- Can be very effective if used consistently and correctly.
- Do not require literacy or advanced education.
- Do not harm men who abstain from sex.
- Do not work when a couple is mistaken about when the fertile time occurs, such as thinking it occurs during monthly bleeding.

Fertility Awareness Methods for Women With HIV

- Women who are infected with HIV, have AIDS, or are on antiretroviral (ARV) therapy can safely use fertility awareness methods.
- Urge these women to use condoms along with fertility awareness methods. Used consistently and correctly, condoms help prevent transmission of HIV and other STIs.

Who Can Use Calendar-Based Methods

Medical Eligibility Criteria for

Calendar-Based Methods

All women can use calendar-based methods. No medical conditions prevent the use of these methods, but some conditions can make them harder to use effectively.

Caution means that additional or special counseling may be needed to ensure correct use of the method.

Delay means that use of a particular fertility awareness method should be delayed until the condition is evaluated or corrected. Give the client another method to use until she can start the calendar-based method.

In the following situations use *caution* with calendar-based methods:

- Menstrual cycles have just started or have become less frequent or stopped due to older age (Menstrual cycle irregularities are common in young women in the first several years after their first monthly bleeding and in older women who are approaching menopause. Identifying the fertile time may be difficult.)

In the following situations *delay* starting calendar-based methods:

- Recently gave birth or is breastfeeding (*Delay* until she has had at least 3 menstrual cycles and her cycles are regular again. For several months after regular cycles have returned, use with *caution.*)

- Recently had an abortion or miscarriage (*Delay* until the start of her next monthly bleeding.)

- Irregular vaginal bleeding

In the following situations *delay* or use *caution* with calendar-based methods:

- Taking any mood-altering drugs such as anti-anxiety therapies (except benzodiazepines), antidepressants (selective serotonin reuptake inhibitors [SSRIs], tricyclic, or tetracyclic), long-term use of certain antibiotics, or long-term use of any nonsteroidal anti-inflammatory drug (such as aspirin, ibuprofen, or paracetamol). These drugs may delay ovulation.

Providing Calendar-Based Methods

When to Start

Once trained, a woman or couple usually can begin using calendar-based methods at any time. Give clients who cannot start immediately another method to use until they can start.

Woman's situation	When to start
Having regular menstrual cycles	**Any time of the month** • No need to wait until the start of next monthly bleeding.
No monthly bleeding	• Delay calendar-based methods until monthly bleeding returns.
After childbirth (whether or not breastfeeding)	• Delay the Standard Days Method until she has had 3 menstrual cycles and the last one was 26–32 days long. • Regular cycles will return later in breastfeeding women than in women who are not breastfeeding.
After miscarriage or abortion	• Delay the Standard Days Method until the start of her next monthly bleeding, when she can start if she has no bleeding due to injury to the genital tract.
Switching from a hormonal method	• Delay starting the Standard Days Method until the start of her next monthly bleeding. • If she is switching from injectables, delay the Standard Days Method at least until her repeat injection would have been given, and then start it at the beginning of her next monthly bleeding.
After taking emergency contraceptive pills	• Delay the Standard Days Method until the start of her next monthly bleeding.

17

Fertility Awareness Methods

Explaining How to Use Calendar-Based Methods

Standard Days Method

IMPORTANT: A woman can use the Standard Days Method if most of her menstrual cycles are 26 to 32 days long. If she has more than 2 longer or shorter cycles within a year, the Standard Days Method will be less effective and she may want to choose another method.

Keep track of the days of the menstrual cycle	• A woman keeps track of the days of her menstrual cycle, counting the first day of monthly bleeding as day 1.
Avoid unprotected sex on days 8–19	• Days 8 through 19 of every cycle are considered fertile days for all users of the Standard Days Method. • The couple avoids vaginal sex or uses condoms or a diaphragm during days 8 through 19. They can also use withdrawal or spermicides, but these are less effective. • The couple can have unprotected sex on all the other days of the cycle—days 1 through 7 at the beginning of the cycle and from day 20 until her next monthly bleeding begins.
Use memory aids if needed	• The couple can use CycleBeads, a color-coded string of beads that indicates fertile and nonfertile days of a cycle, or they can mark a calendar or use some other memory aid.

6 If monthly bleeding does not begin before reaching the last brown bead, her menstrual cycle is longer than 32 days.

1 On day 1—the first day of monthly bleeding—move the rubber ring to the red bead.

2 The next day move the ring to the next bead. Do this every day, even bleeding days.

Each bead represents a day of the menstrual cycle.

5 If monthly bleeding begins again before reaching the dark brown bead, her menstrual cycle is shorter than 26 days.

3 White bead days are days when the woman can become pregnant. She should avoid unprotected sex.

4 Brown bead days are days when pregnancy is unlikely and she can have unprotected sex.

Calendar Rhythm Method

Keep track of the days of the menstrual cycle	• Before relying on this method, a woman records the number of days in each menstrual cycle for at least 6 months. The first day of monthly bleeding is always counted as day 1.
Estimate the fertile time	• The woman subtracts 18 from the length of her shortest recorded cycle. This tells her the estimated first day of her fertile time. Then she subtracts 11 days from the length of her longest recorded cycle. This tells her the estimated last day of her fertile time.
Avoid unprotected sex during fertile time	• The couple avoids vaginal sex, or uses condoms or a diaphragm, during the fertile time. They can also use withdrawal or spermicides, but these are less effective.
Update calculations monthly	• She updates these calculations each month, always using the 6 most recent cycles. Example: – If the shortest of her last 6 cycles was 27 days, 27 − 18 = 9. She starts avoiding unprotected sex on day 9. – If the longest of her last 6 cycles was 31 days, 31 − 11 = 20. She can have unprotected sex again on day 21. – Thus, she must avoid unprotected sex from day 9 through day 20 of her cycle.

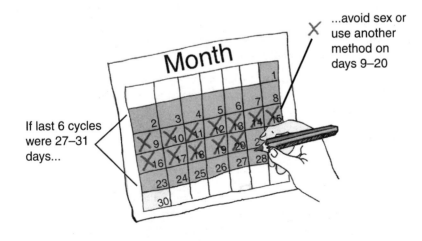

...avoid sex or use another method on days 9–20

If last 6 cycles were 27–31 days...

17

Fertility Awareness Methods

Who Can Use Symptoms-Based Methods

Symptoms-Based Methods

All women can use symptoms-based methods. No medical conditions prevent the use of these methods, but some conditions can make them harder to use effectively.

Caution means that additional or special counseling may be needed to ensure correct use of the method.

Delay means that use of a particular fertility awareness method should be delayed until the condition is evaluated or corrected. Give the client another method to use until she can start the symptoms-based method.

In the following situations use *caution* with symptoms-based methods:

- Recently had an abortion or miscarriage

- Menstrual cycles have just started or have become less frequent or stopped due to older age (Menstrual cycle irregularities are common in young women in the first several years after their first monthly bleeding and in older women who are approaching menopause. Identifying the fertile time may be difficult.)

- A chronic condition that raises her body temperature (for basal body temperature and symptothermal methods)

In the following situations *delay* starting symptoms-based methods:

- Recently gave birth or is breastfeeding (*Delay* until normal secretions have returned—usually at least 6 months after childbirth for breastfeeding women and at least 4 weeks after childbirth for women who are not breastfeeding. For several months after regular cycles have returned, use with *caution*.)

- An acute condition that raises her body temperature (for basal body temperature and symptothermal methods)

- Irregular vaginal bleeding

- Abnormal vaginal discharge

In the following situations *delay* or use *caution* with symptoms-based methods:

- Taking any mood-altering drugs such as anti-anxiety therapies (except benzodiazepines), antidepressants (selective serotonin reuptake inhibitors [SSRIs], tricyclic, or tetracyclic), anti-psychotics (including chlorpromazine, thioridazine, haloperidol, risperdone, clozapine, or lithium), long-term use of certain antibiotics, any nonsteroidal anti-inflammatory drug (such as aspirin, ibuprofen, or paracetamol), or antihistamines. These drugs may affect cervical secretions, raise body temperature, or delay ovulation.

Providing Symptoms-Based Methods

When to Start

Once trained, a woman or couple usually can begin using symptoms-based methods at any time. Women not using a hormonal method can practice monitoring their fertility signs before they start using symptoms-based methods. Give clients who cannot start immediately another method to use until they can start.

Woman's situation	When to start
Having regular menstrual cycles	**Any time of the month** • No need to wait until the start of next monthly bleeding.
No monthly bleeding	• Delay symptoms-based methods until monthly bleeding returns.
After childbirth (whether or not breastfeeding)	• She can start symptoms-based methods once normal secretions have returned. • Normal secretions will return later in breastfeeding women than in women who are not breastfeeding.
After miscarriage or abortion	• She can start symptoms-based methods immediately with special counseling and support, if she has no infection-related secretions or bleeding due to injury to the genital tract.
Switching from a hormonal method	• She can start symptoms-based methods in the next menstrual cycle after stopping a hormonal method.
After taking emergency contraceptive pills	• She can start symptoms-based methods once normal secretions have returned.

Fertility Awareness Methods

Explaining How to Use Symptoms-Based Methods

TwoDay Method

IMPORTANT: If a woman has a vaginal infection or another condition that changes cervical mucus, the TwoDay Method will be difficult to use.

Check for secretions	• The woman checks for cervical secretions every afternoon and/or evening, on fingers, underwear, or tissue paper or by sensation in or around the vagina.
	• As soon as she notices any secretions of any type, color, or consistency, she considers herself fertile that day and the following day.
Avoid sex or use another method on fertile days	• The couple avoids vaginal sex or uses condoms or a diaphragm on each day with secretions and on each day following a day with secretions. They can also use withdrawal or spermicides, but these are less effective.
Resume unprotected sex after 2 dry days	• The couple can have unprotected sex again after the woman has had 2 dry days (days without secretions of any type) in a row.

Basal Body Temperature (BBT) Method

IMPORTANT: If a woman has a fever or other changes in body temperature, the BBT method will be difficult to use.

Take body temperature daily	• The woman takes her body temperature at the same time each morning before she gets out of bed and before she eats anything. She records her temperature on a special graph.
	• She watches for her temperature to rise slightly—0.2° to 0.5° C (0.4° to 1.0° F)—just after ovulation (usually about midway through the menstrual cycle).
Avoid sex or use another method until 3 days after the temperature rise	• The couple avoids vaginal sex, or uses condoms or a diaphragm from the first day of monthly bleeding until 3 days after the woman's temperature has risen above her regular temperature. They can also use withdrawal or spermicides, but these are less effective.
Resume unprotected sex until next monthly bleeding begins	• When the woman's temperature has risen, above her regular temperature and stayed higher for 3 full days, ovulation has occurred and the fertile period has passed.
	• The couple can have unprotected sex on the 4th day and until her next monthly bleeding begins.

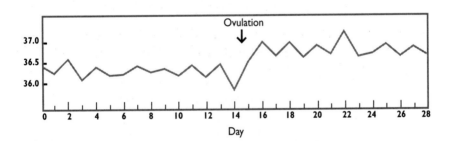

Fertility Awareness Methods

17

IMPORTANT: If a woman has a vaginal infection or another condition that changes cervical mucus, this method may be difficult to use.

Check cervical secretions daily	• The woman checks every day for any cervical secretions on fingers, underwear, or tissue paper or by sensation in or around the vagina.
Avoid unprotected sex on days of heavy monthly bleeding	• Ovulation might occur early in the cycle, during the last days of monthly bleeding, and heavy bleeding could make mucus difficult to observe.
Resume unprotected sex until secretions begin	• Between the end of monthly bleeding and the start of secretions, the couple can have unprotected sex, but not on 2 days in a row. (Avoiding sex on the second day allows time for semen to disappear and for cervical mucus to be observed.) • It is recommended that they have sex in the evenings, after the woman has been in an upright position for at least a few hours and has been able to check for cervical mucus.
Avoid unprotected sex when secretions begin and until 4 days after "peak day"	• As soon as she notices any secretions, she considers herself fertile and avoids unprotected sex. • She continues to check her cervical secretions each day. The secretions have a "peak day"—the last day that they are clear, slippery, stretchy, and wet. She will know this has passed when, on the next day, her secretions are sticky or dry, or she has no secretions at all. She continues to consider herself fertile for 3 days after that peak day and avoids unprotected sex.

Wet and slippery secretions on "peak day"

Resume unprotected sex	• The couple can have unprotected sex on the 4th day after her peak day and until her next monthly bleeding begins.

Symptothermal Method (basal body temperature + cervical secretions + other fertility signs)

Avoid unprotected sex on fertile days

- Users identify fertile and nonfertile days by combining BBT and ovulation method instructions.

- Women may also identify the fertile time by other signs such as breast tenderness and ovulatory pain (lower abdominal pain or cramping around the time of ovulation).

- The couple avoids unprotected sex between the first day of monthly bleeding and either the fourth day after peak cervical secretions or the third full day after the rise in temperature (BBT), whichever happens later.

- Some women who use this method have unprotected sex between the end of monthly bleeding and the beginning of secretions, but not on 2 days in a row.

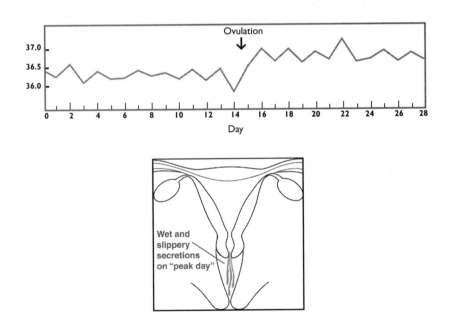

Supporting the User

"Come Back Any Time": Reasons to Return

No routine return visit is required. Providers should invite a woman or couple to meet with them a few times during the first few cycles if they want more help. Assure every client that she is welcome to come back any time—for example, if she has problems, questions, or wants another method; she has any major change in health status; or thinks she might be pregnant. Also if:

- She is having difficulty identifying her fertile days.

- She is having trouble avoiding sex or using another method on the fertile days. For example, her partner does not cooperate.

Helping Continuing Users

Helping Clients at Any Visit

1. Ask clients how they are doing with the method and whether they are satisfied. Ask if they have any questions or anything to discuss.

2. Ask especially if they are having difficulty identifying her fertile days or trouble avoiding unprotected sex on the fertile days.

3. Check whether the couple is using the method correctly. Review observations or records of fertility signs. If needed, plan for another visit.

4. Ask a long-term client if she has had any new health problems since her last visit. Address problems as appropriate.

5. Ask a long-term client about major life changes that may affect her needs—particularly plans for having children and STI/HIV risk. Follow up as needed.

Managing Any Problems

Problems With Use

- Problems with fertility awareness methods affect women's satisfaction and use of the method. They deserve the provider's attention. If the client reports any problems, listen to her concerns and give her advice.

- Offer to help the client choose another method—now, if she wishes, or if problems cannot be overcome.

Inability to abstain from sex during the fertile time

- Discuss the problem openly with the couple and help them feel at ease, not embarrassed.

- Discuss possible use of condoms, diaphragm, withdrawal, or spermicides or sexual contact without vaginal sex during the fertile time.

- If she has had unprotected sex in the past 5 days she can consider ECPs (see Emergency Contraceptive Pills, p. 45).

Calendar-Based Methods

Cycles are outside the 26–32 day range for Standard Days Method

- If she has 2 or more cycles outside the 26 to 32 day range within any 12 months, suggest she use the calendar rhythm method or a symptoms-based method instead.

Very irregular menstrual cycles among users of calendar-based methods

- Suggest she use a symptoms-based method instead.

Symptoms-Based Methods

Difficulty recognizing different types of secretions for the ovulation method

- Counsel the client and help her learn how to interpret cervical secretions.
- Suggest she use the TwoDay Method, which does not require the user to tell the difference among types of secretions.

Difficulty recognizing the presence of secretions for the ovulation method or the TwoDay Method

- Provide additional guidance on how to recognize secretions.
- Suggest she use a calendar-based method instead.

Questions and Answers About Fertility Awareness Methods

1. **Can only well-educated couples use fertility awareness methods?**

   No. Couples with little or no formal schooling can and do use fertility awareness methods effectively. Couples must be highly motivated, well-trained in their method, and committed to avoiding unprotected sex during the fertile time.

2. **Are fertility awareness methods reliable?**

   For many couples, these methods provide reliable information about the fertile days. If the couple avoids vaginal sex, or uses condoms or a diaphragm during the woman's fertile time, fertility awareness methods can be very effective. Using withdrawal or spermicides during the fertile time is less effective.

3. **What is new about the newer fertility awareness methods, the Standard Days Method and the TwoDay Method?**

These new fertility awareness methods are easier to use correctly than some of the older ones. Thus, they could appeal to more couples and be more effective for some people. They are like older methods, however, in that they rely on the same ways of judging when a woman might be fertile—by keeping track of the days of the cycle for the Standard Days Method and by cervical secretions for the TwoDay Method. So far, there are few studies of these methods. A clinical trial found that, as the Standard Days Method was commonly used by women who had most cycles between 26 and 32 days long, there were 12 pregnancies per 100 women over the first year of use. In a clinical trial of the TwoDay Method as it was commonly used, there were 14 pregnancies per 100 women over the first year of use. This rate is based on those who remained in the study. Women who detected secretions on fewer than 5 days or more than 14 days in each cycle were excluded.

4. **How likely is a woman to become pregnant if she has sex during monthly bleeding?**

During monthly bleeding the chances of pregnancy are low but not zero. Bleeding itself does not prevent pregnancy, and it does not promote pregnancy, either. In the first several days of monthly bleeding, the chances of pregnancy are lowest. For example, on day 2 of the cycle (counting from the first day of bleeding as day 1), the chance of getting pregnant is extremely low (less than 1%). As the days pass, the chances of pregnancy increase, whether or not she is still bleeding. The risk of pregnancy rises until ovulation. The day after ovulation the chances of pregnancy begin to drop steadily. Some fertility awareness methods that depend on cervical secretions advise avoiding unprotected sex during monthly bleeding because cervical secretions cannot be detected during bleeding and there is a small risk of ovulation at this time.

5. **How many days of abstinence or use of another method might be required for each of the fertility awareness methods?**

The number of days varies based on the woman's cycle length. The average number of days a woman would be considered fertile—and would need to abstain or use another method—with each method is: Standard Days Method, 12 days; TwoDay Method, 13 days; symptothermal method, 17 days; ovulation method, 18 days.

Withdrawal

Key Points for Providers and Clients

- **Always available in every situation.** Can be used as a primary method or as a backup method.

- **Requires no supplies and no clinic or pharmacy visit.**

- **One of the least effective contraceptive methods.** Some men use this method effectively, however. Offers better pregnancy protection than no method at all.

- **Promotes male involvement and couple communication.**

What Is Withdrawal?

- The man withdraws his penis from his partner's vagina and ejaculates outside the vagina, keeping his semen away from her external genitalia.

- Also known as coitus interruptus and "pulling out."

- Works by keeping sperm out of the woman's body.

How Effective?

Effectiveness depends on the user: Risk of pregnancy is greatest when the man does not withdraw his penis from the vagina before he ejaculates with every act of sex.

- One of the least effective methods, as commonly used.

- As commonly used, about 27 pregnancies per 100 women whose partner uses withdrawal over the first year. This means that 73 of every 100 women whose partners use withdrawal will not become pregnant.

- When used correctly with every act of sex, about 4 pregnancies per 100 women whose partners use withdrawal over the first year.

Return of fertility after use of withdrawal is stopped: No delay

Protection against sexually transmitted infections: None

More effective

Less effective

Side Effects, Health Benefits, and Health Risks

None

Who Can and Cannot Use Withdrawal

Using Withdrawal

- Can be used at any time.

Explaining How to Use

When the man feels close to ejaculating	• He should withdraw his penis from the woman's vagina and ejaculate outside the vagina, keeping his semen away from her external genitalia.
If man has ejaculated recently	• Before sex he should urinate and wipe the tip of his penis to remove any sperm remaining.

Giving Advice on Use

Learning proper use can take time	• Suggest the couple also use another method until the man feels that he can use withdrawal correctly with every act of sex.
Greater protection from pregnancy is available	• Suggest an additional or alternative family planning method. (Couples who have been using withdrawal effectively should not be discouraged from continuing.)
Some men may have difficulty using withdrawal	• Men who cannot sense consistently when ejaculation is about to occur. • Men who ejaculate prematurely.
Can use emergency contraceptive pills (ECPs)	• Explain ECP use in case a man ejaculates before withdrawing (see Emergency Contraceptive Pills, p. 45). Give ECPs if available.

CHAPTER 19

Lactational Amenorrhea Method

Key Points for Providers and Clients

- **A family planning method based on breastfeeding.** Provides contraception for the mother and best feeding for the baby.

- **Can be effective for up to 6 months after childbirth,** as long as monthly bleeding has not returned and the woman is fully or nearly fully breastfeeding.

- **Requires breastfeeding often, day and night.** Almost all of the baby's feedings should be breast milk.

- **Provides an opportunity to offer a woman an ongoing method that she can continue to use after 6 months.**

What Is the Lactational Amenorrhea Method?

- A temporary family planning method based on the natural effect of breastfeeding on fertility. ("Lactational" means related to breastfeeding. "Amenorrhea" means not having monthly bleeding.)

- The lactational amenorrhea method (LAM) requires 3 conditions. All 3 must be met:

  1. The mother's monthly bleeding has not returned

  2. The baby is fully or nearly fully breastfed and is fed often, day and night

  3. The baby is less than 6 months old

- "Fully breastfeeding" includes both exclusive breastfeeding (the infant receives no other liquid or food, not even water, in addition to breast milk) and almost-exclusive breastfeeding (the infant receives vitamins, water, juice, or other nutrients once in a while in addition to breast milk).

- "Nearly fully breastfeeding" means that the infant receives some liquid or food in addition to breast milk, but the majority of feedings (more than three-fourths of all feeds) are breast milk.

- Works primarily by preventing the release of eggs from the ovaries (ovulation). Frequent breastfeeding temporarily prevents the release of the natural hormones that cause ovulation.

How Effective?

More effective

Effectiveness depends on the user: Risk of pregnancy is greatest when a woman cannot fully or nearly fully breastfeed her infant.

- As commonly used, about 2 pregnancies per 100 women using LAM in the first 6 months after childbirth. This means that 98 of every 100 women relying on LAM will not become pregnant.

- When used correctly, less than 1 pregnancy per 100 women using LAM in the first 6 months after childbirth.

Return of fertility after LAM is stopped: Depends on how much the woman continues to breastfeed

Less effective

Protection against sexually transmitted infections: None

Side Effects, Health Benefits, and Health Risks

Side Effects

None. Any problems are the same as for other breastfeeding women.

Known Health Benefits

Helps protect against:

- Risks of pregnancy

Encourages:

- The best breastfeeding patterns, with health benefits for both mother and baby

Known Health Risks

None

Correcting Misunderstandings (see also Questions and Answers, p. 265)

The lactational amenorrhea method:

- Is highly effective when a woman meets all 3 LAM criteria.
- Is just as effective among fat or thin women.
- Can be used by women with normal nutrition. No special foods are required.
- Can be used for a full 6 months without the need for supplementary foods. Mother's milk alone can fully nourish a baby for the first 6 months of life. In fact, it is the ideal food for this time in a baby's life.
- Can be used for 6 months without worry that the woman will run out of milk. Milk will continue to be produced through 6 months and longer in response to the baby's suckling or the mother's expression of her milk.

Who Can Use the Lactational Amenorrhea Method

Medical Eligibility Criteria for the

Lactational Amenorrhea Method

All breastfeeding women can safely use LAM, but a woman in the following circumstances may want to consider other contraceptive methods:

- Has HIV infection including AIDS (see The Lactational Amenorrhea Method for Women With HIV, p. 260)

- Is using certain medications during breastfeeding (including mood-altering drugs, reserpine, ergotamine, anti-metabolites, cyclosporine, high doses of corticosteroids, bromocriptine, radioactive drugs, lithium, and certain anticoagulants)

- The newborn has a condition that makes it difficult to breastfeed (including being small-for-date or premature and needing intensive neonatal care, unable to digest food normally, or having deformities of the mouth, jaw, or palate)

Why Some Women Say They Like the Lactational Amenorrhea Method

- It is a natural family planning method
- It supports optimal breastfeeding, providing health benefits for the baby and the mother
- It has no direct cost for family planning or for feeding the baby

The Lactational Amenorrhea Method for Women With HIV

- Women who are infected with HIV or who have AIDS can use LAM. Breastfeeding will not make their condition worse. There is a chance, however, that mothers with HIV will transmit HIV to their infants through breastfeeding. Without any antiretroviral (ARV) therapy, if infants of HIV-infected mothers are mixed-fed (breast milk and other foods) for 2 years, between 10 and 20 of every 100 will become infected with HIV through breast milk, in addition to those already infected during pregnancy and delivery. Exclusive breastfeeding reduces this risk of HIV infection through breastfeeding by about half. Reducing the length of time of breastfeeding also greatly reduces the risk. For example, breastfeeding for 12 months reduces transmission by 50% compared with breastfeeding for 24 months. HIV transmission through breast milk is more likely among mothers with advanced disease or who are newly infected.

- Women taking ARV therapy can use LAM. In fact, giving ARV therapy to an HIV-infected mother or an HIV-exposed infant very significantly reduces the risk of HIV transmission through breastfeeding.

- HIV-infected mothers should receive the appropriate ARV interventions and should exclusively breastfeed their infants for the first 6 months of life, introduce appropriate complementary foods at 6 months, and continue breastfeeding for the first 12 months. Breastfeeding should then stop only once a nutritionally adequate and safe diet without breast milk can be provided.

- At 6 months—or earlier if her monthly bleeding has returned or she stops exclusive breastfeeding—a woman should begin to use another contraceptive method in place of LAM and continue to use condoms. Urge women with HIV to use condoms along with LAM. Used consistently and correctly, condoms help prevent transmission of HIV and other STIs.

(For further guidance on infant feeding for women with HIV, see Maternal and Newborn Health, Preventing Mother-to-Child Transmission of HIV, p. 294.)

Providing the Lactational Amenorrhea Method

When to Start

Woman's situation	When to start
Within 6 months after childbirth	• Start breastfeeding immediately (within one hour) or as soon as possible after the baby is born. In the first few days after childbirth, the yellowish fluid produced by the mother's breasts (colostrum) contains substances very important to the baby's health.
	• Any time if she has been fully or nearly breastfeeding her baby since birth and her monthly bleeding has not returned.

When Can a Woman Use LAM?

A breastfeeding woman can use LAM to space her next birth and as a transition to another contraceptive method. She may start LAM at any time if she meets all 3 criteria required for using the method.

Ask the mother these 3 questions:

2 Are you regularly giving the baby other food besides breast milk or allowing long periods without breastfeeding, either day or night?

1 Has your monthly bleeding returned?

3 Is your baby more than 6 months old?

If the answer to all of these questions is no...

...she can use LAM. There is only a 2% change of pregnancy at this time. A woman may choose another family planning method at any time—but preferably not a method with estrogen while her baby is less than 6 months old. Methods with estrogen include combined oral contraceptives, monthly injectables, the combined patch, and the combined vaginal ring.

But, when the answer to any one of these questions is yes...

...her chances of pregnancy increase. Advise her to begin using another family planning method and to continue breastfeeding for the child's health.

Explaining How to Use

Breastfeed often	• An ideal pattern is feeding on demand (that is, whenever the baby wants to be fed) and at least 10 to 12 times a day in the first few weeks after childbirth and thereafter 8 to 10 times a day, including at least once at night in the first months.
	• Daytime feedings should be no more than 4 hours apart, and night-time feedings no more than 6 hours apart.
	• Some babies may not want to breastfeed 8 to 10 times a day and may want to sleep through the night. These babies may need gentle encouragement to breastfeed more often.
Start other foods at 6 months	• She should start giving other foods in addition to breast milk when the baby is 6 months old. At this age, breast milk can no longer fully nourish a growing baby.
Plan follow-up visit	• Plan for the next visit while the LAM criteria still apply, so that she can choose another method and continue to be protected from pregnancy.
	• If possible, give her condoms or progestin-only pills now. She can start to use them if the baby is no longer fully or nearly fully breastfeeding, if her monthly bleeding returns, or if the baby reaches 6 months of age before she can come back for another method. Plan for a follow-on method. Give her any supplies now.

Supporting the User

"Come Back Any Time": Reasons to Return

Assure every client that she is welcome to come back any time—for example, if she has problems, questions, or wants another method; she has a major change in health status; or she thinks she might be pregnant. Also, if:

• She no longer meets one or more of the 3 LAM criteria and so cannot keep relying on LAM.

Lactational Amenorrhea Method

Helping Continuing Users

Helping Clients Switch to a Continuing Method

1. A woman can switch to another method any time she wants while using LAM. If she still meets all 3 LAM criteria, it is reasonably certain she is not pregnant. She can start a new method with no need for a pregnancy test, examinations, or evaluation.

2. To continue preventing pregnancy, a woman *must* switch to another method as soon as any one of the 3 LAM criteria no longer applies.

3. Help the woman choose a new method *before* she needs it. If she will continue to breastfeed, she can choose from several hormonal or nonhormonal methods, depending on how much time has passed since childbirth (see Maternal and Newborn Health, Earliest Time That a Woman Can Start a Family Planning Method After Childbirth, p. 293).

Managing Any Problems

Problems With Use

- Problems with breastfeeding or LAM affect women's satisfaction and use of the method. If the client reports any problems, listen to her concerns, give her advice, and, if appropriate, treat.

- Offer to help the client choose another method—now, if she wishes, or if problems cannot be overcome.

- For problems with breastfeeding, see Maternal and Newborn Health, Managing Breastfeeding Problems, p. 295.

Questions and Answers About the Lactational Amenorrhea Method

1. **Can LAM be an effective method of family planning?**

   Yes. LAM is very effective if the woman's monthly bleeding has not returned, she is fully or nearly fully breastfeeding, and her baby is less than 6 months old.

2. **When should a mother start giving her baby other foods besides breast milk?**

   Ideally, when the baby is 6 months old. Along with other foods, breast milk should be a major part of the child's diet through the child's second year or longer.

3. **Can women use LAM if they work away from home?**

   Yes. Women who are able to keep their infants with them at work or nearby and are able to breastfeed frequently can rely on LAM as long as they meet all 3 criteria for LAM. Women who are separated from their infants can use LAM if breastfeeds are less than 4 hours apart. Women can also express their breast milk at least every 4 hours, but pregnancy rates may be slightly higher for women who are separated from their infants. The one study that assessed use of LAM among working women estimated a pregnancy rate of 5 per 100 women during the first 6 months after childbirth, compared with about 2 per 100 women as LAM is commonly used.

4. **What if a woman learns that she has HIV while she is using LAM? Can she continue breastfeeding and using LAM?**

   If a woman is newly infected with HIV, the risk of transmission through breastfeeding may be higher than if she was infected earlier, because there is more HIV in her body. The breastfeeding recommendation is the same as for other HIV-infected women, however. HIV-infected mothers or their infants should receive the appropriate ARV therapy, and mothers should exclusively breastfeed their infants for the first 6 months of life, then introduce appropriate complementary foods and continue breastfeeding for the first 12 months of life. At 6 months— or earlier if her monthly bleeding has returned or she stops exclusive breastfeeding—she should begin to use another contraceptive method in place of LAM and continue to use condoms. (See also Maternal and Newborn Health, Preventing Mother-to-Child Transmission of HIV, p. 294.)

CHAPTER 20

Serving Diverse Groups

Key Points for Providers and Clients

Adolescents

- **Unmarried and married youth may have different sexual and reproductive health needs**. All contraceptives are safe for young people.

Men

- **Correct information can help men make better decisions about their own health and their partner's health, too.** When couples discuss contraception, they are more likely to make plans that they can carry out.

Women Near Menopause

- **To be sure to avoid pregnancy, a woman should use contraception until she has had no monthly bleeding for 12 months in a row.**

Adolescents

Young people may come to a family planning provider not only for contraception but also for advice about physical changes, sex, relationships, family, and problems of growing up. Their needs depend on their particular situations. Some are unmarried and sexually active, others are not sexually active, while still others are already married. Some already have children. Age itself makes a great difference, since young people mature quickly during the adolescent years. These differences make it important to learn about each client first, to understand why that client has come, and to tailor counseling and the offer of services accordingly.

Provide Services with Care and Respect

Young people deserve nonjudgmental and respectful care no matter how young they are. Criticism or unwelcoming attitudes will keep young people away from the care they need. Counseling and services do not encourage young people to have sex. Instead, they help young people protect their health.

To make services friendly to youth, you can:

- Show young people that you enjoy working with them.

- Counsel in private areas where you cannot be seen or overheard. Ensure confidentiality and assure the client of confidentiality.

- Listen carefully and ask open-ended questions such as "How can I help you?" and "What questions do you have?"

- Use simple language and avoid medical terms.

- Use terms that suit young people. Avoid such terms as "family planning," which may seem irrelevant to those who are not married.

- Welcome partners and include them in counseling, if the client desires.

- Try to make sure that a young woman's choices are her own and are not pressured by her partner or her family. In particular, if she is being pressured to have sex, help a young woman think about what she can say and do to resist and reduce that pressure. Practice skills to negotiate condom use.

- Speak without expressing judgment (for example, say "You can" rather than "You should"). Do not criticize even if you do not approve of what the young person is saying or doing. Help young clients make decisions that are in their best interest.

- Take time to fully address questions, fears, and misinformation about sex, sexually transmitted infections (STIs), and contraceptives. Many young people want reassurance that the changes in their bodies and their feelings are normal. Be prepared to answer common questions about puberty, monthly bleeding, masturbation, night-time ejaculation, and genital hygiene.

All Contraceptives Are Safe for Young People

Young people can safely use any contraceptive method.

- Young women are often less tolerant of side effects than older women. With counseling, however, they will know what to expect and may be less likely to stop using their methods.

- Unmarried young people may have more sex partners than older people and so may face a greater risk of STIs. Considering STI risk and how to reduce it is an important part of counseling.

For some contraceptive methods there are specific considerations for young people (see contraceptive method chapters for complete guidance):

Hormonal contraceptives (oral contraceptives, injectables, combined patch, combined vaginal ring, and implants)

- Injectables and the combined ring can be used without others knowing.
- Some young women find regular pill-taking particularly difficult.

Emergency contraceptive pills (ECPs)

- Young women may have less control than older women over having sex and using contraception. They may need ECPs more often.
- Provide young women with ECPs in advance, for use when needed. ECPs can be used whenever she has any unprotected sex, including sex against her will, or a contraceptive mistake has occurred.

Female sterilization and vasectomy

- Provide with great caution. Young people and people with few or no children are among those most likely to regret sterilization.

Male and female condoms

- Protect against both STIs and pregnancy, which many young people need.
- Readily available, and they are affordable and convenient for occasional sex.
- Young men may be less successful than older men at using condoms correctly. They may need practice putting condoms on.

Intrauterine device (copper-bearing and hormonal IUDs)

- IUDs are more likely to come out among women who have not given birth because their uteruses are small.

Diaphragms, spermicides, and cervical caps

- Although among the least effective methods, young women can control use of these methods, and they can be used as needed.

Fertility awareness methods

- Until a young woman has regular menstrual cycles, fertility awareness methods should be used with caution.
- Need a backup method or ECPs on hand in case abstinence fails.

Withdrawal

- Requires the man to know when he is about to ejaculate so he can withdraw in time. This may be difficult for some young men.
- One of the least effective methods of pregnancy prevention, but it may be the only method available—and always available—for some young people.

Men

Important Supporters, Important Clients

To health care providers, men are important for 2 reasons. First, they influence women. Some men care about their partner's reproductive health and support them. Others stand in their way or make decisions for them. Thus, men's attitudes can determine whether women can practice healthy behaviors. In some circumstances, such as avoiding HIV infection or getting help quickly in an obstetric emergency, a man's actions can determine whether a woman lives or dies.

Men are also important as clients. Major family planning methods—male condoms and vasectomy—are used by men. Men also have their own sexual and reproductive health needs and concerns—in particular regarding sexually transmitted infections (STIs)—which deserve the attention of the health care system and providers.

Many Ways to Help Men

Providers can give support and services to men both as supporters of women and as clients.

Encourage Couples to Talk

Couples who discuss family planning—with or without a provider's help—are more likely to make plans that they can carry out. Providers can:

- Coach men and women on how to talk with their partners about sex, family planning, and STIs.
- Encourage joint decision-making about sexual and reproductive health matters.
- Invite and encourage women to bring their partners to the clinic for joint counseling, decision-making, and care.
- Suggest to female clients that they tell their partners about health services for men. Give informational materials to take home, if available.

Provide Accurate Information

To inform men's decisions and opinions, they need correct information and correction of misperceptions. Topics important to men include:

- Family planning methods, both for men and for women, including safety and effectiveness

- STIs including HIV/AIDS—how they are and are not transmitted, signs and symptoms, testing, and treatment

- The benefits of waiting until the youngest child is 2 years old before a woman becomes pregnant again

- Male and female sexual and reproductive anatomy and function

- Safe pregnancy and delivery

Offer Services or Refer

Important services that many men want include:

- Condoms, vasectomy, and counseling about other methods

- Counseling and help for sexual problems

- STI/HIV counseling, testing, and treatment

- Infertility counseling (see Infertility, p. 304)

- Screening for penile, testicular, and prostate cancer

Like women, men of all ages, married or unmarried, have their own sexual and reproductive health needs. They deserve good-quality services and respectful, supportive, and nonjudgmental counseling.

Women Near Menopause

A woman has reached menopause when her ovaries stop releasing eggs (ovulating). Because bleeding does not come every month as menopause approaches, a woman is considered no longer fertile once she has gone 12 months in a row without having any bleeding.

Menopause usually occurs between the ages of 45 and 55. About half of women reach menopause by age 50. By age 55 some 96% of women have reached menopause.

To prevent pregnancy until it is clear that she is no longer fertile, an older woman can use any method, if she has no medical condition that limits its use. By itself, age does not restrict a woman from using any contraceptive method.

Special Considerations About Method Choice

When helping women near menopause choose a method, consider:

Combined hormonal methods (combined oral contraceptives [COCs], monthly injectables, combined patch, combined vaginal ring)

- Women age 35 and older who smoke—regardless of how much—should not use COCs, the patch, or the vaginal ring.

- Women age 35 and older who smoke 15 or more cigarettes a day should not use monthly injectables.

- Women age 35 or older should not use COCs, monthly injectables, the patch, or the vaginal ring if they have migraine headaches (whether with migraine aura or not).

Progestin-only methods (progestin-only pills, progestin-only injectables, implants)

- A good choice for women who cannot use methods with estrogen.

- During use, DMPA decreases bone mineral density slightly. It is not known whether this decrease in bone density increases the risk of bone fracture later, after menopause.

Emergency contraceptive pills

- Can be used by women of any age, including those who cannot use hormonal methods on a continuing basis.

Female sterilization and vasectomy

- May be a good choice for older women and their partners who know they will not want more children.

- Older women are more likely to have conditions that require delay, referral, or caution for female sterilization.

Male and female condoms, diaphragms, spermicides, cervical caps and withdrawal

- Protect older women well, considering women's reduced fertility in the years before menopause.

- Affordable and convenient for women who may have occasional sex.

Intrauterine device (copper-bearing and hormonal IUDs)

- Expulsion rates fall as women grow older, and are lowest in women over 40 years of age.

- Insertion may be more difficult due to tightening of the cervical canal.

Fertility awareness methods

- Lack of regular cycles before menopause makes it more difficult to use these methods reliably.

When a Woman Can Stop Using Family Planning

Because bleeding does not come every month in the time before menopause, it is difficult for a woman whose bleeding seems to have stopped to know when to stop using contraception. Thus, it is recommended to use a family planning method for 12 months after last bleeding in case bleeding occurs again.

Hormonal methods affect bleeding, and so it may be difficult to know if a woman using them has reached menopause. After stopping a hormonal method, she can use a nonhormonal method. She no longer needs contraception once she has had no bleeding for 12 months in a row.

Copper-bearing IUDs can be left in place until after menopause. They should be removed within 12 months after a woman's last monthly bleeding.

Relieving Symptoms of Menopause

Women experience physical effects before, during, and after menopause: hot flashes, excess sweating, difficulty holding urine, vaginal dryness that can make sex painful, and difficulty sleeping.

Providers can suggest ways to reduce some of these symptoms:

- Deep breathing from the diaphragm may make a hot flash go away faster. A woman can also try eating foods containing soy or taking 800 international units per day of vitamin E.

- Eat foods rich in calcium (such as dairy products, beans, fish) and engage in moderate physical activity to help slow the loss of bone density that comes with menopause.

- Vaginal lubricants or moisturizers can be used if vaginal dryness persists and causes irritation. During sex, use a commercially available vaginal lubricant, water, or saliva as a lubricant, if vaginal dryness is a problem.

CHAPTER 21

Sexually Transmitted Infections, Including HIV

Key Points for Providers and Clients

- **People with sexually transmitted infections (STIs) including HIV, can use most family planning methods safely and effectively.**

- **Male and female condoms can prevent STIs** when used consistently and correctly.

- **STIs can be reduced in other ways, too**—limiting number of partners, abstaining from sex, and having a mutually faithful relationship with an uninfected partner.

- **Some STIs have no signs or symptoms in women.** If a woman thinks her partner may have an STI, she should seek care.

- **Some STIs can be treated.** The sooner treated, the less likely to cause long-term problems, such as infertility or chronic pain.

- **In most cases, vaginal discharge comes from infections that are not sexually transmitted.**

Family planning providers can help their clients in various ways to prevent STIs, including infection with the Human Immunodeficiency Virus (HIV). Program managers and providers can choose approaches that fit their clients' needs, their training and resources, and the availability of services for referral.

What Are Sexually Transmitted Infections?

STIs are caused by bacteria and viruses spread through sexual contact. Infections can be found in body fluids such as semen, on the skin of the genitals and areas around them, and some also in the mouth, throat, and rectum. Some STIs cause no symptoms. Others may cause discomfort or pain. If not treated, some can cause pelvic inflammatory disease, infertility, chronic pelvic pain, and cervical cancer. Over time, HIV suppresses the immune system. Some STIs can also greatly increase the chance of becoming infected with HIV.

STIs spread in a community because an infected person has sex with an uninfected person. The more sexual partners a person has, the greater his or her risk of either becoming infected with STIs or transmitting STIs.

Who Is at Risk?

Many women seeking family planning services—women in stable, mutually faithful, long-term relationships—face little risk of getting an STI. Some clients may be at high risk for STIs, however, or have an STI now. Clients who might benefit most from discussion of STI risk include those who do not have steady partners, unmarried clients, and anyone, married or unmarried, who asks or expresses concern about STIs or HIV, or that her partner may have other partners.

The risk of acquiring an STI, including HIV, depends on a person's behavior, the behavior of that person's sexual partner or partners, and how common those diseases are in the community. By knowing what STIs and what sexual behavior are common locally, a health care provider can better help a client assess her or his own risk.

Understanding their own risk for HIV and other STIs helps people decide how to protect themselves and others. Women are often the best judges of their own STI risk, especially when they are told what behaviors and situations can increase risk.

Sexual behavior that can increase exposure to STIs includes:

- Sex with a partner who has STI symptoms
- A sex partner who has recently been diagnosed with or treated for an STI
- Sex with more than one partner—the more partners, the more risk
- Sex with a partner who has sex with others and does not always use condoms
- Where many people in the community are infected with STIs, sex without a condom may be risky with almost any new partner

In certain situations people tend to change sexual partners often, to have many partners, or to have a partner who has other partners—all behaviors that increase the risk of STI transmission. This includes people who:

- Have sex for money, food, gifts, shelter, or favors
- Move to another area for work or travel often for work, such as truck driving
- Have no established long-term sexual relationship, as is common among sexually active adolescents and young adults
- Are the sexual partners of these people

What Causes STIs?

Several types of organisms cause STIs. Those caused by organisms such as bacteria generally can be cured. STIs caused by viruses generally cannot be cured, although they can be treated to relieve symptoms.

STI	Type	Sexual transmission	Nonsexual transmission	Curable?
Chancroid	Bacterial	Vaginal, anal, and oral sex	None	Yes
Chlamydia	Bacterial	Vaginal and anal sex. Rarely, from genitals to mouth	From mother to child during pregnancy	Yes
Gonorrhea	Bacterial	Vaginal and anal sex, or contact between mouth and genitals	From mother to child during delivery	Yes
Hepatitis B	Viral	Vaginal and anal sex, or from penis to mouth	In blood, from mother to child during delivery or in breast milk	No
Herpes	Viral	Genital or oral contact with an ulcer, including vaginal and anal sex; also genital contact in area without ulcer	From mother to child during pregnancy or delivery	No
HIV	Viral	Vaginal and anal sex. Very rarely, oral sex	In blood, from mother to child during pregnancy or delivery or in breast milk	No
Human papilloma-virus	Viral	Skin-to-skin and genital contact or contact between mouth and genitals	From mother to child during delivery	No
Syphilis	Bacterial	Genital or oral contact with an ulcer, including vaginal and anal sex	From mother to child during pregnancy or delivery	Yes
Tricho-moniasis	Parasite	Vaginal, anal, and oral sex	From mother to child during delivery	Yes

More About HIV and AIDS

- HIV is the virus that causes acquired immune deficiency syndrome (AIDS). HIV slowly damages the body's immune system, reducing its ability to fight other diseases.

- People can live with HIV for many years without any signs or symptoms of infection. Eventually, they develop AIDS—the condition when the body's immune system breaks down and is unable to fight certain infections, known as opportunistic infections.

- There is no cure for HIV infection or AIDS, but antiretroviral (ARV) therapy can slow how the disease progresses, improve the health of those with AIDS, and prolong life. ARVs also can reduce mother-to-child transmission at the time of delivery and during breastfeeding. Opportunistic infections can be treated.

- Family planning providers can help with prevention and treatment efforts for HIV/AIDS, particularly in countries where many people are infected with HIV, by:

  - Counseling about ways to reduce risk of infection (see Choosing a Dual Protection Strategy, p. 280).
  - Refer clients for HIV counseling and testing and for HIV care and treatment if the clinic does not offer such services.

Symptoms of Sexually Transmitted Infections

Early identification of STIs is not always possible. For example, chlamydia and gonorrhea often have no noticeable signs or symptoms in women. Early identification, however, is important both to avoid passing on the infection and to avoid more serious long-term health consequences. To help detect STIs early, a provider can:

- Ask whether the client or the client's partner has genital sores or unusual discharge.

- Look for signs of STIs when doing a pelvic or genital examination for another reason.

- Know how to advise a client who may have an STI.

- If the client has signs or symptoms, promptly diagnose and treat, or else refer for appropriate care.

- Advise clients to notice genital sores, warts, or unusual discharge in themselves or in their sexual partners.

Common signs and symptoms that may suggest an STI include:

Symptoms	Possible cause
Discharge from the penis—pus, clear or yellow-green drip	Commonly: Chlamydia, gonorrhea Sometimes: Trichomoniasis
Abnormal vaginal bleeding or bleeding after sex	Chlamydia, gonorrhea, pelvic inflammatory disease
Burning or pain during urination	Chlamydia, gonorrhea, herpes
Lower abdominal pain or pain during sex	Chlamydia, gonorrhea, pelvic inflammatory disease
Swollen and/or painful testicles	Chlamydia, gonorrhea
Itching or tingling in the genital area	Commonly: Trichomoniasis Sometimes: Herpes
Blisters or sores on the genitals, anus, surrounding areas, or mouth	Herpes, syphilis, chancroid
Warts on the genitals, anus, or surrounding areas	Human papillomavirus
Unusual vaginal discharge—changes from normal vaginal discharge in color, consistency, amount, and/or odor	Most commonly: Bacterial vaginosis, candidiasis (not STIs; see Common Vaginal Infections Often Confused With Sexually Transmitted Infections, below) Commonly: Trichomoniasis Sometimes: Chlamydia, gonorrhea

Common Vaginal Infections Often Confused With Sexually Transmitted Infections

The most common vaginal infections are not sexually transmitted. Instead, they usually are due to an overgrowth of organisms normally present in the vagina. Common infections of the reproductive tract that are not sexually transmitted include bacterial vaginosis and candidiasis (also called yeast infection or thrush).

• In most areas these infections are much more common than STIs. Researchers estimate that between 5% and 25% of women have bacterial vaginosis and between 5% and 15% have candidiasis at any given time.

• Vaginal discharge due to these infections may be similar to discharge caused by some STIs such as trichomoniasis. It is important to reassure clients with such symptoms that they may not have an STI—particularly if they have no other symptoms and are at low risk for STIs.

- Bacterial vaginosis and trichomoniasis can be cured with antibiotics such as metronidazole; candidiasis can be cured with anti-fungal medications such as fluconazole. Without treatment, bacterial vaginosis can lead to pregnancy complications and candidiasis can be transmitted to a newborn during delivery.

Washing the external genital area with unscented soap and clean water, and not using douches, detergents, disinfectants, or vaginal cleaning or drying agents are good hygiene practices. They may also help some women avoid vaginal infections.

Preventing Sexually Transmitted Infections

The basic strategies for preventing STIs involve avoiding or reducing the chances of exposure. Family planning providers can talk to clients about how they can protect themselves both from STIs, including HIV, and pregnancy (dual protection).

Choosing a Dual Protection Strategy

Every family planning client needs to think about preventing STIs, including HIV—even people who assume they face no risk. A provider can discuss what situations place a person at increased risk of STIs, including HIV (see Who Is At Risk?, p. 276), and clients can think about whether these risky situations come up in their own lives. If so, they can consider 5 dual protection strategies.

One person might use different strategies in different situations; one couple might use different strategies at different times. The best strategy is the one that a person is able to practice effectively in the situation that she or he is facing. (Dual protection does not necessarily mean just using condoms along with another family planning method.)

Strategy 1: Use a male or female condom correctly with every act of sex.

- One method helps protect against pregnancy and STIs, including HIV.

Strategy 2: Use condoms consistently and correctly plus another family planning method.

- Adds extra protection from pregnancy in case a condom is not used or is used incorrectly.

- May be a good choice for women who want to be sure to avoid pregnancy but cannot always count on their partners to use condoms.

Strategy 3: If both partners know they are not infected, use any family planning method to prevent pregnancy and stay in a mutually faithful relationship.

- Many family planning clients will fall into this group and thus are protected from STIs, including HIV.
- Depends on communication and trust between partners.

Other strategies, which do not involve using contraceptives, include:

Strategy 4: Engage only in safer sexual intimacy that avoids intercourse and otherwise prevents semen and vaginal fluids from coming in contact with each other's genitals.

- Depends on communication, trust, and self-control.
- If this is a person's first-choice strategy, it is best to have condoms on hand in case the couple does have sex.

Strategy 5: Delay or avoid sexual activity (either avoiding sex any time that it might be risky or abstaining for a longer time).

- If this is a person's first-choice strategy, it is best to have condoms on hand in case the couple does have sex.
- This strategy is always available in case a condom is not at hand.

Many clients will need help and guidance to make their dual protection strategy succeed. For example, they may need help preparing to talk with their partners about STI protection, learning how to use condoms and other methods, and handling practical matters such as where to get supplies and where to keep them. If you can help with such matters, offer to help. If not, refer the client to someone who can provide more counseling or skills-building, such as role-playing to practice negotiating condom use.

Contraceptives for Clients with STIs, HIV, and AIDS

People with STIs, HIV, AIDS, or on antiretroviral (ARV) therapy can start and continue to use most contraceptive methods safely. In general, contraceptives and ARV medications do not interfere with each other. There are a few limitations, however. See the table below. (Also, every chapter on a contraceptive method provides more information and considerations for clients with HIV and AIDS, including those taking ARV medications.)

Special Family Planning Considerations for Clients with STIs, HIV, AIDS, or on Antiretroviral Therapy

Method	Has STIs	Has HIV or AIDS	On Anti-retroviral (ARV) Therapy
Intrauterine device (copper-bearing or hormonal IUDs)	Do not insert an IUD in a woman who is at very high individual risk for gonorrhea and chlamydia, or who currently has gonorrhea, chlamydia, purulent cervicitis, or PID. (A current IUD user who becomes infected with gonorrhea or chlamydia or develops PID can safely continue using an IUD during and after treatment.)	A woman with HIV can have an IUD inserted. A woman with AIDS should not have an IUD inserted unless she is clinically well on ARV therapy. (A woman who develops AIDS while using an IUD can safely continue using the IUD.)	Do not insert an IUD if client is not clinically well.
Female sterilization	If client has gonorrhea, chlamydia, purulent cervicitis, or PID, delay sterilization until the condition is treated and cured.	Women who are infected with HIV, have AIDS, or are on antiretroviral therapy can safely undergo female sterilization. Special arrangements are needed to perform female sterilization on a woman with AIDS. Delay the procedure if she is currently ill with AIDS-related illness.	

Method	Has STIs	Has HIV or AIDS	On Anti-retroviral (ARV) Therapy
Vasectomy	If client has scrotal skin infection, active STI, swollen, tender tip of penis, sperm ducts, or testicles, delay sterilization until the condition is treated and cured.	Men who are infected with HIV, have AIDS, or are on antiretroviral therapy can safely undergo vasectomy. Special arrangements are needed to perform vasectomy on a man with AIDS. Delay the procedure if he is currently ill with AIDS-related illness.	
Spermicides (including when used with diaphragm or cervical cap)	Can safely use spermicides.	Should not use spermicides if at high risk of HIV, infected with HIV, or has AIDS.	Should not use spermicides.
Combined oral con-traceptives, combined injectables, combined patch, combined ring	Can safely use combined hormonal methods.	Can safely use combined hormonal methods.	A woman can use combined hormonal methods while taking ARVs unless her treatment includes ritonavir.
Progestin-only pills	Can safely use progestin-only pills.	Can safely use progestin-only pills.	A woman can use progestin-only pills while taking ARVs unless her treatment includes ritonavir.
Progestin-only injectables and implants	No special considerations. Can safely use progestin-only injectables or implants.		

21

Sexually Transmitted Infections, Including HIV

What Is Cervical Cancer?

Cervical cancer results from uncontrolled, untreated growth of abnormal cells in the cervix. A sexually transmitted infection, the human papillomavirus (HPV), causes such cells to develop and grow.

HPV is found on skin in the genital area, in semen, and also in the tissues of the vagina, cervix, and mouth. It is primarily transmitted through skin-to-skin contact. Vaginal, anal, and oral sex also can spread HPV. Over 50 types of HPV can infect the cervix; 6 of them account for nearly all cervical cancers. Other types of HPV cause genital warts.

An estimated 50% to 80% of sexually active women are infected with HPV at least once in their lives. In most cases, the HPV infection clears on its own. In some women, however, HPV persists and causes precancerous growths, which can develop into cancer. Overall, less than 5% of all women with persistent HPV infection get cervical cancer.

Cancer of the cervix usually takes 10 to 20 years to develop, and so there is a long period of opportunity to detect and treat changes and precancerous growths before they become cancer. This is the goal of cervical cancer screening.

Who Is at Greatest Risk?

Some factors make women more likely to be infected by HPV. Others help HPV infection progress to cervical cancer more quickly. A woman with any of these characteristics would benefit especially from screening:

- Started having sex before age 18
- Has many sexual partners now or over the years
- Has a sexual partner who has or has had many other sexual partners
- Had many births (the more births, the greater the risk)
- Has a weak immune system (includes women with HIV/AIDS)
- Smokes cigarettes
- Burns wood indoors (as for cooking)
- Has had other sexually transmitted infections
- Has used combined oral contraceptives for more than 5 years

Screening and Treatment

Screening for cervical cancer is simple, quick, and generally not painful. A Papanicolaou (Pap) smear involves scraping a few cells from the cervix and examining them under a microscope. A woman will need to go to a facility for results and for treatment if an abnormality is found.

Before precancers become cancer, they can be frozen away with a probe filled with dry ice (cryotherapy) or cut away using a hot wire loop (loop electrosurgical excision procedure [LEEP]). Freezing is less effective for larger growths, but LEEP requires electricity and more extensive training. No hospital stay is needed for either type of treatment.

Treatment for cervical cancer includes surgery or radiation therapy, sometimes together with chemotherapy.

Promising New Approaches to Screening and Prevention

An alternative to the Papanicolaou smear is being tested. The cervix is coated with either vinegar or Lugol's iodine, which makes any abnormal cells visible to the provider. This makes possible immediate treatment if needed.

In 2006 the European Union and the United States Food and Drug Administration approved the first vaccine against cervical cancer, precancer, and genital warts. The vaccine protects against infection by 4 types of HPV that account for about 70% of all cervical cancers and an estimated 90% of all genital warts. It is approved for use among females age 9 to 26 years.

Questions and Answers About Sexually Transmitted Infections, Including HIV

1. **Does having another STI place a person at greater risk of infection if they are exposed to HIV?**

    Yes. In particular, infections that cause sores on the genitals such as chancroid and syphilis increase a person's risk of becoming infected if exposed to HIV. Other STIs, too, can increase the risk of HIV infection.

2. **Does using a condom only some of the time offer any protection from STIs, including HIV?**

    For best protection, a condom should be used with every act of sex. In some cases, however, occasional use can be protective. For example, if a person has a regular, faithful partner and has one act of sex outside of the relationship, using a condom for that one act can be very protective. For people who are exposed to STIs, including HIV, frequently, however, using a condom only some of the time will offer limited protection.

3. **Who is more at risk of becoming infected with an STI—men or women?**

    If exposed to STIs, women are more likely to become infected than men due to biological factors. Women have a greater area of exposure (the cervix and the vagina) than men, and small tears may occur in the vaginal tissue during sex, making an easy pathway for infection.

4. **Can HIV be transmitted through hugging? Shaking hands? Mosquito bites?**

    HIV cannot be transmitted through casual contact. This includes closed mouth kissing, hugging, shaking hands, and sharing food, clothing, or toilet seats. The virus cannot survive long outside of the human body. Mosquitoes cannot transmit HIV, either.

5. **Is there any truth to rumors that condoms are coated with HIV?**

    No, these rumors are false. Some condoms are covered with a wet or a powder-like material such as spermicide or cornstarch, but these are materials used for lubrication, to make sex smoother.

6. **Will having sex with a virgin cure someone with an STI, including HIV?**

   No. Instead, this practice only risks infecting the person who has not yet had sex.

7. **Will washing the penis or vagina after sex lower the risk of becoming infected with an STI?**

   Genital hygiene is important and a good practice. There is no evidence, however, that washing the genitals prevents STI infection. In fact, vaginal douching increases a woman's risk of acquiring STIs, including HIV, and pelvic inflammatory disease. If exposure to HIV is certain, treatment with antiretroviral medications (post-exposure prophylaxis), where available, can help reduce HIV transmission. If exposure to other STIs is certain, a provider can treat presumptively for those STIs—that is, treat the client as if he or she were infected.

8. **Does pregnancy place women at increased risk of becoming infected with HIV?**

   Current evidence is conflicting as to whether pregnancy increases a woman's chances of infection if exposed to HIV. If she does become infected with HIV during pregnancy, however, the chances that HIV will be transmitted to her baby during pregnancy, delivery, and childbirth may be at their highest because she will have a high level of virus in her blood. Thus, it is important for pregnant women to protect themselves from HIV and other STIs through condom use, mutual faithfulness, or abstinence. If a pregnant woman thinks that she may have HIV, she should seek HIV testing. Resources may be available to help her prevent transmitting HIV to her baby during pregnancy, delivery, and childbirth.

9. **Is pregnancy especially risky for women with HIV/AIDS and their infants?**

   Pregnancy will not make the woman's condition worse. HIV/AIDS may increase some health risks of pregnancy, however, and may also affect the health of the infant. Women with HIV are at greater risk of developing anemia and infection after vaginal delivery or caesarean section. The level of risk depends on such factors as a woman's health during pregnancy, her nutrition, and the medical care she receives. Also, the risk of these health problems increases as HIV infection progresses into AIDS. Further, women with HIV/AIDS are at greater risk of having preterm births, stillbirths, and low birthweight babies.

10. Does using hormonal contraception increase the risk of becoming infected with HIV?

The best evidence is reassuring. Recent studies among family planning clients in Uganda and Zimbabwe and women in a study in South Africa found that users of DMPA, NET-EN, or combined oral contraceptives were no more likely to become infected with HIV than women using nonhormonal methods. Use of hormonal methods is not restricted for women at high risk for HIV or other STIs.

11. How well do condoms help protect against HIV infection?

On average, condoms are 80% to 95% effective in protecting people from HIV infection when used correctly with every act of sex. This means that condom use prevents 80% to 95% of HIV transmissions that would have occurred without condoms. (It does *not* mean that 5% to 20% of condom users will become infected with HIV.) For example, among 10,000 uninfected women whose partners have HIV, if each couple has vaginal sex just once and has no additional risk factors for infection, on average:

- If all 10,000 did not use condoms, about 10 women would likely become infected with HIV.

- If all 10,000 used condoms correctly, 1 or 2 women would likely become infected with HIV.

The chances that a person who is exposed to HIV will become infected can vary greatly. These chances depend on the partner's stage of HIV infection (early and late stages are more infectious), whether the person exposed has other STIs (increases susceptibility), male circumcision status (uncircumcised men are more likely to become infected with HIV), and pregnancy (women who are pregnant may be at higher risk of infection), among other factors. On average, women face twice the risk of infection, if exposed, that men do.

CHAPTER 22

Maternal and Newborn Health

Key Points for Providers and Clients

- **Wait until the youngest child is at least 2 years old before trying to become pregnant again.** Spacing births is good for the mother's and the baby's health.

- **Make the first antenatal care visit within the first 12 weeks of pregnancy.**

- **Plan ahead for family planning after delivery.**

- **Prepare for childbirth.** Have a plan for normal delivery and an emergency plan, too.

- **Breastfeed for a healthier baby.**

Many health care providers see women who want to become pregnant, who are pregnant, or who have recently given birth. Providers can help women plan pregnancies, plan for contraception after delivery, prepare for childbirth, and care for their babies.

Planning Pregnancy

A woman who wants to have a child can use advice about preparing for safe pregnancy and delivery and having a healthy child:

- It is best to wait at least 2 years after giving birth before stopping contraception to become pregnant.

- At least 3 months before stopping contraception to get pregnant, a woman should begin taking care to eat a balanced diet, and she should continue doing so throughout pregnancy. Folic acid and iron are particularly important.

    - Folic acid is found in such foods as legumes (beans, bean curd, lentils, and peas), citrus fruits, whole grains, and green leafy vegetables. Folic acid tablets may be available.

    - Iron is found in such foods as meat and poultry, fish, green leafy vegetables, and legumes. Iron tablets may be available.

22

Maternal and Newborn Health

- If a woman has, or may have been exposed to a sexually transmitted infection (STI), including HIV, treatment can reduce the chances that her child will be born with an infection. If a woman thinks she has been exposed or might be infected, she should seek testing, if available.

During Pregnancy

The first antenatal care visit should come early in pregnancy, ideally before week 12. For most women, 4 visits during pregnancy are appropriate. Women with certain health conditions or complications of pregnancy may need more visits, however. Provide care or refer for antenatal care.

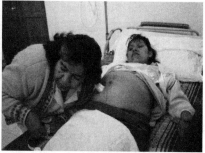

Health Promotion and Disease Prevention

- Counsel women about good nutrition and eating foods that contain iron, folate, vitamin A, calcium, and iodine and avoiding tobacco, alcohol, and drugs (except medications recommended by a health care provider).
- Help pregnant women protect themselves from infections.
  - If she is at risk for STIs, discuss condom use or abstinence during pregnancy (see Sexually Transmitted Infections, Including HIV, p. 275).
  - Ensure that pregnant women are immunized against tetanus.
  - To prevent or treat anemia, where hookworm infection is common provide treatment (antihelminthic therapy) after the first trimester.
- Help pregnant women protect their babies from infections.
  - Test for syphilis as early in pregnancy as possible, and treat as needed.
  - Offer HIV testing and counseling.
- Pregnant women are particularly susceptible to malaria. Provide insecticide-treated bed nets for malaria prevention and effective malaria treatment to every pregnant woman in areas where malaria is widespread, whether or not malaria is diagnosed (presumptive treatment). Monitor pregnant women for malaria and provide immediate treatment when diagnosed.

Planning for Family Planning After Delivery

Help pregnant women and new mothers decide how they will avoid pregnancy after childbirth. Ideally, family planning counseling should start during antenatal care.

- Waiting until her baby is at least 2 years old before a woman tries to become pregnant again is best for the baby and good for the mother, too.

- A woman who is not fully or nearly fully breastfeeding is able to become pregnant as soon as 4 to 6 weeks after childbirth.

- A woman who is fully or nearly fully breastfeeding is able to become pregnant as soon as 6 months postpartum (see Lactational Amenorrhea Method, p. 257).

- For maximum protection, a woman should not wait until the return of monthly bleeding to start a contraceptive method, but instead she should start as soon as guidance allows (see Earliest Time That a Woman Can Start a Family Planning Method After Childbirth, p. 293).

Preparing for Childbirth and Complications

Potentially life-threatening complications develop in about 15% of pregnancies, and all of these women need immediate care. Most complications cannot be predicted, but providers can help women and their families be prepared for them.

- Help women arrange for skilled attendance at birth, and ensure that they know how to contact the skilled birth attendant at the first signs of labor.

- Explain danger signs during pregnancy and childbirth to women and their families (see below).

- Help the woman and her family plan how she will reach emergency care if complications arise: Where will she go? Who will take her there? What transport will they use? How will she pay for medical help? Are there people ready to donate blood?

Danger Signs During Pregnancy and Childbirth

If any of these signs appears, the family should follow their emergency plan and get the woman to emergency care immediately.

- Fever (38° C/101° F or higher)
- Foul-smelling discharge from vagina
- Severe headache/blurred vision
- Decreased or no fetal movements
- Green or brown fluid leaking from vagina

- High blood pressure
- Vaginal bleeding
- Difficulty breathing
- Convulsions, fainting
- Severe abdominal pain

After Childbirth

- Coordinate family planning visits with an infant's immunization schedule.

- Optimal breastfeeding offers triple value: important improvements in child survival and health, better health for mothers, and temporary contraception. Still, any breastfeeding is better than none (except if a woman has HIV). See Preventing Mother-to-Child Transmission of HIV, p. 294.

Guidelines for Best Breastfeeding

1. Begin breastfeeding the newborn as soon as possible— within 1 hour after delivery

- Stimulates uterine contractions that help prevent heavy bleeding.

- Helps the infant to establish suckling early on, which stimulates milk production.

- Colostrum, the yellowish milk produced in the first days after childbirth, provides important nutrients for the child and transfers immunities from mother to child.

- Avoids the risks of feeding the baby contaminated liquids or foods.

2. Fully or nearly fully breastfeed for 6 months

- Mother's milk alone can fully nourish a baby for the first 6 months of life.

3. At 6 months, add other foods to breastfeeding

- After 6 months babies need a variety of foods in addition to breast milk.

- At each feeding breastfeed before giving other foods.

- Breastfeeding can and should continue through the child's second year or longer.

Earliest Time That a Woman Can Start a Family Planning Method After Childbirth

Family Planning Method	Fully or Nearly Fully Breastfeeding	Partially Breastfeeding or Not Breastfeeding
Lactational Amenorrhea Method	Immediately	(Not applicable)
Vasectomy	Immediately or during partner's pregnancy[‡]	
Male or female condoms	Immediately	
Spermicides		
Copper-bearing IUD	Within 48 hours, otherwise wait 4 weeks	
Female sterilization	Within 7 days, otherwise wait 6 weeks	
Levonorgestrel IUD	4 weeks after childbirth	
Diaphragm	6 weeks after childbirth	
Fertility awareness methods	Start when normal secretions have returned (for symptoms-based methods) or she has had 3 regular menstrual cycles (for calendar-based methods). This will be later for breastfeeding women than for women who are not breastfeeding.	
Progestin-only pills	6 weeks after childbirth[§]	Immediately if not breastfeeding[§]
Progestin-only injectables		6 weeks after childbirth if partially breastfeeding[§]
Implants		
Combined oral contraceptives	6 months after childbirth[§]	21 days after childbirth if not breastfeeding[§]
Monthly injectables		6 weeks after childbirth if partially breastfeeding[§]
Combined patch		
Combined vaginal ring		

[‡] *If a man has a vasectomy during the first 6 months of his partner's pregnancy, it will be effective by the time she delivers her baby.*

[§] *Earlier use is not usually recommended unless other, more appropriate methods are not available or not acceptable. See also p. 129, Q&A 8.*

Preventing Mother-to-Child Transmission of HIV

A woman infected with HIV can pass HIV to her child during pregnancy, delivery, or breastfeeding. Preventive antiretroviral (ARV) therapy (prophylaxis) given to the mother during pregnancy and labor can greatly reduce the chances that the baby will be infected while developing in the uterus or during delivery. During breastfeeding, ARV therapy for the mother, for the HIV-exposed infant, or for both, also can significantly reduce the chances of HIV transmission through breast milk.

How can family planning providers help prevent mother-to-child transmission of HIV?

- *Help women avoid HIV infection* (see Sexually Transmitted Infections, Including HIV, Preventing Sexually Transmitted Infections, p. 280).

- *Prevent unintended pregnancies:* Help women who do not want a child to choose a contraceptive method that they can use effectively.

- *Offer HIV counseling and testing:* Offer counseling and testing to all pregnant women, if possible, or offer to refer them to an HIV testing service, so they can learn their HIV status.

- *Refer:* Refer women with HIV who are pregnant, or who want to become pregnant, to services for prevention of mother-to-child transmission, if available.

- *Encourage appropriate infant feeding:* Counsel women with HIV on safer infant feeding practices to reduce the risk of transmission, and help them develop a feeding plan. If possible, refer them to someone trained to counsel on infant feeding.

  - For all women, including women with HIV, breastfeeding, and especially early and exclusive breastfeeding, is an important way to promote the child's survival.

  - HIV-infected mothers and/or their infants should receive the appropriate ARV therapy, and mothers should exclusively breastfeed their infants for the first 6 months of life, then introduce appropriate complementary foods and continue breastfeeding for the first 12 months of life.

  - Breastfeeding should then stop only once a nutritionally adequate and safe diet without breast milk can be provided. When mothers decide to stop breastfeeding, they should stop gradually within one month, and infants should be given safe and adequate replacement feeds to enable normal growth and development. Stopping breastfeeding abruptly is not advised.

  - Even when ARV therapy is not available, breastfeeding (exclusive breastfeeding in the first 6 months of life and continued breastfeeding for the first 12 months of life) may still give infants born to mothers infected with HIV a greater chance of survival while still avoiding HIV infection than not breastfeeding at all.

- In some well-resourced countries with low infant and child mortality rates, however, avoiding all breastfeeding will be appropriate. A woman with HIV should be advised of the national recommendation for infant feeding by HIV-infected mothers and counseled and supported in the feeding practice that best suits her situation.

- An HIV-infected mother should consider replacement feeding if—and only if—all the following conditions are met:
  - safe water and sanitation are assured in the household and community;
  - the mother or caregiver can reliably provide infant formula:
    - o sufficient for normal growth and development of the infant
    - o cleanly and frequently, to avoid diarrhea and malnutrition, and
    - o exclusively in the first 6 months;
  - the family is supportive of this practice; and
  - the mother or caregiver can obtain health care that offers comprehensive child health services.

- If infants and young children are known to be HIV-infected, mothers should be strongly encouraged to exclusively breastfeed for the first 6 months of life and continue breastfeeding up to 2 years or beyond.

- If a woman is temporarily unable to breastfeed—for example, she or the infant is sick, she is weaning, or her supply of ARVs has run out—she may express and heat-treat breast milk to destroy the HIV before feeding it to the infant. Milk should be heated to the boiling point in a small pot and then cooled by letting the milk stand or by placing the pot in a container of cool water. This should be used only short-term, not throughout breastfeeding.

- Women with HIV who are breastfeeding need advice on keeping their nutrition adequate and their breasts healthy. Infection of the milk ducts in the breast (mastitis), a pocket of pus under the skin (breast abscess), and cracked nipples increase the risk of HIV transmission. If a problem does occur, prompt and appropriate care is important (see Sore or cracked nipples, p. 296).

22

Maternal and Newborn Health

Managing Any Breastfeeding Problems

If a client reports any of these common problems, listen to her concerns and give advice.

Baby is not getting enough milk

- Reassure the woman that most women can produce enough breast milk to feed their babies.
- If the newborn is gaining more than 500 grams a month, weighs more than birth weight at 2 weeks, or urinates at least 6 times a day, reassure her that her baby is getting enough breast milk.
- Tell her to breastfeed her newborn about every 2 hours to increase milk supply.
- Recommend that she reduce any supplemental foods and/or liquids if the baby is less than 6 months of age.

Sore breasts

- If her breasts are full, tight, and painful, then she may have engorged breasts. If one breast has tender lumps, then she may have blocked ducts. Engorged breasts or blocked ducts may progress to red and tender infected breasts. Treat breast infection with antibiotics according to clinic guidelines. To aid healing, advise her to:
  - Continue to breastfeed often
  - Massage her breasts before and during breastfeeding
  - Apply heat or a warm compress to breasts
  - Try different breastfeeding positions
  - Ensure that the infant attaches properly to the breast
  - Express some milk before breastfeeding

Sore or cracked nipples

- If her nipples are cracked, she can continue breastfeeding. Assure her that they will heal over time.
- To aid healing, advise her to:
  - Apply drops of breast milk to the nipples after breastfeeding and allow to air-dry.
  - After feeding, use a finger to break suction first before removing the baby from the breast.
  - Do not wait until the breast is full to breastfeed. If full, express some milk first.
- Teach her about proper attachment and how to check for signs that the baby is not attaching properly.
- Tell her to clean her nipples with only water only once a day and to avoid soaps and alcohol-based solutions.
- Examine her nipples and the baby's mouth and buttocks for signs of fungal infection (thrush).

CHAPTER 23

Reproductive Health Issues

Key Points for Providers and Clients

Postabortion Care

- **Fertility returns quickly, within a few weeks, after abortion or miscarriage.** Women need to start using a family planning method almost immediately to avoid unwanted pregnancy.

Violence Against Women

- **Violence is not the woman's fault.** It is very common. Local resources may be available to help.

Infertility

- **Infertility often can be prevented.** Avoiding sexually transmitted infections and receiving prompt treatment for these and other reproductive tract infections can reduce a client's risk of infertility.

Family Planning in Postabortion Care

Women who have just been treated for postabortion complications need easy and immediate access to family planning services. When such services are integrated with postabortion care, are offered immediately postabortion, or are nearby, women are more likely to use contraception when they face the risk of unintended pregnancy.

23

Reproductive Health Issues

Help Women Obtain Family Planning

Counsel with Compassion

A woman who has had postabortion complications needs support. A woman who has faced the double risk of pregnancy and unsafe induced abortion especially needs help and support. Good counseling gives support to the woman who has just been treated for postabortion complications. In particular:

- Try to understand what she has been through
- Treat her with respect and avoid judgment and criticism
- Ensure privacy and confidentiality
- Ask if she wants someone she trusts to be present during counseling

Provide Important Information

A woman has important choices to make after receiving postabortion care. To make decisions about her health and fertility, she needs to know:

- Fertility returns quickly—within 2 weeks after a first-trimester abortion or miscarriage and within 4 weeks after a second-trimester abortion or miscarriage. Therefore, she needs protection from pregnancy almost immediately.

- She can choose among many different family planning methods that she can start at once (see next page). Methods that women should not use immediately after giving birth pose no special risks after treatment for abortion complications.

- She can wait before choosing a contraceptive for ongoing use, but she should consider using a backup method* in the meantime if she has sex. If a woman decides not to use contraceptives at this time, providers can offer information on available methods and where to obtain them. Also, providers can offer condoms, oral contraceptives, or emergency contraceptive pills for women to take home and use later.

- To avoid infection, she should not have sex until bleeding stops—about 5 to 7 days. If being treated for infection or vaginal or cervical injury, she should wait to have sex again until she has fully healed.

- If she wants to become pregnant again soon, encourage her to wait. Waiting at least 6 months may reduce the chances of low birthweight, premature birth, and maternal anemia. A woman receiving postabortion care may need other reproductive health services. In particular, a provider can help her consider if she might have been exposed to sexually transmitted infections.

* Backup methods include abstinence, male or female condoms, spermicides, and withdrawal. She can use spermicides if she has no vaginal or cervical injury. Tell her that spermicides and withdrawal are the least effective contraceptive methods. If possible, give her condoms.

When to Start Contraceptive Methods

- Combined oral contraceptives, progestin-only pills, progestin-only injectables, monthly injectables, combined patch, implants, male condoms, female condoms, and withdrawal can be started immediately in every case, even if the woman has injury to the genital tract or has a possible or confirmed infection.

- IUDs, female sterilization, and fertility awareness methods can be started once infection is ruled out or resolved.

- IUDs, combined vaginal ring, spermicides, diaphragms, cervical caps, female sterilization, and fertility awareness methods can be started once any injury to the genital tract has healed.

Special considerations:

- *IUD* insertion immediately after a second-trimester abortion requires a specifically trained provider.

- *Female sterilization* must be decided upon in advance, and not while a woman is sedated, under stress, or in pain. Counsel carefully and be sure to mention available reversible methods (see Female Sterilization, Because Sterilization Is Permanent, p. 174).

- The *combined vaginal ring, spermicides, diaphragms,* and *cervical caps* can be used immediately even in cases of uncomplicated uterine perforation.

- The *diaphragm* must be refitted after uncomplicated first-trimester miscarriage or abortion. After uncomplicated second-trimester miscarriage or abortion, use should be delayed 6 weeks for the uterus to return to normal size, and then the diaphragm should be refitted.

- *Fertility awareness methods:* A woman can start symptoms-based methods once she has no infection-related secretions or bleeding due to injury to the genital tract. She can start calendar-based methods with her next monthly bleeding, if she is not having bleeding due to injury to the genital tract.

Violence Against Women

Every family planning provider probably sees many women who have experienced violence. Violence against women is common everywhere, and in some places it is very common. In a recent study of 10 countries more than 1 of every 10 women and up to about 7 of every 10 women reported that they had experienced physical or sexual violence in their lifetimes. Physical violence includes a wide range of behaviors, including hitting, slapping, kicking, and beating. Sexual violence includes unwanted sexual contact or attention, coercive sex, and forced sex (rape). Violence against women can be psychological, too, such as controlling behavior, intimidation, humiliation, isolating a woman from family and friends, and restricting her access to resources.

Women experiencing violence have special health needs, many of them related to sexual and reproductive health. Violence can lead to a range of health problems including injuries, unwanted pregnancy, sexually transmitted infections (STIs) including HIV, decreased sexual desire, pain during sex, and chronic pelvic pain. For some women, violence may start or become worse during pregnancy, placing her fetus at risk as well. Furthermore, a man's violence or the threat of violence can deprive a woman of her right to make her own choice about whether to use family planning or what method to use. Therefore, providers of reproductive health care may be more likely than other health care providers to see abused women among their usual clientele.

What Can Providers Do?

1. **Help women feel welcome, safe, and free to talk.** Help women feel comfortable speaking freely about any personal issue, including violence. Ensure every woman that her visit will be confidential.

   Give women opportunities to bring up violence, such as asking a woman about her partner's attitudes toward her using family planning, asking whether she foresees any problems with using family planning, and asking simply if there is anything else she would like to discuss.

2. **Ask women about abuse whenever violence is suspected.** While most women will not bring up that they are being abused, many will talk if asked about violence. Asking all clients if they are experiencing violence is recommended only when providers are well-trained in counseling about violence, privacy and confidentiality can be ensured, and there are sufficient resources available to respond adequately to identified cases of violence. Until then, providers can ask whenever abuse is suspected, thereby focusing resources on those who need immediate care.

Be alert to symptoms, injuries, or signs that suggest violence. Providers may suspect violence when depression, anxiety, chronic headaches, pelvic pain, or vague stomach pains have not improved over time with treatment. Another sign of violence may be when the client's story about how an injury occurred does not fit the type of injury she has. Suspect violence with any injury during pregnancy, especially to the abdomen or breasts.

Some tips for bringing up the subject of violence:

- To increase trust, explain why you are asking—because you want to help.

- Use language that is comfortable for you and best fits your own style.

- Do not ask such questions when a woman's partner or anyone else is present or when privacy cannot be ensured.

- You can say, "Domestic violence is a common problem in our community so we have been asking our clients about abuse."

- You can ask such questions as:

  - "Your symptoms may be due to stress. Do you and your partner tend to fight a lot? Have you ever gotten hurt?"

  - "Does your partner ever want sex when you do not? What happens in such situations?"

  - "Are you afraid of your partner?"

3. **Counsel in a nonjudgmental, sensitive, supportive manner.**
   An important service for women in violent relationships is counseling. Counseling about violence should be tailored to a woman's particular circumstances. Women may be at different stages of willingness to seek change. This will affect whether and how a woman will accept help.

Some women will not be ready to discuss their situation with a health care provider. The point of counseling is not to find out for sure whether the client is experiencing violence, but rather to address the issue with compassion and let her know that you care.

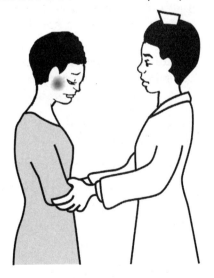

- If she does not want to talk about the violence, assure her that you are available whenever she needs you. Tell her what options and resources are available should she ever want them.

- If she wants to talk about her experience of violence, you can:
  - Ensure confidentiality, and keep the woman's situation confidential. Tell only those who need to know (such as security staff), and do that only with the client's permission.
  - Acknowledge her experience. Listen, offer support, and avoid making judgments. Respect her ability and her right to make her own choices about her life.
  - Try to relieve the woman's possible feelings of shame and self-blame: "No one ever deserves to be hit." "You don't deserve the abuse, and it's not your fault."
  - Explain that violence is a common problem: "This happens to many women." "You are not alone, and help is available."
  - Explain that violence is not likely to stop on its own: "Abuse tends to continue, and often it becomes worse and happens more often."

4. **Assess a woman's immediate danger, help her develop a safety plan, and refer her to community resources.** If the woman faces immediate danger, help her consider various courses of action. If not in immediate danger, help her develop a longer-term plan.

- Help her assess her present situation:
  - "Is he here at the health facility now?"
  - "Are you or your children in danger now?"
  - "Do you feel safe to go home?"
  - "Is there a friend or relative who can help you with the situation at home?"

- Help her protect herself and her children if the violence recurs. Suggest that she keep a bag packed with important documents and a change of clothes so she can leave quickly if need be. Suggest that she have a signal to let children know when to seek help from neighbors.

- Make and keep up-to-date a list of resources available to help victims of abuse, including police, counseling services, and women's organizations that can provide emotional, legal, and perhaps even financial support. Give a copy of the list to the client.

5. **Provide appropriate care.** Tailor your care and counseling to a woman's circumstances.

- Treat any injuries or see that she gets treatment.

- Evaluate risk of pregnancy and provide emergency contraception if appropriate and wanted.

- Offer emergency contraceptive pills for future use (see Emergency Contraceptive Pills, p. 45).

- If she wants, give her a contraceptive method that can be used without a partner's knowledge, such as an injectable.

- Help women think about whether they could safely propose condom use, without risking further violence.

- In cases of rape:
  - First collect any samples that could be used as evidence (such as torn or stained clothing, hair, and blood or semen stains).
  - Provide or refer for HIV and STI testing and treatment. Some women may need such services repeatedly.
  - Consider post-exposure prophylaxis for HIV, if available, and presumptive treatment for gonorrhea, chlamydia, syphilis, and other, locally common STIs.

6. **Document the woman's condition.** Carefully document the woman's symptoms or injuries, the cause of the injuries, and her history of abuse. Clearly record the identity of the abuser, his relationship to the victim, and any other details about him. These notes could be helpful for future medical follow-up and legal action, if taken.

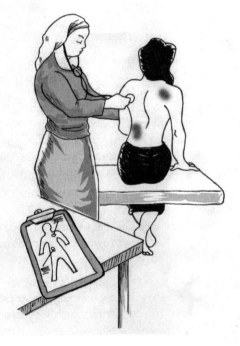

Infertility

What Is Infertility?

Infertility is the inability to produce children. Although often the woman is blamed, infertility occurs in both men and women. On average, infertility affects 1 of every 10 couples. A couple is considered infertile after having 12 months of unprotected sex without pregnancy. A couple can be infertile whether or not the woman has been pregnant in the past.

Among couples with no fertility problems, 85% of women will become pregnant over one year. On average, pregnancy occurs after 3 to 6 months of unprotected sex. There is great variation around this average, however.

Pregnancy wastage is another form of infertility: A woman can become pregnant, but miscarriage or stillbirth prevents a live birth.

What Causes Infertility?

Different factors or conditions can reduce fertility, such as:

- Infectious diseases (sexually transmitted infections [STIs], including HIV, other reproductive tract infections; mumps that develop after puberty in men)
- Anatomical, endocrine, genetic, or immune system problems
- Aging
- Medical procedures that bring infection into a woman's upper reproductive tract

STIs are a major cause of infertility. Left untreated, gonorrhea and chlamydia can infect fallopian tubes, the uterus, and ovaries. This is known as pelvic inflammatory disease (PID). Clinical PID is painful, but sometimes PID has no symptoms and goes unnoticed (silent PID). Gonorrhea and chlamydia can scar women's fallopian tubes, blocking eggs from traveling down the tubes to meet sperm. Men can have scarring and blockage in the sperm duct (epididymis) and urethra from untreated gonorrhea and chlamydia (see Female Anatomy, p. 364, and Male Anatomy, p. 367).

Other reasons for male infertility include a natural inability either to produce any sperm at all or enough sperm to cause pregnancy. Less commonly, sperm are malformed and die before reaching an egg. Among women, natural inability to become pregnant often is due to blocked fallopian tubes or inability to ovulate.

Fertility is also related to age. As a woman gets older, her ability to become pregnant naturally deceases over time. Emerging evidence suggests that, similarly, men, as they age, produce sperm that is less able to fertilize an egg.

Postpartum and postabortion infections also can cause PID, which may lead to infertility. This happens when the surgical instruments used for medical procedures are not properly disinfected or sterilized. A woman can also develop PID if an infection present in the lower reproductive tract is carried into the upper reproductive tract during a medical procedure.

Preventing Infertility

Infertility is often preventable. Providers can:

- Counsel clients about STI prevention (see Sexually Transmitted Infections, Including HIV, Preventing Sexually Transmitted Infections, p. 280). Encourage clients to seek treatment as soon as they think they might have an STI or might have been exposed.

- Treat or refer clients with signs and symptoms of STIs and clinical PID (see Sexually Transmitted Infections, Including HIV, Symptoms of Sexually Transmitted Infections, p. 278). Treating these infections helps preserve fertility.

- Avoid infection by following proper infection-prevention practices when performing medical procedures that pass instruments from the vagina into the uterus, such as IUD insertion (see Infection Prevention in the Clinic, p. 312).

Contraceptives Do Not Cause Infertility

- With most contraceptive methods, there is no delay in the return of fertility after use is stopped. The return of fertility after injectable contraceptives are stopped usually takes longer than with most other methods (see Progestin-Only Injectables, Questions 6 and 7, p. 79, and Monthly Injectables, Questions 10 and 11, p. 100). In time, however, women who have used injectables are as fertile as they were before using the method, taking aging into account.

- Among women with current gonorrhea or chlamydia, IUD insertion slightly increases the risk of pelvic inflammatory disease in the first 20 days after insertion. Still, research has not found that former IUD users are more likely to be infertile than other women (see Copper-Bearing IUD, Question 4, p. 155).

Counseling Clients With Fertility Problems

Counsel both partners together, if possible. Men often blame women for infertility when they themselves might be responsible. Tell couples:

- A man is just as likely to have fertility problems as a woman. It may not be possible to find who is infertile and what caused the infertility.

- Try for pregnancy for at least 12 months before worrying about infertility.

- The most fertile time of a woman's cycle is several days before and at the time an egg is released from the ovary (see The Menstrual Cycle, p. 366). Suggest they have sex often during this time. Fertility awareness methods can help couples identify the most fertile time of each cycle (see Fertility Awareness Methods, p. 239). Teach or refer if the couple wants to try this.

- If after one year the suggestions above have not helped, refer both partners for evaluation, if available. The couple also may want to consider adoption.

CHAPTER 24

Family Planning Provision

Importance of Selected Procedures for Providing Family Planning Methods

The classifications below of examinations and tests apply to people who are presumed to be healthy. For a person with a known medical condition or other special condition, refer to the Medical Eligibility Criteria for Contraceptive Use, p. 324.

Class A: Essential and mandatory in all circumstances for safe and effective use of the contraceptive method.

Class B: Contributes substantially to safe and effective use. If the test or examination cannot be done, however, the risk of not performing it should be weighed against the benefits of making the contraceptive method available.

Class C: Does not contribute substantially to safe and effective use of the contraceptive method.

Specific situation	Combined oral contraceptives	Monthly injectables	Progestin-only pills	Progestin-only injectables	Implants	IUDs	Male and female condoms	Diaphragms and cervical caps	Spermicides	Female sterilization	Vasectomy
Breast examination by provider	C	C	C	C	C	C	C	C	C	C	NA
Pelvic/genital examination	C	C	C	C	C	A	C	A	C	A	A
Cervical cancer screening	C	C	C	C	C	C	C	C	C	C	NA
Routine laboratory tests	C	C	C	C	C	C	C	C	C	C	C
Hemoglobin test	C	C	C	C	C	B	C	C	C	B	C
STI risk assessment: medical history and physical examination	C	C	C	C	C	A*	C	C†	C†	C	C
STI/HIV screening: laboratory tests	C	C	C	C	C	B*	C	C†	C†	C	C
Blood pressure screening	‡	‡	‡	‡	‡	C	C	C	C	A	C§

* If a woman has a very high individual likelihood of exposure to gonorrhea or chlamydia, she generally should not have an IUD inserted unless other methods are not available or not acceptable. If she has current purulent cervicitis, gonorrhea, or chlamydia, she should not have an IUD inserted until these conditions are resolved and she is otherwise medically eligible.

† Women at high risk of HIV infection or AIDS should not use spermicides. Using diaphragms and cervical caps with spermicide is not usually recommended for such women unless other more appropriate methods are not available or acceptable.

NA=Not applicable

‡ Desirable, but in settings where the risks of pregnancy are high, and hormonal methods are among the few methods widely available, women should not be denied use of hormonal methods solely because their blood pressure cannot be measured.

§ For procedures performed using only local anesthesia.

24

Family Planning Provision

Successful Counseling

Good counseling helps clients choose and use family planning methods that suit them. Clients differ, their situations differ, and they need different kinds of help. The best counseling is tailored to the individual client.

Client Type	Usual Counseling Tasks
Returning clients with no problems	• Provide more supplies or routine follow-up • Ask a friendly question about how the client is doing with the method
Returning clients with problems	• Understand the problem and help resolve it—whether the problem is side effects, trouble using the method, an uncooperative partner, or another problem
New clients with a method in mind	• Check that the client's understanding is accurate • Support the client's choice, if client is medically eligible • Discuss how to use method and how to cope with any side effects
New clients with no method in mind	• Discuss the client's situation, plans, and what is important to her about a method • Help the client consider methods that might suit her. If needed, help her reach a decision • Support the client's choice, give instructions on use, and discuss how to cope with any side effects

Give time to clients who need it. Many clients are returning with no problems and need little counseling. Returning clients with problems and new clients with no method in mind need the most time, but usually they are few.

Tips for Successful Counseling

- Show every client respect, and help each client feel at ease.
- Encourage the client to explain needs, express concerns, ask questions.
- Let the client's wishes and needs guide the discussion.
- Be alert to related needs such as protection from sexually transmitted infections including HIV, and support for condom use.
- Listen carefully. Listening is as important as giving correct information.
- Give just *key* information and instructions. Use words the client knows.
- Respect and support the client's informed decisions.
- Bring up side effects, if any, and take the client's concerns seriously.

- Check the client's understanding.
- Invite the client to come back any time for any reason.

Counseling has succeeded when:

- Clients feel they got the help they wanted
- Clients know what to do and feel confident that they can do it
- Clients feel respected and appreciated
- Clients come back when they need to
- And, most important, clients use their methods effectively and with satisfaction.

Counseling Tool Available from WHO

The *Decision-Making Tool for Family Planning Clients and Providers*, another of the World Health Organization's 4 cornerstones of family planning guidance, helps clients and providers in counseling sessions with choosing and learning to use family planning methods. This tool is an illustrated flip chart. It offers help tailored for each type of client mentioned in the table on previous page. Key information from this handbook can be found in the *Decision-Making Tool*, worded in a way that may be helpful for counseling.

To see the *Decision-Making Tool* and to download it from the Internet, go to http://www.who.int/reproductivehealth/publications/ family_planning/9241593229index/en/index.html.

Who Provides Family Planning?

Many different people can learn to inform and advise people about family planning and to provide family planning methods. Countries and programs have various guidelines about who can offer which methods and where, and some have rules that differ depending on whether the client is starting a new method or is continuing a method. Still, in countries around the world these people commonly provide family planning:

- Nurses, nurse-midwives, nurse-practitioners
- Auxiliary nurse-midwives
- Midwives
- Physicians, including gynecologists and obstetricians
- Physicians' assistants, physicians' associates
- Pharmacists, pharmacists' assistants, chemists
- Primary health care providers, community health care providers
- Community-based health workers and community members serving as community-based distributors
- Specifically trained traditional birth attendants
- Shopkeepers and vendors
- Volunteers, experienced users of family planning, peer educators, and community leaders

Specific training helps all these people do a better job at providing family planning. Training needs to cover skills in informing and counseling clients about choosing and using specific methods, including their side effects, as well as teaching any specific technical skills such as how to give injections or insert an IUD. Checklists can help a wide range of providers and managers in various ways, such as screening clients for medical eligibility criteria, making sure all steps in a process are carried out (such as infection prevention), and assuring good quality of services.

Method	Who can provide?
Oral contraceptives, combined patch, combined vaginal ring	• All providers with training, including brief specific training.
Emergency contraceptive pills	• All providers.

Method	Who can provide?
Injectables	• Anyone trained to give injections and to handle needles and syringes properly, including appropriate disposal. This includes community-based health care providers.
Implants	• Anyone with training in medical procedures and training in insertion of the specific implants being used, including physicians, nurses, nurse-midwives, nurse-practitioners, midwives, physicians' assistants and associates.
Intrauterine device (copper-bearing and hormonal IUDs)	• Anyone with training in medical procedures and specific training in IUD screening, insertion, and removal including physicians, nurses, nurse-midwives, midwives, nurse-practitioners, physicians' assistants and associates, and medical students. Training is different for the copper-bearing IUD and the hormonal IUD. In some countries pharmacists sell IUDs—the woman takes the IUD to a health care provider who inserts it.
Female sterilization	• Anyone with specific training in the procedure, including general physicians, specialized physicians (such as gynecologists and surgeons), medical assistants or medical students under supervision. Laparoscopy is best performed by experienced and specifically trained surgeons.
Vasectomy	• Anyone with specific training in the procedure, including physicians, medical officers, nurse-midwives, nurse practitioners, midwives, physicians' assistants and associates.
Male and female condoms and spermicides	• All providers.
Diaphragms and cervical caps	• Any provider specifically trained to perform pelvic examinations and to choose the right size diaphragm or cervical cap for each woman.
Fertility awareness methods	• Anyone specifically trained to teach fertility awareness. Experienced users of these methods often make the best teachers.
Withdrawal, lactational amenorrhea method	• These methods do not require a provider. Still, knowledgeable and supportive health care providers can help clients use these methods most effectively.

24

Family Planning Provision

Infection Prevention in the Clinic

Infection-prevention procedures are simple, effective, and inexpensive. Germs (infectious organisms) of concern in the clinic include bacteria (such as staphylococcus), viruses (particularly HIV and hepatitis B), fungi, and parasites. In the clinic, infectious organisms can be found in blood, body fluids with visible blood, or tissue. (Feces, nasal secretions, saliva, sputum, sweat, tears, urine, and vomit are not considered potentially infectious unless they contain blood.) The organisms can be passed through mucous membranes or broken skin, such as cuts and scratches, and by needlesticks with used needles and other puncture wounds. Infectious organisms can pass from clinics to communities when waste disposal is not proper or staff members do not wash their hands properly before leaving the clinic.

Basic Rules of Infection Prevention

These rules apply the universal precautions for infection prevention to the family planning clinic.

Wash hands

- *Hand washing may be the single most important infection-prevention procedure.*

- Wash hands before and after examining or treating each client. (Hand washing is not necessary if clients do not require an examination or treatment.)

- Use clean water and plain soap, and rub hands for at least 10 to 15 seconds. Be sure to clean between the fingers and under fingernails. Wash hands after handling soiled instruments and other items or touching mucous membranes, blood, or other body fluids. Wash hands before putting on gloves, after taking off gloves, and whenever hands get dirty. Wash hands when you arrive at work, after you use the toilet or latrine, and when you leave work. Dry hands with a paper towel or a clean, dry cloth towel that no one else uses, or air-dry.

Process instruments that will be reused

- High-level disinfect or sterilize instruments that touch intact mucous membranes or broken skin.

- Sterilize instruments that touch tissue beneath the skin (see The 4 Steps of Processing Equipment, p. 315).

Wear gloves	• Wear gloves for any procedure that risks touching blood, other body fluids, mucous membranes, broken skin, soiled items, dirty surfaces, or waste. Wear surgical gloves for surgical procedures such as insertion of implants. Wear single-use examination gloves for procedures that touch intact mucous membranes or generally to avoid exposure to body fluids. Gloves are not necessary for giving injections.
	• Change gloves between procedures on the same client and between clients.
	• Do not touch clean equipment or surfaces with dirty gloves or bare hands.
	• Wash hands before putting on gloves. Do not wash gloved hands instead of changing gloves. Gloves are not a substitute for hand washing.
	• Wear clean utility gloves when cleaning soiled instruments and equipment, handling waste, and cleaning blood or body fluid spills.
Do pelvic examinations only when needed	• Pelvic examinations are not needed for most family planning methods—only for female sterilization, the IUD, diaphragm, and cervical cap (see Importance of Selected Procedures for Providing Family Planning Methods, p. 307). Pelvic examinations should be done only when there is a reason—such as suspicion of sexually transmitted infections, when the examination could help with diagnosis or treatment.
For injections, use new auto-disable syringes and needles	• Auto-disable syringes and needles are safer and more reliable than standard single-use disposable syringes and needles, and any disposable syringes and needles are safer than sterilizing reusable syringes and needles. Reusable syringes and needles should be considered only when single-use injection equipment is not available and if programs can document the quality of sterilization.
	• Cleaning the client's skin before the injection is not needed unless the skin is dirty. If it is, wash with soap and water and dry with a clean towel. Wiping with an antiseptic has no added benefit.
Wipe surfaces with chlorine solution	• Wipe examination tables, bench tops, and other surfaces that come in contact with unbroken skin with 0.5% chlorine solution after each client.

Dispose of single-use equipment and supplies properly and safely 	• Use personal protective equipment—goggles, mask, apron, and closed protective shoes—when handling wastes. • Needles and syringes meant for single use must not be reused. Do not take apart the needle and syringe. Used needles should not be broken, bent, or recapped. Put used needles and syringes immediately into a puncture-proof container for disposal. (If needles and syringes will not be incinerated, they should be decontaminated by flushing with 0.5% chlorine solution before they are put into the puncture-proof container.) The puncture-proof sharps container should be sealed and either burned, incinerated, or deeply buried when three-fourths full. • Dressings and other soiled solid waste should be collected in plastic bags and, within 2 days, burned and buried in a deep pit. Liquid wastes should be poured down a utility sink drain or a flushable toilet, or poured into a deep pit and buried. • Clean waste containers with detergent and rinse with water. • Remove utility gloves and clean them whenever they are dirty and at least once every day. • Wash hands before and after disposing of soiled equipment and waste.
Wash linens	• Wash linens (for example, bedding, caps, gowns, and surgical drapes) by hand or machine and line-dry or machine-dry. When handling soiled linens, wear gloves, hold linens away from your body, and do not shake them.

Little Risk of HIV Infection in the Clinic

Health care providers may be exposed to HIV through needle sticks, mucous membranes, or broken skin, but the risk of infection is low:

• Needle sticks or cuts cause most infections in health care settings. The average risk of HIV infection after a needle stick exposure to HIV-infected blood is 3 infections per 1,000 needle sticks.

• The risk after exposure of the eye, nose, or mouth to HIV-infected blood is estimated to be about 1 infection per 1,000 exposures.

Following universal precautions is the best way that providers can avoid workplace exposure to HIV and other fluid-borne infections.

Make Infection Prevention a Habit

With each and every client, a health care provider should think, "What infection prevention is needed?" Any client or provider may have an infection without knowing it and without obvious symptoms. Infection prevention is a sign of good health care that can attract clients. For some clients cleanliness is one of the most important signs of quality.

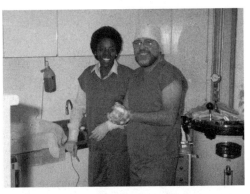

The 4 Steps of Processing Equipment

1. *Decontaminate to kill infectious organisms such as HIV and hepatitis B* and to make instruments, gloves, and other objects safer for people who clean them. Soak in 0.5% chlorine solution for 10 minutes. Rinse with clean cool water or clean immediately.

2. *Clean to remove body fluids, tissue, and dirt.* Wash or scrub with a brush with liquid soap or detergent and water. Avoid bar soap or powdered soap, which can stay on the equipment. Rinse and dry. While cleaning, wear utility gloves and personal protective equipment—goggles, mask, apron, and enclosed shoes.

3. *High-level disinfect or sterilize.*

   - High-level disinfect to kill all infectious organisms except some bacterial endospores (a dormant, resistant form of bacteria) by boiling, by steaming, or with chemicals. High-level disinfect instruments or supplies that touch intact mucous membranes or broken skin, such as vaginal specula, uterine sounds, and gloves for pelvic examinations.

   - Sterilize to kill all infectious organisms, including bacterial endospores, with a high-pressure steam autoclave, a dry-heat oven, chemicals, or radiation. Sterilize instruments such as scalpels and needles that touch tissue beneath the skin. If sterilization is not possible or practical (for example, for laparoscopes), instruments must be high-level disinfected.

4. *Store instruments and supplies to protect them from contamination.* They should be stored in a high-level disinfected or sterilized container in a clean area away from clinic traffic. The equipment used to sterilize and high-level disinfect instruments and supplies also must be guarded against contamination.

24

Family Planning Provision

Managing Contraceptive Supplies

Good-quality reproductive health care requires a continuous supply of contraceptives and other commodities. Family planning providers are the most important link in the contraceptive supply chain that moves commodities from the manufacturer to the client.

Accurate and timely reports and orders from providers help supply chain managers determine what products are needed, how much to buy, and where to distribute them. Clinic staff members do their part when they properly manage contraceptive inventory, accurately record and report what is provided to clients, and promptly order new supplies. In some facilities one staff member is assigned all the logistics duties. In other facilities different staff members may help with logistics as needed. Clinic staff members need to be familiar with, and work within, whatever systems are in place to make certain that they have the supplies they need.

Logistics Responsibilities in the Clinic

Each supply chain operates according to specific procedures that work in a specific setting, but typical contraceptive logistics responsibilities of clinic staff include these common activities:

Daily

- Track the number and types of contraceptives dispensed to clients using the appropriate recording form (typically called a "daily activity register").

- Maintain proper storage conditions for all supplies: clean, dry storage, away from direct sun and protected from extreme heat.

- Provide contraceptives to clients by "First Expiry, First Out" management of the stock of supplies. "First Expiry, First Out," or FEFO, sees to it that products with the earliest labeled expiry dates are the first products issued or dispensed. FEFO clears out older stock first to prevent waste due to expiry.

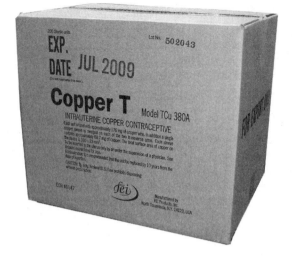

Regularly (monthly or quarterly, depending on the logistics system)

- Count the amount of each method on hand in the clinic and determine the quantity of contraceptives to order (often done with a clinic pharmacist). This is a good time to inspect the supplies, looking for such problems as damaged containers and packages, IUD or implant packaging that has come open, or discoloration of condoms.

- Work with any community-based distribution agents supervised by clinic staff, reviewing their consumption records and helping them complete their order forms. Issue contraceptive supplies to community-based agents based on their orders.

- Report to and make requests of the family planning program coordinator or health supplies officer (typically at the district level), using the appropriate reporting and ordering form or forms. The quantity that is ordered is the amount that will bring the stock up to the level that will meet expected need until the next order is received. (A plan should be made in advance to place emergency orders or borrow supplies from neighboring facilities if there are sudden increases in demand, potential for running out of inventory, or large losses, for example, if a warehouse is flooded.)

- Receive the ordered contraceptive supplies from the clinic pharmacist or other appropriate person in the supply chain. Receipts should be checked against what was ordered.

24

Family Planning Provision

APPENDIX A

Contraceptive Effectiveness

Rates of Unintended Pregnancies per 100 Women

Family planning method	First-Year Pregnancy Rates (Trussell[a])		12-month Pregnancy Rates (Cleland & Ali[b])	Key
	Consistent and correct use	As commonly used	As commonly used	
Implants	0.05	0.05		**0–0.9** Very effective
Vasectomy	0.1	0.15		
Levonorgestrel IUD	0.2	0.2		
Female sterilization	0.5	0.5		**1–9** Effective
Copper-bearing IUD	0.6	0.8	2	
LAM (for 6 months)	0.9[c]	2[c]		
Monthly injectables	0.05	3		**10–25** Moderately effective
Progestin-only injectables	0.3	3	2	
Combined oral contraceptives	0.3	8	7	
Progestin-only oral pills	0.3	8		
Combined patch	0.3	8		**26–32** Less effective
Combined vaginal ring	0.3	8		
Male condoms	2	15	10	
Ovulation method	3			
TwoDay Method	4			
Standard Days Method	5			
Diaphragms with spermicide	6	16		
Female condoms	5	21		
Other fertility awareness methods		25	24	
Withdrawal	4	27	21	
Spermicides	18	29		
Cervical caps	26[d], 9[e]	32[d],16[e]		
No method	85	85	85	

[a] Rates largely from the United States. Source: Trussell J. Contraceptive efficacy. In: Hatcher R et al., editors. Contraceptive technology. 19th revised ed. 2007. Rates for monthly injectables and cervical cap are from Trussell J. Contraceptive failure in the United States. Contraception. 2004;70(2): 89–96.

[b] Rates from developing countries. Source: Cleland J and Ali MM. Reproductive consequences of contraceptive failure in 19 developing countries. Obstetrics and Gynecology. 2004;104(2): 314–320.

[c] Rate for consistent and correct use of LAM is a weighted average from 4 clinical studies cited in Trussell (2007). Rate for LAM as commonly used is from Kennedy KI et al. Consensus statement: Lactational amenorrhea method for family planning. International Journal of Gynecology and Obstetrics. 1996;54(1): 55–57.

[d] Pregnancy rate for women who have given birth

[e] Pregnancy rate for women who have never given birth

Signs and Symptoms of Serious Health Conditions

The table below lists signs and symptoms of some serious health conditions. These conditions are mentioned under Health Risks or Managing Any Problems in the chapters on contraceptive methods. These conditions occur rarely to extremely rarely among users of the method. They also occur rarely among people of reproductive age generally. Still, it is important to recognize possible signs of these conditions and to take action or refer for care if a client reports them. In some cases, clients who develop one of these conditions may need to choose another contraceptive method.

Condition	Description	Signs and Symptoms
Deep vein thrombosis	A blood clot that develops in the deep veins of the body, generally in the legs	Persistent, severe pain in one leg, sometimes with swelling or red skin.
Ectopic pregnancy	Pregnancy in which the fertilized egg implants in tissue outside the uterus, most commonly in a fallopian tube but sometimes in the cervix or abdominal cavity	In the early stages of ectopic pregnancy, symptoms may be absent or mild, but eventually they become severe. A combination of these signs and symptoms should increase suspicion of ectopic pregnancy: • Unusual abdominal pain or tenderness • Abnormal vaginal bleeding or no monthly bleeding—especially if a change from her usual bleeding pattern • Light-headedness or dizziness • Fainting
Heart attack	Occurs when the blood supply to the heart is blocked, usually due to a build-up of cholesterol and other substances in the coronary arteries	Chest discomfort or uncomfortable pressure; fullness, squeezing, or pain in the center of the chest that lasts longer than a few minutes or that comes and goes; spreading pain or numbness in one or both arms, back, jaw, or stomach; shortness of breath; cold sweats; nausea.

Condition	Description	Signs and Symptoms
Liver disorders	Infection with hepatitis inflames the liver; cirrhosis scars tissue, which blocks blood flow through the liver	Yellow eyes or skin (jaundice) and abdominal swelling, tenderness, or pain, especially in the upper abdomen.
Pelvic inflammatory disease (PID)	An infection of the upper genital tract, caused by various types of bacteria	Lower abdominal pain; pain during sex, pelvic examination, or urination; abnormal vaginal bleeding or discharge; fever; cervix bleeds when touched. In a pelvic examination, signs of PID include tenderness in the ovaries or fallopian tubes, yellowish cervical discharge containing mucus and pus, bleeding easily when the cervix is touched with a swab, or a positive swab test, and tenderness or pain when moving the cervix and uterus during pelvic examination.
Pulmonary embolism	A blood clot that travels through the bloodstream to the lungs	Sudden shortness of breath, that may worsen with a deep breath, cough that may bring up blood, fast heart rate, and a light-headed feeling.
Ruptured ectopic pregnancy	When a fallopian tube breaks due to an ectopic pregnancy	Sudden sharp or stabbing pain in lower abdomen, sometimes on one side. Possible right shoulder pain. Usually, within hours the abdomen becomes rigid and the woman goes into shock.
Severe allergic reaction to latex	When a person's body has a strong reaction to contact with latex	Rash over much of the body, dizziness brought on by a sudden drop in blood pressure, difficult breathing, loss of consciousness (anaphylactic shock).
Stroke	When arteries to the brain become blocked or burst, preventing normal blood flow and leading to the death of brain tissue	Numbness or weakness of the face, arm or leg, especially on one side of the body; confusion or trouble speaking or understanding; trouble seeing in one or both eyes; trouble walking, dizziness, loss of balance or coordination; severe headache with no other known cause. Signs and symptoms develop suddenly.
Toxic shock syndrome	A severe reaction throughout the body to toxins released by bacteria	High fever, body rash, vomiting, diarrhea, dizziness, muscle aches. Signs and symptoms develop suddenly.

Medical Conditions That Make Pregnancy Especially Risky

Some common medical conditions make pregnancy riskier to a woman's health. The effectiveness of her contraceptive method thus has special importance. For a comparison of the effectiveness of family planning methods, see Contraceptive Effectiveness, p. 319.

Some methods depend more on their users for effectiveness than do others. Mostly, the methods that require correct use with every act of sex or abstaining during fertile days are the less effective methods, as commonly used:

- Spermicides
- Withdrawal
- Fertility awareness methods
- Cervical caps
- Diaphragms
- Female condoms
- Male condoms

If a woman says that she has any of the common conditions listed below:

- She should be told that pregnancy could be especially risky to her health and in some cases, to the health of her baby.
- During counseling, focus special attention on the effectiveness of methods. Clients who are considering a method that requires correct use with every act of sex should think carefully whether they can use it effectively.

Reproductive Tract Infections and Disorders

- Breast cancer
- Endometrial cancer
- Ovarian cancer
- Some sexually transmitted infections (gonorrhea, chlamydia)
- Some vaginal infections (bacterial vaginosis)

Cardiovascular Disease

- High blood pressure (systolic blood pressure higher than 160 mm Hg or diastolic blood pressure higher than 100 mm Hg)
- Complicated valvular heart disease
- Ischemic heart disease (heart disease due to narrowed arteries)
- Stroke

Other Infections

- HIV/AIDS (see Sexually Transmitted Infections Including HIV, Question 9, p. 287)
- Tuberculosis
- Schistosomiasis with fibrosis of the liver

Endocrine Conditions

- Diabetes if insulin dependent, with damage to arteries, kidneys, eyes, or nervous system (nephropathy, retinopathy, neuropathy), or of more than 20 years' duration

Anemia

- Sickle cell disease

Gastrointestinal Conditions

- Severe (decompensated) cirrhosis of the liver
- Malignant (cancerous) liver tumors (hepatoma)

APPENDIX D

Medical Eligibility Criteria for Contraceptive Use

The table on the following pages summarizes the World Health Organization Medical Eligibility Criteria for using contraceptive methods. These criteria are the basis for the Medical Eligibility Criteria checklists in Chapters 1 through 19.

Categories for Temporary Methods

Category	With Clinical Judgment	With Limited Clinical Judgment
1	Use method in any circumstances	Yes (Use the method)
2	Generally use method	
3	Use of method not usually recommended unless other more appropriate methods are not available or not acceptable	No (Do not use the method)
4	Method not to be used	

Note: In the table beginning on the next page, category 3 and 4 conditions are shaded to indicate that the method should not be provided where clinical judgment is limited.

For vasectomy, male and female condoms, spermicides, diaphragms, cervical caps, and lactational amenorrhea method, see p. 333. For fertility awareness methods, see p. 334.

Categories for Female Sterilization

Accept (A)	There is no medical reason to deny the method to a person with this condition or in this circumstance.
Caution (C)	The method is normally provided in a routine setting, but with extra preparation and precautions.
Delay (D)	Use of the method should be delayed until the condition is evaluated and/or corrected. Alternative, temporary methods of contraception should be provided.
Special (S)	The procedure should be undertaken in a setting with an experienced surgeon and staff, equipment needed to provide general anesthesia, and other backup medical support. The capacity to decide on the most appropriate procedure and anesthesia support also is needed. Alternative, temporary methods of contraception should be provided if referral is required or there is otherwise any delay.

	= Use the method
▨	= Do not use the method
I	= Initiation of the method
C	= Continuation of the method
—	= Condition not listed; does not affect eligibility for method
NA	= Not applicable

Condition

Condition	Combined oral contraceptives	Monthly injectables	Combined patch and combined vaginal ring	Progestin-only pills	Progestin-only injectables	Implants	Emergency contraceptive pills*	Copper-bearing intrauterine device	Levonorgestrel intrauterine device	Female sterilization*
PERSONAL CHARACTERISTICS AND REPRODUCTIVE HISTORY										
Pregnant	NA	NA	NA	NA	NA	NA	NA	4	4	D
Age	Menarche to < 40 years			Menarche to < 18 years				Menarche to < 20 years		Young age
	1	1	1	1	2	1	—	2	2	C
	≥ 40 years			18 to 45 years				≥ 20 years		
	2	2	2	1	1	1	—	1	1	
				> 45						
				1	2	1	—			
Parity										
Nulliparous (has not given birth)	1	1	1	1	1	1	—	2	2	A
Parous (has given birth)	1	1	1	1	1	1	—	1	1	A
Breastfeeding										
< 6 weeks postpartum	4	4	4	3[a]	3[a]	3[a]	1	b	b	*
≥ 6 weeks to < 6 months postpartum (primarily breastfeeding)	3	3	3	1	1	1	1	b	b	A
≥ 6 months postpartum	2	2	2	1	1	1	1	b	b	A
Postpartum (not breastfeeding)										
< 21 days	3	3	3	1	1	1	—	b	b	
With other added VTE risk factors	3/4**	3/4**	3/4**							*
21–42 days	2	2	2	1	1	1	—	b	b	
With other added VTE risk factors	2/3**	2/3**	2/3**							
>42 days	1	1	1	1	1	1	—	1	1	A
Postabortion										
First trimester	1	1	1	1	1	1	—	1	1	
Second trimester	1	1	1	1	1	1	—	2	2	*
Immediate post-septic abortion	1	1	1	1	1	1	—	4	4	

* For additional conditions relating to emergency contraceptive pills and female sterilization, see p. 332. *(Continued)*

**Category depends on the number, severity, and combination of risk factors for venous thromboembolism (VTE).

a In settings where pregnancy morbidity and mortality risks are high and this method is one of few widely available contraceptives, it may be made accessible to breastfeeding women immediately postpartum.

b Postpartum IUD use: For the copper-bearing IUD, insertion at <48 hours is category 1. For the LNG-IUD, insertion at <48 hours is category 3 for breastfeeding women and category 1 for women not breastfeeding. For all women and both IUD types, insertion from 48 hours to <4 weeks is category 3; ≥4 weeks, category 1; and puerperal sepsis, category 4.

D

Medical Eligibility Criteria for Contraceptive Use

	= Use the method = Do not use the method I = Initiation of the method C = Continuation of the method — = Condition not listed; does not affect eligibility for method NA = Not applicable	Combined oral contraceptives	Monthly injectables	Combined patch and combined vaginal ring	Progestin-only pills	Progestin-only injectables	Implants	Emergency contraceptive pills*	Copper-bearing intrauterine device	Levonorgestrel intrauterine device	Female sterilization*
Condition											
Past ectopic pregnancy		1	1	1	2	1	1	1	1	1	A
History of pelvic surgery		1	1	1	1	1	1	—	1	1	C*
Smoking											
Age < 35 years		2	2	2	1	1	1	—	1	1	A
Age ≥ 35 years											
<15 cigarettes/day		3	2	3	1	1	1	—	1	1	A
≥15 cigarettes/day		4	3	4	1	1	1	—	1	1	A
Obesity											
≥ 30 kg/m² body mass index		2	2	2	1	1†	1	—	1	1	C
Blood pressure measurement unavailable		NA^c	NA^c	NA^c	NA^c	NA^c	NA^c	—	NA	NA	NA
CARDIOVASCULAR DISEASE											
Multiple risk factors for arterial cardiovascular disease (older age, smoking, diabetes, and hypertension)		3/4^d	3/4^d	3/4^d	2	3	2	—	1	2	S
Hypertension^e											
History of hypertension, where blood pressure CANNOT be evaluated (including hypertension in pregnancy)		3	3	3	2^c	2^c	2^c	—	1	2	NA
Adequately controlled hypertension, where blood pressure CAN be evaluated		3	3	3	1	2	1	—	1	1	C
Elevated blood pressure (properly measured)											
Systolic 140–159 or diastolic 90–99		3	3	3	1	2	1	—	1	1	C^f
Systolic ≥ 160 or diastolic ≥ 100^g		4	4	4	2	3	2	—	1	2	S^f
Vascular disease		4	4	4	2	3	2	—	1	2	S

† From menarche to age <18 years, ≥30 kg/m² body mass index is category 2 for DMPA, category 1 for NET-EN.

^{c} In settings where pregnancy morbidity and mortality risks are high and this method is one of few widely available contraceptives, women should not be denied access simply because their blood pressure cannot be measured.

^{d} When multiple major risk factors exist, any of which alone would substantially increase the risk of cardiovascular disease, use of the method may increase her risk to an unacceptable level. However, a simple addition of categories for multiple risk factors is not intended. For example, a combination of factors assigned a category 2 may not necessarily warrant a higher category.

^{e} Assuming no other risk factors for cardiovascular disease exist. A single reading of blood pressure is not sufficient to classify a woman as hypertensive.

^{f} Elevated blood pressure should be controlled before the procedure and monitored during the procedure.

Legend:

- ☐ = Use the method
- ▨ (shaded) = Do not use the method
- **I** = Initiation of the method
- **C** = Continuation of the method
- — = Condition not listed; does not affect eligibility for method
- NA = Not applicable

Condition

Condition	Combined oral contraceptives	Monthly injectables	Combined patch and combined vaginal ring	Progestin-only pills	Progestin-only injectables	Implants	Emergency contraceptive pills*	Copper-bearing intrauterine device	Levonorgestrel intrauterine device	Female sterilization*
History of high blood pressure during pregnancy (where current blood pressure is measurable and normal)	2	2	2	1	1	1	—	1	1	A
Deep venous thrombosis (DVT)/Pulmonary embolism (PE)										
History of DVT/PE	4	4	4	2	2	2	*	1	2	A
Acute DVT/PE	4	4	4	3	3	3	*	1	3	D
DVT/PE and on anticoagulant therapy	4	4	4	2	2	2	*	1	2	S
Family history of DVT/PE (first-degree relatives)	2	2	2	1	1	1	*	1	1	A
Major surgery										
With prolonged immobilization	4	4	4	2	2	2	—	1	2	D
Without prolonged immobilization	2	2	2	1	1	1	—	1	1	A
Minor surgery without prolonged immobilization	1	1	1	1	1	1	—	1	1	A
Known thrombogenic mutations (e.g., Factor V Leiden, Prothrombin mutation; Protein S, Protein C, and Antithrombin deficiencies)[g]	4	4	4	2	2	2	*	1	2	A
Superficial venous thrombosis										
Varicose veins	1	1	1	1	1	1	—	1	1	A
Superficial thrombophlebitis	2	2	2	1	1	1	—	1	1	A
Ischemic heart disease[g]				I / C		I / C			I / C	
Current	4	4	4	2 / 3	3	2 / 3	*	1	2 / 3	D
History of	4	4	4	2 / 3	3	2 / 3	*	1	2 / 3	C
Stroke (history of cerebrovascular accident)[g]	4	4	4	2 / 3	3	2 / 3	*	1	2	C
Known hyperlipidemias	2/3[h]	2/3[h]	2/3[h]	2	2	2	—	1	2	A
Valvular heart disease										
Uncomplicated	2	2	2	1	1	1	—	1	1	C[i]
Complicated [‡,g]	4	4	4	1	1	1	—	2[i]	2[i]	S*

‡ Pulmonary hypertension, atrial fibrillation, history of subacute bacterial endocarditis.

g This condition may make pregnancy an unacceptable health risk. Women should be advised that because of relatively higher pregnancy rates, as commonly used, spermicides, withdrawal, fertility awareness methods, cervical caps, diaphragms, or female or male condoms may not be the most appropriate choice.

h Assess according to the type and severity of hyperlipidemia and the presence of other cardiovascular risk factors.

i Prophylactic antibiotics are advised before providing the method.

(Continued)

Medical Eligibility Criteria for Contraceptive Use

D

	Combined oral contraceptives	Monthly injectables	Combined patch and combined vaginal ring	Progestin-only pills	Progestin-only injectables	Implants	Emergency contraceptive pills*	Copper-bearing intrauterine device	Levonorgestrel intrauterine device	Female sterilization*

Legend:
- ☐ = Use the method
- ▨ = Do not use the method
- **I** = Initiation of the method
- **C** = Continuation of the method
- ⊟ = Condition not listed; does not affect eligibility for method
- NA = Not applicable

Condition

Systemic lupus erythematosus

Condition	Combined oral contraceptives	Monthly injectables	Combined patch and combined vaginal ring	Progestin-only pills	Progestin-only injectables (I / C)	Implants	Emergency contraceptive pills*	Copper-bearing IUD (I / C)	Levonorgestrel IUD	Female sterilization*
Positive (or unknown) antiphospholipid antibodies	4	4	4	3	3 / 3	3	—	1 / 1	3	S
Severe thrombocytopenia	2	2	2	2	3 / 2	2	—	3 / 2	2	S
Immunosuppresive treatment	2	2	2	2	2 / 2	2	—	2 / 1	2	S
None of the above	2	2	2	2	2 / 2	2	—	1 / 1	2	C

NEUROLOGICAL CONDITIONS

Headaches[j] — Initiation / Continuation shown for each method where applicable

Condition	Combined oral contraceptives (I / C)	Monthly injectables (I / C)	Combined patch/ring (I / C)	Progestin-only pills (I / C)	Progestin-only injectables (I / C)	Implants (I / C)	Emergency contraceptive pills*	Copper-bearing IUD	Levonorgestrel IUD (I / C)	Female sterilization*
Nonmigrainous (mild or severe)	1 / 2	1 / 2	1 / 2	1 / 1	1 / 1	1 / 1	—	1	1 / 1	A
Migraine							2			
Without aura — Age < 35	2 / 3	2 / 3	2 / 3	1 / 2	2 / 2	2 / 2	—	1	2 / 2	A
Without aura — Age ≥ 35	3 / 4	3 / 4	3 / 4	1 / 2	2 / 2	2 / 2	—	1	2 / 2	A
With aura, at any age	4 / 4	4 / 4	4 / 4	2 / 3	2 / 3	2 / 3	—	1	2 / 3	A
Epilepsy	1[k]	1[k]	1[k]	1[k]	1[k]	1[k]	—	1	1	C

DEPRESSIVE DISORDERS

Condition	Combined oral contraceptives	Monthly injectables	Combined patch/ring	Progestin-only pills	Progestin-only injectables	Implants	Emergency contraceptive pills*	Copper-bearing IUD	Levonorgestrel IUD	Female sterilization*
Depressive disorders	1[l]	1[l]	1[l]	1[l]	1[l]	1[l]	—	1	1[l]	C

REPRODUCTIVE TRACT INFECTIONS AND DISORDERS

Vaginal bleeding patterns

Condition	Combined oral contraceptives	Monthly injectables	Combined patch/ring	Progestin-only pills	Progestin-only injectables	Implants	Emergency contraceptive pills*	Copper-bearing IUD (I / C)	Levonorgestrel IUD (I / C)	Female sterilization*
Irregular pattern without heavy bleeding	1	1	1	2	2	2	—	1	1 / 1	A
Heavy or prolonged bleeding (including regular and irregular patterns)	1	1	1	2	2	2	—	2	1 / 2	A
Unexplained vaginal bleeding (suspicious for serious condition), before evaluation	2	2	2	2	3	3	—	4 / 2	4 / 2	D
Endometriosis	1	1	1	1	1	1	—	2	1	S
Benign ovarian tumors (including cysts)	1	1	1	1	1	1	—	1	1	A
Severe dysmenorrhea	1	1	1	1	1	1	—	2	1	A
Trophoblast disease										
ß-hCG regression	1	1	1	1	1	1	—	3	3	A
ß-hCG elevation[g]	1	1	1	1	1	1	—	4	4	D
Cervical ectropion	1	1	1	1	1	1	—	1	1	A

[j] Category is for women without any other risk factors for stroke.
[k] If taking anticonvulsants, refer to section on drug interactions, p. 332.
[l] Certain medications may interact with the method, making it less effective.

Key	
☐	= Use the method
▧	= Do not use the method
I	= Initiation of the method
C	= Continuation of the method
—	= Condition not listed; does not affect eligibility for method
NA	= Not applicable

Condition

Condition	Combined oral contraceptives	Monthly injectables	Combined patch and combined vaginal ring	Progestin-only pills	Progestin-only injectables	Implants	Emergency contraceptive pills*	Copper-bearing intrauterine device	Levonorgestrel intrauterine device	Female sterilization*
Cervical intraepithelial neoplasia (CIN)	2	2	2	1	2	2	—	1	2	A
Cervical cancer (awaiting treatment)	2	2	2	1	2	2	—	I 4 / C 2	I 4 / C 2	D
Breast disease										
Undiagnosed mass	2	2	2	2	2	2	—	1	2	A
Benign breast disease	1	1	1	1	1	1	—	1	1	A
Family history of cancer	1	1	1	1	1	1	—	1	1	A
Breast cancer										
Current[g]	4	4	4	4	4	4	—	1	4	C
Past, no evidence of disease for at least 5 years	3	3	3	3	3	3	—	1	3	A
Endometrial cancer[g]	1	1	1	1	1	1	—	I 4 / C 2	I 4 / C 2	D
Ovarian cancer[g]	1	1	1	1	1	1	—	3 2	3 2	D
Uterine fibroids										
Without distortion of the uterine cavity	1	1	1	1	1	1	—	1	1	C
With distortion of the uterine cavity	1	1	1	1	1	1	—	4	4	C
Anatomical abnormalities										
Distorted uterine cavity	—	—	—	—	—	—	—	4	4	—
Other abnormalities not distorting the uterine cavity or interfering with IUD insertion (including cervical stenosis or lacerations)	—	—	—	—	—	—	—	2	2	—
Pelvic inflammatory disease (PID)										
Past PID (assuming no current risk factors for STIs)								I C	I C	
With subsequent pregnancy	1	1	1	1	1	1	—	1 1	1 1	A
Without subsequent pregnancy	1	1	1	1	1	1	—	2 2	2 2	C
Current PID	1	1	1	1	1	1	—	4 2[m]	4 2[m]	D
Sexually transmitted infections (STIs)[g]								I C	I C	
Current purulent cervicitis, chlamydia, or gonorrhea	1	1	1	1	1	1	—	4 2	4 2	D
Other STIs (excluding HIV and hepatitis)	1	1	1	1	1	1	—	2 2	2 2	A

[m]Treat PID using appropriate antibiotics. There is usually no need to remove the IUD if the client wishes to continue use.

(Continued)

	= Use the method
▢	= Do not use the method
I	= Initiation of the method
C	= Continuation of the method
—	= Condition not listed; does not affect eligibility for method
NA	= Not applicable

Condition	Combined oral contraceptives	Monthly injectables	Combined patch and combined vaginal ring	Progestin-only pills	Progestin-only injectables	Implants	Emergency contraceptive pills*	Copper-bearing intrauterine device		Levonorgestrel intrauterine device		Female sterilization*
Vaginitis (including trichomonas vaginalis and bacterial vaginosis)	1	1	1	1	1	1	—	2	2	2	2	A
Increased risk of STIs	1	1	1	1	1	1	—	$\frac{2}{3^n}$	2	$\frac{2}{3^n}$	2	A
HIV/AIDS[g]								**I**	**C**	**I**	**C**	
High risk of HIV	1	1	1	1	1	1	—	2	2	2	2	A
HIV-infected	1	1	1	1	1	1	—	2	2	2	2	A
AIDS	1	1	1	1	1	1	—	3	2	3	2	S[o]
Treated with NRTIs	1	1	1	1	1	1	—	$\frac{2}{3^p}$	2	$\frac{2}{3^p}$	2	—
Treated with NNRTIs	2	2	2	2	DMPA 1 NET-EN 2	2	—	$\frac{2}{3^p}$	2	$\frac{2}{3^p}$	2	—
Treated with ritonavir-boosted protease inhibitors	3	3	3	3	DMPA 1 NET-EN 2	2	—	$\frac{2}{3^p}$	2	$\frac{2}{3^p}$	2	—
OTHER INFECTIONS												
Schistosomiasis												
Uncomplicated	1	1	1	1	1	1	—	1		1		A
Fibrosis of liver (if severe, see cirrhosis, next page)[g]	1	1	1	1	1	1	—	1		1		C
Tuberculosis[g]								**I**	**C**	**I**	**C**	
Non-pelvic	1	1	1	1	1	1	—	1	1	1	1	A
Known pelvic	1	1	1	1	1	1	—	4	3	4	3	S
Malaria	1	1	1	1	1	1	—	1		1		A
ENDOCRINE CONDITIONS												
Diabetes												
History of gestational diabetes	1	1	1	1	1	1	—	1		1		A[q]
Non-vascular diabetes												
Non-insulin dependent	2	2	2	2	2	2	—	1		2		C[i,q]
Insulin dependent[g]	2	2	2	2	2	2	—	1		2		C[i,q]

[n] The condition is category 3 if a woman has a very high individual likelihood of exposure to gonorrhea or chlamydia.
[o] Presence of an AIDS-related illness may require a delay in the procedure.
[p] AIDS is category 2 for insertion for those clinically well on antiretroviral therapy; otherwise, category 3 for insertion.
[q] If blood glucose is not well controlled, referral to a higher-level facility is recommended.

□ = Use the method
▒ = Do not use the method
I = Initiation of the method
C = Continuation of the method
— = Condition not listed; does not affect eligibility for method
NA = Not applicable

Condition	Combined oral contraceptives	Monthly injectables	Combined patch and combined vaginal ring	Progestin-only pills	Progestin-only injectables	Implants	Emergency contraceptive pills*	Copper-bearing intrauterine device	Levonorgestrel intrauterine device	Female sterilization*
With kidney, eye, or nerve damage[g]	3/4[r]	3/4[r]	3/4[r]	2	3	2	—	1	2	S
Other vascular disease or diabetes of >20 years' duration[g]	3/4[r]	3/4[r]	3/4[r]	2	3	2	—	1	2	S
Thyroid disorders										
Simple goiter	1	1	1	1	1	1	—	1	1	A
Hyperthyroid	1	1	1	1	1	1	—	1	1	S
Hypothyroid	1	1	1	1	1	1	—	1	1	C
GASTROINTESTINAL CONDITIONS										
Gall bladder disease										
Symptomatic										
Treated by cholecystectomy	2	2	2	2	2	2	—	1	2	A
Medically treated	3	2	3	2	2	2	—	1	2	A
Current	3	2	3	2	2	2	—	1	2	D
Asymptomatic	2	2	2	2	2	2	—	1	2	A
History of cholestasis										
Pregnancy-related	2	2	2	1	1	1	—	1	1	A
Past combined oral contraceptives-related	3	2	3	2	2	2	—	1	2	A
Viral hepatitis	I / C	I / C	I / C							
Acute or flare	I: 3/4[r]; C: 2	I: 3; C: 2	I: 3/4[r,s]; C: 2	1	1	1	2	1	1	D
Carrier	1	1	1	1	1	1	—	1	1	A
Chronic	1	1	1	1	1	1	—	1	1	A
Cirrhosis										
Mild (compensated)	1	1	1	1	1	1	—	1	1	A
Severe (decompensated)[g]	4	3	4	3	3	3	—	1	3	S[t]
Liver tumors										
Focal nodular hyperplasia	2	2	2	2	2	2	—	1	2	A
Hepatocellular adenoma	4	3	4	3	3	3	—	1	3	C[t]
Malignant (hepatoma)[g]	4	3/4	4	3	3	3	—	1	3	C[t]

[r] Assess according to severity of condition.

(Continued)

[s] In women with symptomatic viral hepatitis, withhold these methods until liver function returns to normal or 3 months after she becomes asymptomatic, whichever is earlier.

[t] Liver function should be evaluated.

Legend	Condition	Combined oral contraceptives	Monthly injectables	Combined patch and combined vaginal ring	Progestin-only pills	Progestin-only injectables	Implants	Emergency contraceptive pills*	Copper-bearing intrauterine device	Levonorgestrel intrauterine device	Female sterilization*

☐ = Use the method
▨ = Do not use the method
I = Initiation of the method
C = Continuation of the method
— = Condition not listed; does not affect eligibility for method
NA = Not applicable

Condition	Combined oral contraceptives	Monthly injectables	Combined patch and combined vaginal ring	Progestin-only pills	Progestin-only injectables	Implants	Emergency contraceptive pills*	Copper-bearing intrauterine device	Levonorgestrel intrauterine device	Female sterilization*
ANEMIAS										
Thalassemia	1	1	1	1	1	1	—	2	1	C
Sickle cell disease[g]	2	2	2	1	1	1	—	2	1	C
Iron-deficiency anemia	1	1	1	1	1	1	—	2	1	D/C[u]
DRUG INTERACTIONS (for antiretroviral drugs, see HIV/AIDS)										
Anticonvulsant therapy										
Certain anticonvulsants (phenytoin, carbamazepine, barbiturates, primidone, topiramate, oxcarbazepine)	3[I]	2	3[I]	3[I]	DMPA 1 NET-EN 2	2[I]	—	1	1	—
Lamotrigine	3[§]	3[§]	3[§]	1	1	1	—	1	1	—
Antimicrobial therapy										
Broad-spectrum antibiotics	1	1	1	1	1	1	—	1	1	—
Antifungals and antiparasitics	1	1	1	1	1	1	—	1	1	—
Rifampicin or rifabutin therapy	3[I]	2	3[I]	3[I]	DMPA 1 NET-EN 2	2	—	1	1	—

§ Combined hormonal contraceptives may reduce the effectiveness of lamotrigine.
u For hemoglobin < 7 g/dl, delay. For hemoglobin ≥ 7 to < 10 g/dl, caution.

*Additional conditions relating to emergency contraceptive pills:

Category 1: Repeated use; rape.

Category 2: History of severe cardiovascular complications (ischemic heart disease, cerebrovascular attack, or other thromboembolic conditions, and angina pectoralis).

*Additional conditions relating to female sterilization:

Caution: Diaphragmatic hernia; kidney disease; severe nutritional deficiencies; previous abdominal or pelvic surgery; concurrent with elective surgery.

Delay: Abdominal skin infection; acute respiratory disease (bronchitis, pneumonia); systemic infection or gastroenteritis; emergency surgery (without previous counseling); surgery for an infectious condition; certain postpartum conditions (7 to 41 days after childbirth); severe pre-eclampsia/eclampsia; prolonged rupture of membranes (24 hours or more); fever during or immediately after delivery; sepsis after delivery; severe hemorrhage; severe trauma to the genital tract; cervical or vaginal tear at time of delivery); certain postabortion conditions (sepsis, fever, or severe hemorrhage; severe trauma to the genital tract; cervical or vaginal tear at time of abortion; acute hematometra); subacute bacterial endocarditis; unmanaged atrial fibrillation.

Special arrangements: Coagulation disorders; chronic asthma, bronchitis, emphysema, or lung infection; fixed uterus due to previous surgery or infection; abdominal wall or umbilical hernia; postpartum uterine rupture or perforation; postabortion uterine perforation.

Conditions relating to vasectomy:

No special considerations: High risk of HIV, HIV-infected, sickle cell disease.

Caution: Young age; depressive disorders; diabetes; previous scrotal injury; large varicocele or hydrocele; cryptorchidism (may require referral); lupus with positive (or unknown) antiphospholipid antibodies; lupus and on immunosuppressive treatment.

Delay: Active STIs (excluding HIV and hepatitis); scrotal skin infection; balanitis; epididymitis or orchitis; systemic infection or gastroenteritis; filariasis; elephantiasis; intrascrotal mass.

Special arrangements: AIDS (AIDS-related illness may require delay); coagulation disorders; inguinal hernia; lupus with severe thrombocytopenia.

Conditions relating to male and female condoms, spermicides, diaphragms, cervical caps, and the lactational amenorrhea method:

All other conditions listed on the previous pages that do not appear here are a category 1 or NA for male and female condoms, spermicides, diaphragms, and cervical caps and not listed in the Medical Eligibility Criteria for the Lactational Amenorrhea Method.

	= Use the method
▨	= Do not use the method
—	= Condition not listed; does not affect eligibility for method

NA = Not applicable

Condition	Male and female condoms	Spermicides	Diaphragms	Cervical caps	Lactational amenorrhea method[‡‡]
REPRODUCTIVE HISTORY					
Parity					
Nulliparous (has not given birth)	1	1	1	1	—
Parous (has given birth)	1	1	2	2	—
< 6 weeks postpartum	1	1	NA[v]	NA[v]	—
CARDIOVASCULAR DISEASE					
Complicated valvular heart disease (pulmonary hypertension, risk of atrial fibrillation, history of subacute bacterial endocarditis)[g]	1	1	2	2	—
REPRODUCTIVE TRACT INFECTIONS AND DISORDERS					
Cervical intraepithelial neoplasia	1	1	1	4	—
Cervical cancer	1	2	1	4	—
Anatomical abnormalities	1	1	NA[w]	NA[x]	—
HIV/AIDS[g]					
High risk of HIV	1	4	4	4	—
HIV-infected	1	3	3	3	C[y]
AIDS	1	3	3	3	C[y]

[v] Wait to fit/use until uterine involution is complete.

[w] Diaphragm cannot be used in certain cases of uterine prolapse.

[x] Cap use is not appropriate for a client with severely distorted cervical anatomy.

[y] Caution: women with HIV or AIDS should receive appropriate ARV therapy and exclusively breastfeed for the first 6 months of a baby's life, introduce appropriate complementary foods at 6 months, and continue breastfeeding through 12 months.

(Continued)

Medical Eligibility Criteria for Contraceptive Use

D

Condition	Male and female condoms	Spermicides	Diaphragms	Cervical caps	Lactational amenorrhea method#
<div>☐ = Use the method</div><div>▨ = Do not use the method</div><div>— = Condition not listed; does not affect eligibility for method</div>					
OTHERS					
History of toxic shock syndrome	1	1	3	3	—
Urinary tract infection	1	1	2	2	—
Allergy to latex[z]	3	1	3	3	—

[z] Does not apply to plastic condoms, diaphragms, and cervical caps.

#Additional conditions relating to lactational amenorrhea method:

Medication used during breastfeeding: To protect infant health, breastfeeding is not recommended for women using such drugs as anti-metabolites, bromocriptine, certain anticoagulants, corticosteroids (high doses), cyclosporine, ergotamine, lithium, mood-altering drugs, radioactive drugs, and reserpine.

Conditions affecting the newborn that may make breastfeeding difficult: Congenital deformities of the mouth, jaw, or palate; newborns who are small-for-date or premature and needing intensive neonatal care; and certain metabolic disorders.

Conditions relating to fertility awareness methods:

Condition A = Accept C = Caution D = Delay	Symptoms-based methods	Calendar-based methods
Age: post menarche or perimenopause	C	C
Breastfeeding < 6 weeks postpartum	D	D[aa]
Breastfeeding ≥ 6 weeks postpartum	C[bb]	D[bb]
Postpartum, not breastfeeding	D[cc]	D[aa]
Postabortion	C	D[dd]
Irregular vaginal bleeding	D	D
Vaginal discharge	D	A
Taking drugs that affect cycle regularity, hormones, and/or fertility signs	D/C[ee]	D/C[ee]
Diseases that elevate body temperature		
Acute	D	A
Chronic	C	A

[aa] Delay until she has had 3 regular menstrual cycles.
[bb] Use caution after monthly bleeding or normal secretions return (usually at least 6 weeks after childbirth).
[cc] Delay until monthly bleeding or normal secretions return (usually < 4 weeks postpartum).
[dd] Delay until she has had one regular menstrual cycle.
[ee] Delay until the drug's effect has been determined, then use caution.

Glossary

abscess A pocket of **pus** surrounded by inflammation, caused by a bacterial infection and marked by persistent pain.

acquired immune deficiency syndrome (AIDS) The condition, due to infection with **human immunodeficiency virus** (HIV), when the body's immune system breaks down and is unable to fight certain infections.

AIDS See **acquired immune deficiency syndrome**.

amenorrhea See **vaginal bleeding**.

anaphylactic shock See Severe allergic reaction to latex, Appendix B, p. 321.

anemia A condition in which the body lacks adequate **hemoglobin**, commonly due to iron deficiency or excessive blood loss. As a result, tissues do not receive adequate oxygen.

antiretroviral (ARV) therapy A group of drugs used to treat people with **acquired immune deficiency syndrome (AIDS)**. There are several ARV classes, which work against HIV in different ways. Patients may take a combination of several drugs at once.

atrial fibrillation A heart rhythm disorder in which the upper heart chambers contract in an abnormal or disorganized manner.

aura See **migraine aura**.

backup method A contraceptive method used when mistakes are made with using an ongoing method of contraception, or to help ensure that a woman does not become pregnant when she first starts to use a contraceptive method. Include abstinence, male or female condoms, spermicides, and withdrawal.

bacterial endocarditis Infection that occurs when bacteria from the bloodstream colonize damaged heart tissue or valves.

bacterial vaginosis A common condition caused by overgrowth of bacteria normally found in the **vagina**. Not a sexually transmitted infection.

balanitis Inflammation of the tip of the **penis**.

benign breast disease Growth of abnormal but noncancerous breast tissue.

benign ovarian tumor Noncancerous growth that develops on or in the ovary.

blood pressure The force of the blood against the walls of blood vessels. Generally, normal systolic (pumping) blood pressure is less than 140 mm Hg, and normal diastolic (resting) blood pressure is less than 90 mm Hg (see **hypertension**).

bone density A measure of how dense and strong a bone is. When old bone breaks down faster than new bone tissue is formed, bones become less dense, increasing risk of fractures.

breakthrough bleeding See **vaginal bleeding**.

breast cancer Malignant (cancerous) growth that develops in breast tissue.

breastfeeding Feeding an infant with milk produced by the breasts (see also Lactational Amenorrhea Method, p. 257). Breastfeeding patterns include:

exclusive breastfeeding Giving the infant only breast milk with no supplementation of any type—not even water—except for perhaps vitamins, minerals, or medication.

fully breastfeeding Giving the infant breast milk almost exclusively but also water, juice, vitamins, or other nutrients infrequently.

nearly fully breastfeeding Giving the infant some liquid or food in addition to breast milk, but more than three-fourths of feedings are breastfeeds.

partially breastfeeding Any breastfeeding less than nearly fully breastfeeding, giving the infant more supplementation with other liquids or food. Less than three-fourths of feedings are breastfeeds.

G

Glossary

candidiasis A common vaginal infection caused by a yeast-like fungus. Also known as yeast infection or thrush. Not a sexually transmitted infection.

cardiovascular disease Any disease of the heart, blood vessels, or blood circulation.

cerebrovascular disease Any disease of the blood vessels of the brain.

cervical cancer Malignant (cancerous) growth that occurs in the **cervix**, usually due to persistent infection with certain types of **human papillomavirus**.

cervical ectropion A nonserious condition in which the mucus-producing cells found in the cervical canal begin to grow on the area around the opening of the **cervix**.

cervical intraepithelial neoplasia (CIN) Abnormal, precancerous cells in the cervix. Mild forms may go away on their own, but more severe abnormalities may progress to **cervical cancer** if not treated. Also called cervical dysplasia or precancer.

cervical laceration See **laceration**.

cervical mucus A thick fluid plugging the opening of the **cervix**. Most of the time it is thick enough to prevent **sperm** from entering the **uterus**. At the midpoint of the **menstrual cycle**, however, the mucus becomes thin and watery, and sperm can more easily pass through.

cervical stenosis When the cervical opening is narrower than normal.

cervicitis See **purulent cervicitis**.

cervix The lower portion of the **uterus** extending into the upper **vagina** (see Female Anatomy, p. 364).

chancroid A **sexually transmitted infection** caused by a bacterium, which causes an ulcer to grow on the genitals.

chlamydia A **sexually transmitted infection** caused by a bacterium. If left untreated, it can cause infertility.

cholecystectomy Surgical removal of the gallbladder.

cholestasis Reduced flow of bile secreted by the liver.

cirrhosis (of the liver) See Liver disorders, Appendix B, p. 321.

cryptorchidism Failure of one or both **testes** to descend into the **scrotum** after birth.

decontaminate (medical equipment) To remove infectious organisms in order to make instruments, gloves, and other objects safer for people who clean them.

deep vein thrombosis See Deep vein thrombosis, Appendix B, p. 320.

depression A mental condition typically marked by dejection, despair, lack of hope, and sometimes either extreme tiredness or agitation.

diabetes (diabetes mellitus) A chronic disorder that occurs when blood glucose levels become too high because the body does not produce enough insulin or cannot use the insulin properly.

disinfection See **high-level disinfection**.

dual protection Avoiding both pregnancy and **sexually transmitted infection**.

dysmenorrhea Pain during **vaginal bleeding**, commonly known as menstrual cramps.

eclampsia A condition of late pregnancy, labor, and the period immediately after delivery characterized by convulsions. In serious cases, sometimes followed by coma and death.

ectopic pregnancy See Ectopic pregnancy, Appendix B, p. 320.

ejaculation The release of **semen** from the **penis** at orgasm.

elephantiasis A chronic and often extreme swelling and hardening of skin and tissue just beneath the skin, especially of the legs and **scrotum**, due to an obstruction in the lymphatic system (see **filariasis**).

embryo The product of fertilization of an egg (**ovum**) by a **sperm** during the first 8 weeks of development.

endometrial cancer Malignant (cancerous) growth in the lining of the **uterus**.

endometriosis A condition in which tissue of the **endometrium** grows outside the **uterus**. Tissue may attach itself to the reproductive organs or to other organs in the abdominal cavity. Can cause pelvic pain and impair fertility.

endometrium The membrane that lines the inner surface of the **uterus**. It thickens and is then shed once a month, causing **monthly bleeding**. During pregnancy, this lining is not shed but instead changes and produces hormones, helping to support the pregnancy (see Female Anatomy, p. 364).

engorgement (breast engorgement) A condition during breastfeeding that occurs when more milk accumulates in the breasts than the infant consumes. May make breasts feel full, hard, tender, and warm. Can be prevented (or relieved) by breastfeeding often and on demand.

epididymis A coiled tube (duct) attached to and lying on the **testes**. Developing **sperm** reach maturity and develop their swimming capabilities within this duct. The matured sperm leave the epididymis through the **vas deferens** (see Male Anatomy, p. 367).

epididymitis Inflammation of the **epididymis**.

epilepsy A chronic disorder caused by disturbed brain function. May involve convulsions.

estrogen Hormone responsible for female sexual development. Natural estrogens, especially the **hormone** estradiol, are secreted by a mature ovarian **follicle**, which surrounds the egg (**ovum**). Also, a group of synthetic drugs that have effects similar to those of natural estrogen; some are used in some hormonal contraceptives.

expulsion When a contraceptive implant or intrauterine device fully or partially comes out of place.

fallopian tube Either of a pair of slender ducts that connect the **uterus** to the region of each **ovary**. **Fertilization** of an egg (**ovum**) by **sperm** usually takes place in one of the fallopian tubes (see Female Anatomy, p. 364).

fertilization Union of an **ovum** with a **sperm**.

fetus The product of **fertilization** from the end of the 8th week of pregnancy until birth (see **embryo**).

fibroid See **uterine fibroid.**

fibrosis The excess formation of fibrous tissue, as in reaction to organ damage.

filariasis A chronic parasitic disease caused by filarial worms. May lead to inflammation and permanent clogging of channels in the lymphatic system and **elephantiasis**.

fixed uterus A **uterus** that cannot be moved out of place, often as a result of **endometriosis**, past surgery, or infection.

follicle A small round structure in the **ovary,** each of which contains an egg (**ovum**). During **ovulation** a follicle on the surface of the ovary opens and releases a mature egg.

foreskin Hood of skin covering the end of the **penis** (see Male Anatomy, p. 367).

fully breastfeeding See **breastfeeding**.

gallbladder diseases Conditions that affect the gallbladder, a sac located under the liver that stores bile used in fat digestion. May include inflammation, infection, or obstruction, gallbladder cancer, or gall stones (when the components of bile solidify within the organ).

gastroenteritis Inflammation of the stomach and intestine.

genital herpes A disease caused by a virus, spread by sexual contact.

genital warts Growths on the **vulva**, the vaginal wall, and the **cervix** in women, and on the **penis** in men. Caused by certain types of **human papillomavirus**.

gestational trophoblast disease Disease during pregnancy involving abnormal cell growth of the trophoblast, the outermost layer of cells of the developing **embryo**, which develops into the **placenta**.

goiter A noncancerous enlargement of the thyroid.

gonorrhea A **sexually transmitted infection** caused by a bacterium. If not treated, can cause **infertility**.

heart attack See Heart attack, Appendix B, p. 320. See also **ischemic heart disease**.

heavy bleeding See **vaginal bleeding**.

hematocrit The percentage of whole blood that is made up of red blood cells. Used as a measurement of **anemia**.

hematoma A bruise or area of skin discoloration caused by broken blood vessels beneath the skin.

hematometra An accumulation of blood in the **uterus**, which may occur following spontaneous or induced abortion.

hemoglobin The iron-containing material in red blood cells that carries oxygen from the lungs to the tissues of the body.

hepatitis See Liver disorders, Appendix B, p. 321.

hernia The projection of an organ, part of an organ, or any bodily structure through the wall that normally contains it.

herpes See **genital herpes**.

high-level disinfection (medical instruments) To destroy all living microorganisms except some forms of bacteria. Compare with **sterilize**.

HIV See **human immunodeficiency virus**.

hormone A chemical substance formed in one organ or part of the body and carried in the blood to another organ or part, where it works through chemical action. Also, manufactured chemical substances that function as hormones.

human immunodeficiency virus (HIV) The virus that causes **acquired immune deficiency syndrome** (AIDS).

human papillomavirus (HPV) A common, highly contagious virus spread by sexual activity and skin-to-skin contact in the genital area. Certain subtypes of HPV are responsible for most cases of **cervical cancer**; others cause **genital warts**.

hydrocele The collection of fluid in a body cavity, especially in the **testes** or along the **spermatic cord** (see Male Anatomy, p. 367).

hyperlipidemia High level of fats in the blood that increases the risk of heart disease.

hypertension Higher **blood pressure** than normal; 140 mm Hg or higher (systolic) or 90 mm Hg or higher (diastolic).

hyperthyroidism Too much production of thyroid **hormones**.

hypothyroidism Not enough production of thyroid **hormones**.

implantation The embedding of the **embryo** into the **endometrium** of the **uterus** where it establishes contact with the woman's blood supply for nourishment.

infertility The inability of a couple to produce living children.

informed choice A freely made decision based on clear, accurate, and relevant information. A goal of family planning counseling.

infrequent bleeding See **vaginal bleeding**.

inguinal hernia A **hernia** in the groin.

intercourse See **sex**.

irregular bleeding See **vaginal bleeding**.

ischemic heart disease, ischemia Ischemia is reduced blood flow to tissues of the body. When this reduced flow is in the arteries of the heart, it is called ischemic heart disease.

jaundice Abnormal yellowing of the skin and eyes. Usually a symptom of **liver disease**.

labia The inner and outer lips of the **vagina**, which protect the internal female organs (see Female Anatomy, p. 365).

laceration A wound or irregular tear of the flesh anywhere on the body, including the **cervix** and **vagina**.

laparoscope A device consisting of a tube with lenses for viewing the inside of an organ or body cavity. Used in diagnosis and in some female sterilization procedures.

laparoscopy A procedure performed with a laparoscope.

latex allergy When a person's body has a reaction to contact with latex, including persistent or recurring severe redness, itching, or swelling. In extreme cases, may lead to anaphylactic shock (see Severe allergic reaction to latex, Appendix B, p. 321).

lesion A disturbed or diseased area of skin or other body tissue.

liver disease Includes tumors, **hepatitis**, and **cirrhosis**.

mastitis An inflammation of breast tissue due to infection that may cause fever, redness, and pain.

menarche The beginning of cycles of **monthly bleeding**. Occurs during puberty after girls start producing **estrogen** and **progesterone**.

menopause The time in a woman's life when monthly bleeding stops permanently. Occurs when a woman's **ovaries** stop producing eggs (ova). A woman is considered menopausal after she has had no bleeding for 12 months.

menorrhagia See **vaginal bleeding**.

menses, menstrual period, menstruation See **monthly bleeding**.

menstrual cycle A repeating series of changes in the **ovaries** and **endometrium** that includes **ovulation** and **monthly bleeding.** Most women have cycles that each last between 24 and 35 days (see The Menstrual Cycle, p. 366).

migraine aura A nervous system disturbance that affects sight and sometimes touch and speech (see Identifying Migraine Headaches and Auras, p. 368).

migraine headache A type of severe, recurrent headache (see Identifying Migraine Headaches and Auras, p. 368).

minilaparotomy A female sterilization technique performed by bringing the **fallopian tubes** to a small incision in the abdomen and then usually tying and cutting them.

miscarriage Natural loss of pregnancy during the first 20 weeks.

monthly bleeding Monthly flow of bloody fluid from the **uterus** through the **vagina** in adult women, which takes place between **menarche** and **menopause**. Also, the monthly vaginal flow of bloody fluid that women have while using combined hormonal contraceptives (a withdrawal bleed).

mucous membrane Membrane lining passages and cavities of the body that come in contact with air.

nearly fully breastfeeding See **breastfeeding**.

nephropathy Kidney disease, including damage to the small blood vessels in the kidneys from long-standing diabetes.

neuropathy Nervous system or nerve disease, including nerve degeneration due to damage to the small blood vessels in the nervous system from long-standing diabetes.

nonsteroidal anti-inflammatory drug (NSAID) A class of drugs used to reduce pain, fever, and swelling.

orchitis Inflammation of a **testis** (see Male Anatomy, p. 367).

ovarian cyst Fluid-filled sac that develops in the **ovary** or on its surface. Usually disappears on its own but may rupture and cause pain and complications.

ovaries A pair of female sex glands that store and release ova (see **ovum**) and produce the sex **hormones estrogen** and **progesterone** (see Female Anatomy, p. 364).

ovulation The release of an **ovum** from an **ovary**.

ovum Reproductive egg cell produced by the **ovaries**.

partially breastfeeding See **breastfeeding**.

pelvic inflammatory disease See Pelvic inflammatory disease, Appendix B, p. 321.

pelvic tuberculosis Infection of the pelvic organs by **tuberculosis** bacteria from the lungs.

pelvis The skeletal structure located in the lower part of the human torso, resting on the legs and supporting the spine. In females, also refers to the hollow portion of the pelvic bone structure through which the **fetus** passes during birth.

penis The male organ for urination and sexual intercourse (see Male Anatomy, p. 367).

perforation A hole in the wall of an organ or the process of making the hole, as with a medical instrument.

placenta The organ that nourishes a growing **fetus**. The placenta (afterbirth) is formed during pregnancy and comes out of the **uterus** within a few minutes after the birth of a baby.

postpartum After childbirth; the first 6 weeks after childbirth.

pre-eclampsia **Hypertension** with either excess protein in the urine, or local or generalized swelling, or both (but without convulsions) after 20 weeks of pregnancy. May progress to **eclampsia**.

premature birth A birth that occurs before 37 weeks of pregnancy.

preventive measures Actions taken to prevent disease, such as washing hands or providing drugs or other therapy.

progesterone A steroid **hormone** that is produced by the **ovary** after **ovulation**. Prepares the **endometrium** for **implantation** of a fertilized egg (**ovum**), protects the **embryo,** enhances development of the **placenta**, and helps prepare the breasts for **breastfeeding**.

progestin (progestogen) Any of a large group of synthetic drugs that have effects similar to those of **progesterone.** Some are used in hormonal contraceptives.

prolonged bleeding See **vaginal bleeding**.

prolonged rupture of membranes Occurs when the fluid-filled sac surrounding a pregnant woman's fetus breaks 24 hours or more before delivery of the infant.

prophylaxis See **preventive measures**.

prostate Male reproductive organ where some of the **semen** is produced (see Male Anatomy, p. 367).

puerperal sepsis Infection of the reproductive organs during the first 42 days **postpartum** (puerperium).

pulmonary embolism See Pulmonary embolism, Appendix B, p. 321.

pulmonary hypertension Continuous **hypertension** in the pulmonary artery, impeding blood flow from the heart to the lungs.

purulent cervicitis Inflammation of the **cervix** accompanied by a **pus**-like discharge. Often indicates infection with gonorrhea or chlamydia.

pus A yellowish-white fluid formed in infected tissue.

retinopathy Disease of the retina (nerve tissue lining the back of the eye), including damage to the small blood vessels to the retina from long-standing diabetes.

ruptured ectopic pregnancy See Ruptured ectopic pregnancy, Appendix B, p. 321.

schistosomiasis A parasitic disease caused by a flatworm living in a snail host. People become infected while wading or bathing in water containing larvae of the infected snails.

scrotum The pouch of skin behind the **penis** that contains the **testes** (see Male Anatomy, p. 367).

semen The thick, white fluid produced by a man's reproductive organs and released through the **penis** during **ejaculation**. Contains **sperm** unless the man has had a vasectomy.

seminal vesicles Male organs where **sperm** mixes with **semen** (see Male Anatomy, p. 367).

sepsis The presence of various **pus**-forming and disease-causing organisms, or poisonous substances that they produce, in the blood or body tissues.

septic abortion Induced or **spontaneous abortion** involving infection.

sex, sexual intercourse Sexual activity in which the penis is inserted into a body cavity.

   anal Sex involving the anus.

   oral Sex involving the mouth.

   vaginal Sex involving the vagina.

sexually transmitted infection (STI) Any of a group of bacterial, fungal, and viral infections and parasites that are transmitted during sexual activity.

sickle cell anemia, sickle cell disease Hereditary, chronic form of **anemia**. Blood cells take on an abnormal sickle or crescent shape when deprived of oxygen.

speculum A medical tool used to widen a body opening to better see inside. A speculum is inserted into the vagina to help see the cervix.

sperm The male sex cell. Sperm are produced in the **testes** of an adult male, mixed with **semen** in the **seminal vesicles**, and released during **ejaculation** (see Male Anatomy, p. 367).

spermatic cord A cord consisting of the **vas deferens,** arteries, veins, nerves, and lymphatic vessels that passes from the groin down to the back of each **testis** (see Male Anatomy, p. 367).

spontaneous abortion See **miscarriage**.

spotting See **vaginal bleeding**.

sterilize (medical equipment) To destroy all microorganisms, including spores that are not killed by **high-level disinfection**.

stroke See Stroke, Appendix B, p. 321.

superficial thrombophlebitis Inflammation of a vein just beneath the skin due to a blood clot.

syphilis A **sexually transmitted infection** caused by a bacterium. If untreated, may progress to systemic infection, causing general paralysis and dementia or be transmitted to the fetus during pregnancy or childbirth.

tampon A plug of cotton or other absorbent material used to absorb fluids, such as a plug inserted in the vagina to absorb bloody flow during **monthly bleeding**.

testes, testicles The 2 male reproductive organs that produce **sperm** and the **hormone** testosterone. Located in the **scrotum**. (Testis if referring to one of the testes; see Male Anatomy, p. 367).

thalassemia An inherited type of **anemia**.

thromboembolic disorder (or disease) Abnormal clotting of blood in the blood vessels.

thrombogenic mutations Any of several genetic disorders that causes abnormal thickening or clotting of the blood.

thrombophlebitis Inflammation of a vein due to the presence of a blood clot (see **thrombosis**).

thrombosis Formation of a blood clot inside a blood vessel.

thrush See **candidiasis**.

thyroid disease Any disease of the thyroid (see **hyperthyroid, hypothyroid**).

toxic shock syndrome See Toxic shock syndrome, Appendix B, p. 321.

trichomoniasis A **sexually transmitted infection** caused by a protozoan.

G

Glossary

trophoblast disease See **gestational trophoblastic disease**.

tuberculosis A contagious disease caused by a bacterium. Most commonly infects the respiratory system; also infects the organs in a woman's **pelvis**, and then known as **pelvic tuberculosis**.

urethra Tube through which urine is released from the body (see Female Anatomy, p. 365 and Male Anatomy, p. 367). In men, **semen** also passes through the urethra.

uterine fibroid Noncancerous tumor that grows in the muscle of the **uterus**.

uterine perforation Puncturing of the wall of the **uterus**, which may occur during an induced abortion or with insertion of an intrauterine device.

uterine rupture A tear of the **uterus**, typically during labor or late pregnancy.

uterus The hollow, muscular organ that carries the **fetus** during pregnancy. Also called the womb (see Female Anatomy, p. 364).

vagina The passage joining the outer sexual organs with the **uterus** in females (see Female Anatomy, p. 364).

vaginal bleeding Any bloody vaginal discharge (pink, red, or brown) that requires the use of sanitary protection (pads, cloths, or tampons). Different vaginal bleeding patterns include:

  amenorrhea No bleeding at all at expected bleeding times.

  breakthrough bleeding Any bleeding outside of expected bleeding times (i.e., outside of regular monthly bleeding) that requires use of sanitary protection.

  heavy bleeding (menorrhagia) Bleeding that is twice as heavy as a woman's usual bleeding.

  infrequent bleeding Fewer than 2 bleeding episodes over 3 months.

  irregular bleeding Spotting and/or breakthrough bleeding that occurs outside of expected bleeding times (i.e., outside of regular monthly bleeding).

  menstrual bleeding, monthly bleeding. Bleeding that takes place, on average, for 3-7 days about every 28 days.

  prolonged bleeding Bleeding that lasts longer than 8 days.

  spotting Any bloody vaginal discharge outside of expected bleeding times that requires no sanitary protection.

vaginal mucus The fluid secreted by glands in the **vagina**.

vaginitis Inflammation of the **vagina**. May be due to infection by bacteria, viruses, or fungi, or to chemical irritation. Not a sexually transmitted infection.

valvular heart disease Health problems due to improperly functioning heart valves.

varicose veins Enlarged, twisted veins, most commonly seen in veins just beneath the skin of the legs.

vas deferens (vas, vasa) 2 muscular tubes that transport **sperm** from the **testes** to the **seminal vesicles**. These tubes are cut or blocked during a vasectomy (see Male Anatomy, p. 367).

vascular disease Any disease of the blood vessels.

vulva The exterior female genitals.

warts See **genital warts**.

withdrawal bleed See **monthly bleeding**.

womb See **uterus**.

yeast infection See **candidiasis**.

Index

A

abdominal bloating and discomfort...61, 75, 177

abdominal pain...50, 137, 139, 146, 200, 279, 291, 301, 320–321

    as side effect...27, 47, 102, 111, 119

    management of...40, 44, 125, 130, 151, 152, 177, 179

abdominal surgery...171

abnormal vaginal bleeding...See unexplained vaginal bleeding

abscess...126, 171, 178, 194

abstinence...252, 254, 287, 290...See also periodic abstinence

acetaminophen...See paracetamol

acne

    as side effect...2, 111, 158, 164

    management of...3, 19, 125

adolescence, adolescent...154, 242, 246, 267–271, 276

allergic reaction...See latex allergy

amenorrhea...See no monthly bleeding

anal sex...205, 209, 277, 284

anaphylactic shock...207, 321

anatomical abnormalities...137, 304, 329, 333

anemia...See iron-deficiency anemia, sickle cell anemia, thalassemia

anesthesia, anesthetic...176, 180, 181, 195

    general...166, 169, 187, 324

    local...120–121, 166, 175–176, 191

anti-anxiety therapies...242, 246

anti-nausea medications...51

antibiotics...139, 156, 242, 247, 280, 328

    and contraceptive effectiveness...242, 247, 332

    before IUD insertion...139, 156

    for abscess, infection...126, 178, 194

    for pelvic inflammatory disease...151, 156, 329

anticoagulants...259, 334

anticonvulsants...20, 41, 127, 328, 332

antidepressants...242, 246

antiretroviral therapy...209, 282–283, 287, 294

    not limiting method use...9, 30, 55, 67, 88, 115, 136, 138, 171, 188, 283, 330, 332

antiseptic...126, 142, 144, 147, 178, 194, 313

artery damage due to diabetes...77, 97

ARVs...See antiretroviral therapy

aspirin...242, 247

    as treatment...18, 19, 39, 40, 76, 96, 125, 126, 194

    to be avoided...143, 150, 177, 192

aura...See migraine auras, migraine headaches

B

bacteria...205, 277, 312, 315, 321

bacterial infection...151

bacterial vaginosis...226, 234, 279–280, 322, 330...See also vaginal conditions

balanitis...188, 333

barbiturates...8, 9, 20, 29, 30, 41, 114, 115, 127, 332

basal body temperature...239–240, 249

benign breast disease...329

birth defects...3, 22, 42, 47, 54, 80, 83, 98, 129, 133, 223, 235

birth spacing...82, 289–291

birth weight...295

bleeding...See vaginal bleeding

blocked or narrowed arteries...41, 77, 128, 323

    as medical eligibility criterion...7, 66, 67, 86, 170, 327, 332

blood clot...3, 20, 23, 41, 77, 97, 100, 128, 194, 320, 321...See also deep vein thrombosis

    as medical eligibility criterion...7, 29, 30, 66, 67, 86, 114, 115, 160, 161, 170

Index

E

eclampsia...169, 332

econazole...207

ectopic pregnancy...28, 55, 113, 134, 152, 320, 321, 325

    diagnosis and care...40, 126–127, 152, 179

    reducing risk of...27, 44, 112, 129, 133, 156, 167, 182

effectiveness, contraceptive... See contraceptive effectiveness

ejaculation...203, 212, 238, 255–256, 363, 367

electrocoagulation...176

elephantiasis...188, 333

eligibility criteria...See medical eligibility criteria for each contraceptive method

emergency contraception...52, 142, 362...See also emergency contraceptive pills

emergency contraceptive pills...45–58, 73, 74, 94, 95, 204, 206, 209, 216, 217, 225, 231, 256, 269, 272, 302

    contraceptive effectiveness...46

    medical eligibility criteria...48

    using oral contraceptive pills as...54, 56–58

emphysema...171, 332

endometrial cancer...3, 4, 62, 79, 132, 322, 329, 362

endometriosis...3, 62, 159, 169, 328

endometrium...157, 364, 366

epididymis...188, 304

epididymitis...188, 333

epilepsy...170, 328

erection...185, 206, 210, 361, 363

ergotamine...259, 334

estrogen...15, 364...See also ethinyl estradiol

    in combined hormonal contraceptives...1, 24, 81, 98, 101, 105

    in emergency contraceptive pills...45–46, 50, 54–59

ethinyl estradiol...50, 54, 56–58, 76, 124

expulsion

    of an IUD...142, 152–153, 273

    of implants...112, 126

extended use of combined oral contraceptives...18, 19, 21

eye damage due to diabetes...See vision damage due to diabetes

F

fainting, faintness...40, 127, 152, 178, 179, 191, 291, 320, 362

fallopian tube...137, 165, 181, 304, 364, 366

fatigue...47, 150, 371

female condom...See condoms, female

female sterilization...148, 165–182, 269, 273, 299

    contraceptive effectiveness...165–166

    medical eligibility criteria...168–171

fertility...182, 197, 257, 298, 304–306

fertility awareness methods...148, 239–254, 269, 273, 299...See also calendar-based methods, symptoms-based methods

    contraceptive effectiveness...240

    medical eligibility criteria...242, 246–247

fertilization...364

fever...139, 146, 151, 154, 178, 234, 249, 291, 321, 332

fibroid...See uterine fibroids

fibrosis...170, 323, 330

filariasis...188, 333

follicle...See ovarian follicle

follow-up visit...23, 128, 139, 146–147, 177, 192, 263

forced sex...49, 300, 303, 332

forceps...147, 153, 191

fungal infection...296

G

gall bladder disease...9, 20, 85, 331

gastroenteritis...171, 188, 332–333

genital herpes...200, 277, 279

genital irritation...102, 103, 202, 207, 213, 219, 225, 228, 231, 233, 235, 274

genital lesions, sores, ulcers...137, 222, 226, 233, 277, 278 genital warts...279, 284–285

gloves...210, 312–315

goiter...331

gonorrhea...136, 169, 277, 278, 279, 282–283, 303, 304–305, 307, 322, 330

    and IUD use...132, 136–137, 138–139, 151, 154

    protection against...200, 226, 236

griseofulvin...332

H

hair growth...3, 365

hand washing...71, 92, 224, 230, 231, 312–314

headaches, migraine...See migraine headaches

headaches, ordinary...150

    as side effect...2, 13, 27, 34, 47, 61, 71, 83, 91, 102, 106, 111, 119, 158, 164

    management of...18, 39, 76, 96, 125

heart attack...3, 7, 66, 86, 320

heart disease...8, 20, 41, 66, 87, 97, 170, 198, 323, 328, 333...See also blocked or narrowed arteries, heart attack

heavy or prolonged bleeding...250, 292, 328, 359

    as side effect...27, 61, 71, 83, 102, 106, 132, 143, 158

    management of...19, 39, 76–77, 96, 124–125, 149

hematoma...185, 190

hematometra...332

hemoglobin...150, 152, 170, 171, 186, 307, 332

hemorrhage...169, 332

hepatitis...6, 29, 65, 85, 93, 114, 160, 171, 277, 312, 315, 321, 330, 331, 333...See also liver disease

hernia...169, 170, 188, 332–333

herpes...See genital herpes

high-level disinfection...142, 312, 315

high blood pressure...See blood pressure

HIV/AIDS...226, 275–288...See also antiretroviral therapy

    and safe method use...9, 30, 67, 88, 115, 138, 171, 188, 241, 260

    limitations on method use...282–283

    prevention of...200, 209, 212, 260, 265, 280, 294–295

hormone-free week...18, 19, 103, 107

HPV...See human papillomavirus

human immunodeficiency virus...See HIV/AIDS

human papillomavirus...4, 279, 284–285

hydrocele...187, 333

hypertension...See blood pressure

hyperthyroidism...171, 331

hypothyroidism...170, 331

I

ibuprofen...143, 242, 247

    as treatment...17, 18, 19, 38, 39, 40, 75, 76, 95, 96, 124, 125, 126, 145, 149, 150, 177, 192, 194

Implanon...109, 110, 111, 116, 118, 120, 130, 360...See also implants

implants...109–130, 148, 269, 272, 299, 360

    contraceptive effectiveness...110

    medical eligibility criteria...114–115

    side effects and management...111, 124–128

impotence...202, 210

infant...See newborn health

infection...See also liver infection, reproductive tract infection, sexually transmitted infection, urinary tract infection

    and female sterilization...166, 169, 171, 177, 178

    and implants...112, 123, 126, 129

    and IUD...132, 134–139, 141, 142, 151, 155, 156, 159, 163

    and vasectomy...185, 187–188, 190, 193, 194

infection prevention...120–121, 142, 156, 175, 191, 229, 305, 310, 312, 312–315, 315

Index

undescended testicles...187–188

unexplained vaginal bleeding...40, 127, 152, 179, 279, 320

    as medical eligibility criterion...66, 67, 114, 115, 135, 169

    management of...19, 41, 77, 97, 127, 153

United States Food and Drug Administration...55, 63, 209, 285

upper respiratory infection...102

upset stomach...See nausea

urinary tract infection...222, 226, 233, 234, 334

urination...371...See also see burning or pain with urination

uterine cavity...137, 179, 329

uterine fibroids...62, 169, 329

uterine involution...227, 299, 333

uterine perforation...132, 137, 142, 147, 159, 169, 299, 332

uterine rupture...169, 332

uterus...137, 155, 157, 169, 182, 332, 364, 366, 370–371

V

vaginal bleeding...23, 154...See also heavy or prolonged bleeding, infrequent bleeding, irregular bleeding, monthly bleeding, no monthly bleeding, unexplained vaginal bleeding

vaginal discharge...106, 139, 146, 151, 154, 231, 234, 238, 246, 279, 291

vaginal dryness, vaginal lubricant...274

vaginal infection...134, 207, 219, 233–234, 248, 250, 279–280, 322

vaginal itching...See itching

vaginal ring...See combined vaginal ring

vaginal secretions...204, 223

vaginal sex...205, 208–209, 224, 240, 244–245, 248–249, 252–253, 288

vaginal sponge...236

vaginal tear...286, 332

vaginal wetness...239

vaginal yeast infection...See candidiasis

vaginitis...102, 106, 330

vaginosis...See bacterial vaginosis

varicocele...187, 333

varicose veins...5, 23, 28, 84, 100, 113, 327

vas, vas deferens, vasa deferens...183, 184, 190, 191, 195, 367

vascular disease...323, 327, 331

vasectomy...149, 183–198, 269, 273

    contraceptive effectiveness...183–184

    medical eligibility criteria...187–188

violence against women...300–303

viral hepatitis...See hepatitis

vision damage due to diabetes...20, 77, 97, 323

    as medical eligibility criterion...7, 9, 65, 67, 86, 88, 170, 331

voluntary surgical contraception...See female sterilization, vasectomy

vomiting...8, 87, 146, 151, 234, 312, 321, 362, 368, 371

    and pill effectiveness...15, 17, 36, 38

    as side effect...47, 102

    management of...51

vulva...137

W

waste, waste disposal...312–314, 316, 365

weak, weakness...150, 167, 181, 185, 195, 202, 321, 368

weight, weight change...22, 78, 167, 180, 195, 371

    and duration of implant effectiveness...110, 123, 130, 360

    as side effect...2, 13, 61, 63, 71, 83, 91, 111, 158, 359

    management of...19, 75, 96, 125

withdrawal...148, 255–256, 269, 273, 299

    contraceptive effectiveness...255

    medical eligibility criteria...256

Y

yeast infection...See candidiasis

youth...See adolescence, adolescent

Methodology

This handbook, one of the World Health Organization's family planning cornerstones, provides evidence-based guidance developed through worldwide collaboration. The World Health Organization (WHO) Department of Reproductive Health and Research invited more than 30 organizations to participate in its preparation. The INFO Project at the Johns Hopkins Bloomberg School of Public Health/Center for Communication Programs led the handbook development process.

This handbook is the successor to *The Essentials of Contraceptive Technology* (Johns Hopkins School of Public Health, Population Information Program, 1997). While *Essentials* served as a starting point, new evidence-based guidance has been incorporated and new content has been added (see What's New in This Handbook?, p. viii).

Guidance in this book comes from several similar consensus processes:

- The *Medical Eligibility Criteria for Contraceptive Use* and the *Selected Practice Recommendations for Contraceptive Use*. WHO expert Working Groups developed these guidelines.

- For additional questions specific to this handbook, WHO convened an expert Working Group that met in Geneva on 21–24 June 2005. To discuss topics needing special attention, several subgroups met between October 2004 and June 2005. At the June 2005 meeting the full expert Working Group reviewed and endorsed the subgroups' recommendations.

- Content not addressed in these consensus processes was developed through collaboration between researchers at the INFO Project and technical experts. Then, a group of experts and, finally, representatives of the collaborating organizations had the opportunity to review the entire text.

The 2011 Update of the Handbook

- This 2011 update incorporates all guidance from the latest expert Working Group meeting in April 2008 for the *Medical Eligibility Criteria* and the *Selected Practice Recommendations,* and two Technical Consultations related to these guidelines in October 2008 and January 2010.

- Further guidance has also been incorporated from an expert Working Group meeting on HIV and infant feeding in October 2009 and a Technical Consultation on community-based provision of injectable contraceptives in June 2009.

- In addition to the new guidance available, this update also corrects any errors and brings up to date available information on brands of contraceptives. Selected members of the expert Working Group that met in 2005, experts who contributed to the handbook, and WHO staff have contributed to and reviewed the update. They include: Mario Festin, Mary Lyn Gaffield, Lucy Harber, Douglas Huber, Roy Jacobstein, Sarah Johnson, Kirsten Krueger, Enriquito Lu, Ward Rinehart, James Shelton, Jeff Spieler, and Irina Yacobson.

Future Handbook Updates

- This handbook will be reviewed every 3 to 4 years to determine the need for revisions. New WHO guidance will be incorporated into electronic versions as it becomes available.

Some definitions used in this handbook

Effectiveness: Rates are largely the percentages of US women estimated to have unintended pregnancies during the first year of use, unless noted otherwise.

Side effects: Conditions reported by at least 5% of users in selected studies, regardless of evidence of causality or biological plausibility, listed in order of frequency with the most common at the top.

Terms describing health risks (percentage of users experiencing a risk):
Common: $\geq$15% and <45%
Uncommon: $\geq$1% and <15%
Rare: $\geq$0.1% and <1% (<1 per 100 and $\geq$1 per 1,000)
Very rare: $\geq$0.01% and <0.1% (<1 per 1,000 and $\geq$1 per 10,000)
Extremely rare: <0.01% (<1 per 10,000)

Sources for WHO guidelines and reports of consultations

Community-based health workers can safely and effectively administer injectable contraceptives. Geneva, WHO, 2010. http://www.who.int/reproductivehealth/publications/family_planning/WHO_CBD_brief/en/index.html
Guidelines on HIV and infant feeding. 2010. Principles and recommendations for infant feeding in the context of HIV and a summary of evidence. Geneva, WHO, 2010. http://www.who.int/child_adolescent_health/documents/9789241599535/en/index.html
Medical Eligibility Criteria for Contraceptive Use (4th ed.) Geneva, WHO, 2010. http://www.who.int/reproductivehealth/publications/family_planning/9789241563888/en/index.html
Selected Practice Recommendations for Contraceptive Use (2nd ed.) Geneva, WHO, 2004. http://www.who.int/reproductivehealth/publications/family_planning/9241562846index/en/index.html
Selected Practice Recommendations for Contraceptive Use: 2008 Update. Geneva, WHO, 2008. http://www.who.int/reproductivehealth/publications/family_planning/9241562846index/en/index.html
Statement on combined hormonal contraceptive use during the postpartum period. Geneva, WHO, 2010. http://www.who.int/reproductivehealth/publications/family_planning/rhr_10_15/en/index.html
Technical consultation on hormonal contraception use during lactation and effects on the newborn. Geneva, WHO, 2010. http://www.who.int/reproductivehealth/publications/family_planning/RHR_10_05/en/index.html

(More on processes, sources, selection criteria, and terminology used in this book can be found online at http://www.fphandbook.org/.)

Methodology

Illustration and Photo Credits

Illustrations by Rafael Avila and Rita Meyer, unless otherwise noted below. All adaptations by Rafael Avila.

p. 5   David Alexander, Center for Communication Programs (CCP), courtesy of Photoshare

p. 30   DELIVER

p. 34   Cheikh Fall, CCP, courtesy of Photoshare

p. 37   Lauren Goodsmith, courtesy of Photoshare

p. 46   Francine Mueller, CCP

p. 60   David Alexander, CCP, courtesy of Photoshare

p. 63   PATH

p. 82   Schering AG

p. 99   CCP, courtesy of Photoshare

p. 102   Ortho-McNeil Pharmaceutical

p. 106   David Alexander, CCP, courtesy of Photoshare

p. 112   David Alexander, CCP, courtesy of Photoshare

p. 113   David Alexander, CCP, courtesy of Photoshare

p. 119   Organon USA

p. 120   Indonesia Ministry for Population, National Family Planning Coordinating Board

p. 121   Indonesia Ministry for Population, National Family Planning Coordinating Board

p. 122   JHPIEGO. Source: Bluestone B, Chase R, and Lu ER, editors. IUD Guidelines for Family Planning Service Programs. 3rd ed. Baltimore: JHPIEGO; 2006. (adapted)

p. 133   David Alexander, CCP, courtesy of Photoshare

p. 142   David Alexander, CCP, courtesy of Photoshare

p. 144   JHPIEGO. Source: Bluestone B, Chase R, and Lu ER, editors. IUD Guidelines for Family Planning Service Programs. 3rd ed. Baltimore: JHPIEGO; 2006. (adapted)

p.145   JHPIEGO. Source: Bluestone B, Chase R, and Lu ER, editors. IUD Guidelines for Family Planning Service Programs. 3rd ed. Baltimore: JHPIEGO; 2006. (adapted)

p. 159   David Alexander, CCP, courtesy of Photoshare

p. 175   EngenderHealth (adapted)

p. 176   EngenderHealth (adapted)

p. 191   EngenderHealth (adapted)

p. 212   David Alexander, CCP, courtesy of Photoshare

Credits

Comparing Contraceptives

Comparing Combined Methods

Charac-teristic	Combined Oral Contra-ceptives	Monthly Inject-ables	Combined Patch	Combined Vaginal Ring
How it is used	Pill taken orally.	Intramuscular injection.	Patch worn on upper outer arm, back, abdomen or buttocks. Not on breasts.	Ring inserted in the vagina.
Frequen-cy of use	Daily.	Monthly: Injection every 4 weeks.	Weekly: Patch is changed every week for 3 weeks. No patch worn 4th week.	Monthly: Ring kept in place for 3 weeks and taken out during 4th week.
Effective-ness	Depends on user's ability to take a pill every day.	Least dependent on the user. User must return to clinic every 4 weeks (plus or minus 7 days).	Requires user's attention once a week.	Depends on user keeping the ring in place all day, not leaving it out for more than 3 hours at a time.
Bleeding patterns	Typically, irregular bleeding for the first few months and then lighter and more regular bleeding.	Irregular bleeding or no monthly bleeding is more common than with COCs. Some also have prolonged bleeding in the first few months.	Similar to COCs, but irregular bleeding is more common in the first few cycles than with COCs.	Similar to COCs, but irregular bleeding is less common than with COCs.
Privacy	No physical signs of use but others may find the pills.	No physical signs of use.	Patch may be seen by partner or others.	Some partners may be able to feel the ring.

Comparing Injectables

Charac-teristic	DMPA	NET-EN	Monthly Injectables
Time between injections	3 months.	2 months.	1 month.
How early or late a client can have the next injection	2 weeks early, 4 weeks late.	2 weeks.	7 days.
Injection technique	Deep intramuscular injection into the hip, upper arm, or buttock. (Also, see Progestin-Only Injectables, New Formulation of DMPA, p. 63.)	Deep intramuscular injection into the hip, upper arm, or buttock. May be slightly more painful than DMPA.	Deep intramuscular injection into the hip, upper arm, buttock, or outer thigh.
Typical bleeding patterns in first year	Irregular and prolonged bleeding at first, then no bleeding or infrequent bleeding. About 40% of users have no monthly bleeding after 1 year.	Irregular or prolonged bleeding in first 6 months but shorter bleeding episodes than with DMPA. After 6 months bleeding patterns are similar to those with DMPA. 30% of users have no monthly bleeding after 1 year.	Irregular, frequent, or prolonged bleeding in first 3 months. Mostly regular bleeding patterns by 1 year. About 2% of users have no monthly bleeding after 1 year.
Average weight gain	1–2 kg per year.	1–2 kg per year.	1 kg per year.
Pregnancy rate, as commonly used	About 3 pregnancies per 100 women in the first year.	Assumed to be similar to DMPA.	
Average delay in time to pregnancy after stopping injections	4 months longer than for women who used other methods.	1 month longer than for women who used other methods.	1 month longer than for women who used other methods.

Comparing Implants

Characteristic	Jadelle	Implanon	Sino-Implant (II)	Norplant
Type of progestin	Levonorg-estrel.	Etonogestrel.	Levonor-gestrel.	Levonor-gestrel.
Number	2 rods.	I rod.	2 rods.	6 capsules.
Lifespan	Up to 5 years.	3 years.	4 years, may be extended to 5.	Up to 7 years.
Effectiveness and Client's Weight (see also Implants, Question 9, p. 130)	80 kg or more: Becomes less effective after 4 years of use.	Weight has no known impact on effectiveness.	80 kg or more: Becomes less effective after 4 years of use.	80 kg or more: Becomes less effective after 4 years of use. 70–79 kg: Becomes less effective after 5 years of use.
Availability	Expected to replace Norplant by 2011.	Primarily available in Europe, Asia and Africa. Also approved for use in United States.	Primarily available in Asia and Africa.	Being phased out of use (see Implants, p. 130, Q&A 11).

Comparing Condoms

Characteristic	Male Condoms	Female Condoms
How to wear	Rolled on the man's penis. Fits the penis tightly.	Inserted into the woman's vagina. Loosely lines the vagina and does not constrict the penis.
When to put on	Put on erect penis right before sex.	Can be inserted up to 8 hours before sex.

Continued on next page

Characteristic	Male Condoms	Female Condoms
Material	Most made of latex; some of synthetic materials or animal membranes.	Most made of a thin, synthetic film; a few are latex.
How it feels during sex	Change feeling of sex.	Fewer complaints of changed feeling of sex than with male condoms.
Noise during sex	May make a rubbing noise during sex.	May rustle or squeak during sex.
Lubricants to use	Users can add lubricants: • Water-based or silicone-based only. • Applied to outside of condom.	Users can add lubricants: • Water-based, silicone-based, or oil-based. • Before insertion, applied to outside of condom. • After insertion, applied to inside of condom or to the penis.
Breakage or slippage	Tend to break more often than female condoms.	Tend to slip more often than male condoms.
When to remove	Require withdrawing from the vagina before the erection subsides.	Can remain in vagina after erection subsides. Requires removal before woman stands.
What it protects	Cover and protect most of the penis, protect the woman's internal genitalia.	Cover both the woman's internal and external genitalia and the base of the penis.
How to store	Store away from heat, light, and dampness.	Plastic condoms are not harmed by heat, light or dampness.
Reuse	Cannot be reused.	Reuse not recommended (see Female Condoms, p. 220, Q&A 5).
Cost and availability	Generally low cost and widely available.	Usually more expensive and less widely available than male condoms.

Comparing IUDs

Characteristic	Copper-Bearing IUD	Levonorgestrel IUD
Effectiveness	Nearly equal. Both are among the most effective methods.	
Length of use	Approved for 10 years.	Approved for 5 years.
Bleeding patterns	Longer and heavier monthly bleeding, irregular bleeding, and more cramping or pain during monthly bleeding.	More irregular bleeding and spotting in the first few months. After one year no monthly bleeding is more common. Causes less bleeding than copper-bearing IUDs over time.
Anemia	May contribute to iron-deficiency anemia if a woman already has low iron blood stores before insertion.	May help prevent iron-deficiency anemia.
Main reasons for discontinuation	Increased bleeding and pain.	No monthly bleeding and hormonal side effects.
Noncontraceptive benefits	May help protect against endometrial cancer.	Effective treatment for long and heavy monthly bleeding (alternative to hysterectomy). May also help treat painful monthly bleeding. Can be used as the progestin in hormone replacement therapy.
Postpartum use	Can be inserted up to 48 hours postpartum.	Can be inserted after 4 weeks postpartum.
Use as emergency contraception	Can be used within 5 days after unprotected sex.	Not recommended.
Insertion	Requires specific training but easier to insert than levonorgestrel IUD.	Requires specific training and a unique, more difficult insertion technique. Women may experience faintness, pain, and nausea or vomiting at insertion more than with the copper-bearing IUD.
Cost	Less expensive.	More expensive.

Correctly Using a Male Condom

1. Use a new condom for each act of sex

2. Before any contact, place the condom on tip of erect penis with rolled side out

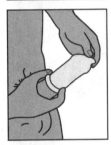

3. Unroll the condom all the way to base of penis

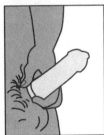

4. After ejaculation, hold rim of condom in place, and withdraw penis while it is still erect

5. Dispose of the used condom safely

Job Aids/Tools

Female Anatomy
and How Contraceptives Work in Women
Internal Anatomy

Womb (uterus)

Where a fertilized egg grows and develops into a fetus. *IUDs* are placed in the uterus, but they prevent fertilization in the fallopian tubes. *Copper-bearing IUDs* also kill sperm as they move into the uterus.

Ovary

Where eggs develop and one is released each month. The *lactational amenorrhea method (LAM)* and *hormonal methods*, especially those with estrogen, prevent the release of eggs. *Fertility awareness methods* require avoiding unprotected sex around the time when an ovary releases an egg.

Uterine lining (endometrium)

Lining of the uterus, which gradually thickens and then is shed during monthly bleeding.

Cervix

The lower portion of the uterus, which extends into the upper vagina. It produces mucus. *Hormonal methods* thicken this mucus, which helps prevent sperm from passing through the cervix. Some *fertility awareness methods* require monitoring cervical mucus. The *diaphragm, cervical cap,* and *sponge* cover the cervix so that sperm cannot enter.

Fallopian tube

An egg travels along one of these tubes once a month, starting from the ovary. Fertilization of the egg (when sperm meets the egg) occurs in these tubes. *Female sterilization* involves cutting or clipping the fallopian tubes. This prevents sperm and egg from meeting. *IUDs* cause a chemical change that damages sperm before they can meet the egg in the fallopian tube.

Vagina

Joins the outer sexual organs with the uterus. The *combined ring* is placed in the vagina, where it releases hormones that pass through the vaginal walls. The *female condom* is placed in the vagina, creating a barrier to sperm. *Spermicides* inserted into the vagina kill sperm.

External Anatomy

Pubic hair
Hair that grows during puberty
and surrounds the female organs

**Inner lips
(labia minora)**
Two folds of skin, inside
the outer lips, that
extend from the clitoris

Clitoris
Sensitive ball of tissue
creating sexual pleasure

Urethra
Opening where
liquid waste (urine)
leaves the body

**Outer lips
(labia majora)**
Two folds of skin, one on
either side of the vaginal
opening, that protect the
female organs

Vaginal opening
The man's penis is inserted here
during sexual intercourse. Blood
flows from here during monthly
bleeding.

Anus
Opening where solid
waste (feces) leaves the
body

The Menstrual Cycle

1 *Days 1–5:*
Monthly bleeding

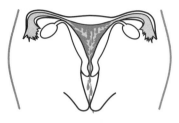

Usually lasts from 2–7 days, often about 5 days

If there is no pregnancy, the thickened lining of the womb is shed. It leaves the body through the vagina. This monthly bleeding is also called menstruation. Contractions of the womb at this time can cause cramps. Some women bleed for a short time (for example, 2 days), while others bleed for up to 8 days. Bleeding can be heavy or light. If the egg is fertilized by a man's sperm, the woman may become pregnant, and monthly bleeding stops.

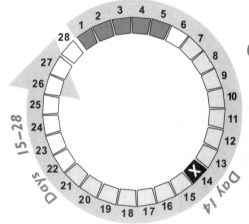

2 *Day 14:*
Release of egg

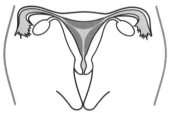

Usually occurs between days 7 and 21 of the cycle, often around day 14

Usually, one of the ovaries releases one egg in each cycle (usually once a month). The egg travels through a fallopian tube towards the womb. It may be fertilized in the tube at this time by a sperm cell that has travelled from the vagina.

3 *Days 15–28:*
Thickening of the womb lining

Usually about 14 days long, after ovulation

The lining of the uterus (endometrium) becomes thicker during this time to prepare for a fertilized egg. Usually there is no pregnancy, and the unfertilized egg cell dissolves in the reproductive tract.

Male Anatomy

and How Contraceptives Work in Men

Penis
Male sex organ made of spongy tissue. When a man becomes sexually excited, it grows larger and stiffens. Semen, containing sperm, is released from the penis (ejaculation) at the height of sexual excitement (orgasm). A *male condom* covers the erect penis, preventing sperm from entering the woman's vagina. *Withdrawal* of the penis from the vagina avoids the release of semen into the vagina.

Urethra
Tube through which semen is released from the body. Liquid waste (urine) is released through the same tube.

Seminal vesicles
Where sperm is mixed with semen.

Foreskin
Hood of skin covering the end of the penis. Circumcision removes the foreskin.

Prostate
Organ that produces some of the fluid in semen.

Scrotum
Sack of thin loose skin containing the testicles.

Testicles
Organs that produce sperm.

Vas deferens
Each of the 2 thin tubes that carry sperm from the testicles to the seminal vesicles. *Vasectomy* involves cutting or blocking these tubes so that no sperm enters the semen.

Job Aids/Tools

Identifying Migraine Headaches and Auras

Identifying women who suffer from migraine headaches and/or auras is important because migraines, and aura in particular, are linked to higher risk of stroke. Some hormonal contraceptives can increase that risk further.

Migraine Headaches

- Recurring, throbbing, severe head pain, often on one side of the head, that can last from 4 to 72 hours.

- Moving about often makes the migraine headache worse.

- Nausea, vomiting, and sensitivity to light or noise may also occur.

Migraine Auras

- Nervous system disruptions that affect sight and sometimes touch and speech.

- Almost all auras include a bright area of lost vision in one eye that increases in size and turns into a crescent shape with zigzag edges.

- About 30% of auras also include a feeling of "pins and needles" in one hand that spreads up the arm and to one side of the face. Some auras also include trouble with speaking. Seeing spots or flashing lights, or having blurred vision, which often occurs during migraine headaches, is not aura.

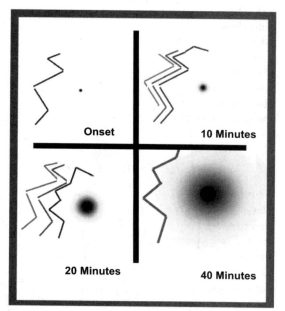

Onset | 10 Minutes

20 Minutes | 40 Minutes

People describe visual auras as bright, shimmering lines or waves around a bright area of lost vision that increase in size and turn into a crescent shape with zigzag edges. The black spot represents how the area of lost vision increases in size over time.

- Auras develop slowly over several minutes and go away within an hour, typically before the headache starts. (In contrast, a sudden blackout in one eye, particularly with a feeling of "pins and needles" or weakness in the opposite arm or leg, may indicate a stroke.)

Identifying Migraine Headaches

For women who want a hormonal method[‡§] or are using one.

If a woman reports having very bad headaches, ask her these questions to tell the difference between a migraine headache and an ordinary headache. If she answers "yes" to any 2 of these questions, she probably suffers from migraine headaches. Continue to Identifying Migraine Auras, below.

1. Do your headaches make you feel sick to your stomach?

2. When you have a headache, do light and noise bother you a lot more than when you do not have a headache?

3. Do you have headaches that stop you from working or carrying out your usual activities for one day or more?

Identifying Migraine Auras

Ask this question to identify the most common migraine aura.
If a woman answers "yes," she probably suffers from migraine auras.

1. Have you ever had a bright light in your eyes lasting 5 to 60 minutes, loss of clear vision usually to one side, and then a headache? (Women with such aura often bring one hand up beside their heads when describing the vision change. In some cases the bright light is not followed by a headache.)

If her headaches are not migraines and she does not have aura, she can start or continue hormonal methods if she is otherwise medically eligible. Any later changes in her headaches should be evaluated, however.

Can a Woman With Migraines and/or Aura Use a Hormonal Method?

In situations where clinical judgment is limited:

Yes = Yes, can use No = No, do not use
I = Initiation C = Continuation

	Combined methods[‡]		Progestin-only methods[§]	
Migraine headaches	I	C	I	C
Without aura				
Age < 35	Yes	No	Yes	Yes
Age ≥ 35	No	No	Yes	Yes
With aura, at any age	No	No	Yes	No

[†] *Methods with estrogen and progestin: combined oral contraceptives, monthly injectables, combined patch, and combined vaginal ring*
[§] *Methods with progestin only: progestin-only pills, progestin-only injectables, and implants*

Job Aids/Tools

Further Options to Assess for Pregnancy

A woman can start a hormonal contraceptive method or, in most cases, an IUD any time it is reasonably certain that she is not pregnant. This includes a certain number of days after the start of monthly bleeding, depending on the method. At other times in a woman's monthly cycle, the checklist on p. 372 often can be used to be reasonably certain she is not pregnant.

A woman who answers "no" to all questions in the pregnancy checklist may or may not be pregnant. In most situations, such a woman will need to use a backup method* and wait either until her next monthly bleeding to start her method of choice or until it becomes clear that she is pregnant.

In some cases, however, some providers may want to assess for pregnancy by other means. To do so, providers can follow one of the sets of instructions below, as appropriate for their situation and training. These options are especially useful when there are likely explanations—other than pregnancy—that a woman has not had monthly bleeding for several months. Such reasons include:

- She has given birth more than 6 months ago and is still breastfeeding.
- She continues to have no monthly bleeding after recently stopping a progestin-only injectable.
- She has a chronic health condition that stops monthly bleeding.

Assessing for Pregnancy

If a pregnancy test is available:

- Give her a urine pregnancy test or refer her to a facility with such tests. If the pregnancy test is negative, give her the contraceptive method she wants.

If a pregnancy test is not available but a provider can conduct a bimanual pelvic examination:

- Take a history from the woman, including when she had her last monthly bleeding and whether she has signs or symptoms of pregnancy (see symptoms on next page).
- Conduct a bimanual pelvic examination to determine the size of her uterus so that you can make a comparison later.
- Give her a backup method to use and teach her how to use it consistently and correctly. Ask her to return in about 4 weeks or when she has monthly bleeding, whichever comes first.

---

* Backup methods include abstinence, male and female condoms, spermicides, and withdrawal. Tell her that spermicides and withdrawal are the least effective contraceptive methods. If possible, give her condoms.

When she returns:

- If she returns with monthly bleeding, give her the contraceptive method she wants.

- If she returns still without monthly bleeding after 4 weeks, conduct a second pelvic examination.

  - A woman who previously had regular monthly bleeding and now has no bleeding is most likely pregnant and would have some enlargement of the uterus.

  - If there is no enlargement of the uterus, no other signs or symptoms of pregnancy, and she has used a backup method consistently and correctly, give her the contraceptive method that she wants. She may need to continue her backup method for the first few days of use, as specified for each method.

If neither a pregnancy test nor a bimanual examination is available:

- The provider can give the woman a backup method and ask her to return during her next monthly bleeding or in 12 to 14 weeks, whichever comes first.

When she returns:

- If she returns with monthly bleeding, give her the contraceptive method she wants.

- If she returns still without monthly bleeding after 12 to 14 weeks:

  - If she is pregnant, the uterus can be felt externally, through the lower abdominal wall, coming up from below.

  - If there is no enlargement of the uterus and no other signs or symptoms of pregnancy, and she has used a backup method consistently and correctly, give her the contraceptive method that she wants. She may need to continue her backup method for the first few days of use, as specified for each method.

Tell her to return to the clinic any time if she thinks that she might be pregnant, or if she has signs or symptoms of pregnancy (see below). If you suspect an underlying health problem as the reason for a prolonged absence of monthly bleeding, refer for assessment and care.

Signs and Symptoms of Pregnancy

- Nausea
- Breast tenderness
- Fatigue
- Vomiting

- Increased frequency of urination
- Increased sensitivity to odors
- Mood changes
- Weight gain

Pregnancy Checklist

Ask the client questions 1–6. As soon as the client answers "yes" to any question, stop and follow the instructions below.

NO		YES
	1 Did you have a baby less than 6 months ago, are you fully or nearly-fully breastfeeding, and had no monthly bleeding since then?	
	2 Have you abstained from sexual intercourse since your last monthly bleeding or delivery?	
	3 Have you had a baby in the last 4 weeks?	
	4 Did your last monthly bleeding start within the past 7 days (or within the past 12 days if the client is planning to use an IUD)?	
	5 Have you had a miscarriage or abortion in the last 7 days (or within the past 12 days if the client is planning to use an IUD)?	
	6 Have you been using a reliable contraceptive method consistently and correctly?	

If the client answered "**no**" to *all* questions, pregnancy cannot be ruled out. The client should wait for her next monthly bleeding or use a pregnancy test.

If the client answered "**yes**" to *at least one* of the questions, and she has no signs or symptoms of pregnancy, you can give her the method she has chosen.